The Defenders of
Rorke's Drift
The Zulu War, 1879

James W. Bancroft

BARNTHORN
PUBLISHING

Published by Barnthorn Publishing Limited.

www.barnthornpublishing.co.uk

ISBN: 978-1-917120-28-9

THE DEFENCE OF RORKE'S DRIFT

Tension between British authority and various factions in South Africa had been building up, and the 2nd Battalion, 24th (2nd Warwickshire) Regiment of Foot joined their 1st Battalion in South Africa to take part in the Ninth Cape Frontier War. The area of unrest was the north-eastern Cape, where the Gaika and Gcaleka tribes were causing problems. The campaign followed the usual pattern of how the British dealt with such disturbances. The rebels used the bushy terrain and hill caves for refuge, and lines of troops formed up and entered the shrub to flush them out. By June 1878, Sindali, the chief of the Gaikas, had been killed, and the Gcaleka chief, Kreli, had been captured. The rebels lost heart and the uprising ended. These sweeping skirmishes in the Perie Bush gave most of the British troops their first experience of active service in South Africa.

However, the main threat to stability in the region came from the highly disciplined army of fearless Zulu warriors. Lord Garnet Wolseley stated: 'These Zulus are a great danger to our Colony.' The British Government knew that they had to be subdued before there could be any progress towards a united nation under one flag, which would be easier for administration and the hard-pressed British Army.

On 11 January 1879, the Third (Central) Column of a British invasion force crossed the Buffalo River border between Natal and Zululand at Rorke's Drift to offer battle to King Cetshwayo's formidable army of Zulu warriors, leaving B Company, 2nd Battalion, 24th Regiment, to garrison the field hospital and storehouse which had been established there.

A base camp was set up at a place known as iSandlwana, and on 22 January the commander-in-chief, Lord Chelmsford, took about half of his force forward into hostile territory to try to locate the enemy, leaving six companies of the 24th Regiment and various colonial units to defend the ill-prepared camp. Later that day a large Zulu army, which outnumbered them by about 20 to 1, swarmed down on them in a devastating surprise attack, which overwhelmed

1

the British and forced the 24th Regiment to have to stand and fight to the last in hopeless disorder and without any possibility of escape.

An estimated 3,000 warriors pushed on into Natal to attack the garrison at Rorke's Drift, but the British had been warned of the impending onslaught and had constructed a makeshift barricade around the perimeter and posted men inside the hospital to defend it. The Zulus launched ferocious assaults throughout the night, setting fire to the hospital and trying to force their way into the compound, but the Brits held out until a relief column arrived early on the following morning.

16 men were initially awarded medals for their courage (one being cancelled later). The 11 Victoria Crosses for the defence has never been equalled since, and the seven awarded to the 24th (2nd Warwickshire) Regiment is the most to one regiment for a single action.

Lieutenant Chard wrote the following concise report of the action, dated 25 January 1879, which can be found at reference WO 32/7737 in the Public Records Office:

I have the honour to report that on the 22 Inst: I was left in command at Rorke's Drift by Major Spalding who went to Helpmekaar to hurry on the Company 24th Regiment ordered to protect the ponts.

About 3:15 pm. on that day, I was at the ponts when two men came riding from Zululand at a gallop, and shouted to be taken across the river–I was informed by one of them, Lieutenant Adendorff of Lonsdale's Regiment (who remained to assist in the defence) of the disaster at iSandlwana camp, and that the Zulus were advancing on Rorke's Drift. The other a carbineer rode off to take the news to Helpmekaar.

Almost immediately I received a message from Lieutenant Bromhead, Commanding the company 24th Regiment at the Camp near the commissariat stores, asking me to come up at once.

I gave the order to inspan, strike tents, put all stores, etc, into the waggon and at once rode up to the commissariat store and found that a note had been received from the third column to state that the enemy were advancing in force against our post, which we were to strengthen and hold at all costs.

2

Lieutenant Bromhead was most actively engaged in loopholing and barricading the store building and hospital and connecting the defence of the two buildings by walls of mealie bags and two waggons that were on the ground.

I held a hurried consultation with him and with Mr. Dalton of the Commissariat (who was actively superintending the work of defence, and whom I cannot sufficiently thank for his most valuable services), entirely approving of the arrangements made. I went round the position and then rode down to the Ponts and brought up the guard of one sergeant and six men, wagon, etc.

I desire here to mention the offer of the punt man Daniells and Sergt. Milne 3rd Buffs, to moor the ponts in the middle of the stream and defend them from their decks with a few men. We arrived at the post about 3:30 pm. Shortly after an officer of Dunford's Horse arrived and asked for orders; I requested him to send a detachment to observe the drifts and ponts, to throw out outposts in the direction of the enemy, and check his advance as much as possible, falling back upon the post when forced to retire and assisting in its defence. I requested Lieutenant Bromhead to post his men, and having seen his and every man at his post, the work once more went on.

About 4:20 pm. the sound of firing was heard behind the hill to our south. The officer of Durnford's returned, reporting the enemy close upon us, and that his men would not obey his orders, but were going off to Helpmakaar, and I saw them, apparently about 100 in number, going off in that direction. About the same time Captain Stephenson's detachment of Natal Native Contingent left us, as did that officer himself. I saw that our line of defence was too extended for the small number of men now left us, and at once commenced a retrenchment of biscuit boxes.

We had not completed a wall two boxes high when about 4:30 pm. 500 or 600 of the enemy came in sight around the hill to our south and advanced at a run against our south wall. They were met by a well sustained fire, but notwithstanding their heavy loss continued the advance to within 50 yards of the wall, when they met with such a heavy fire from the wall, and cross fire from the store, that they were checked, but taking advantage of the cover afforded by the cook house, ovens, etc, kept up a heavy fire. The greater number, however, without stopping, moved to the left around the hospital and made a rush at our north-west wall of mealie bags, but after a short but desperate struggle they were driven back with heavy loss into the bush around the work.

The main body of the enemy were close behind and had lined the ledge of rock and caves overlooking us about 400 yards to our south from where they kept up a constant fire, and advancing somewhat more to their left than the first attack, occupied the garden, hollow road and bush in great force. Taking advantage of the bush which we had not time to cut down, the enemy were able to advance under cover close to our wall, and in this part soon held one side of the wall, while we held the other, a series of desperate assaults were made extending from the hospital along the wall as far as the bush reached, but each was most splendidly met and repulsed by our men with the bayonet; Corporal Schiess N.N.C. greatly distinguishing himself by his conspicuous gallantry.

The fire from the rocks behind us, though badly directed, took us completely in reverse, and was so heavy that we suffered very severely; and at about 6:00 pm we were forced to retire behind the retrenchment of biscuit boxes.

All this time the enemy had been attempting to force the hospital and shortly after set fire to its roof. The garrison of the hospital defended it room by room, bringing out all the sick who could be moved before they retired, Privates Williams, Hook, R. Jones and W. Jones of the 24th Regiment, being the last men to leave, holding the doorway with the bayonet their own ammunition being expended. From the want of interior communication and the burning of the house it was impossible to save all–With most heartfelt sorrow I regret we could not save these poor fellows from their terrible fate.

Seeing the hospital burning and the desperate attempts of the enemy to fire the roof of the stores, we converted two mealie bag heaps, into a sort of redoubt, which gave a second line of fire all round; Assistant Commissary Dunne working hard at this though much exposed, and rendering valuable assistance.

As darkness came on we were completely surrounded and after several attempts had been gallantly repulsed, were eventually forced to retire to the middle and then inner wall of the kraal on our east. The position we then retained throughout. A desultory fire was kept up all night, and several assaults were attempted and repulsed; our men firing with the greatest coolness did not waste a single shot; the light afforded by the burning hospital being of great help to us.

About 4:00 am, 23rd instant, the firing ceased and at daybreak the enemy were out of sight over the hill to the south west.

We patrolled the grounds collecting the arms of the dead Zulus, and strengthened our defences as much as possible.

We were removing the thatch from the roof of the stores when about 7:00 am, a large body of the enemy appeared on the hills to the south west. I sent a friendly Kaffir, who had come in shortly before with a note to the officer commanding at Helpmekaar asking for help.

About 8:00 am, the third column appeared in sight, the enemy who had been gradually advancing, falling back as they approached.

I consider the enemy who attacked us to have numbered about 3,000 (three thousand). We killed about 350 (three hundred and fifty).

Of the steadiness and gallant behaviour of the whole garrison I cannot speak too highly. I wish especially to bring to your notice the conduct of Lieutenant Bromhead 2/24th Regiment, and the splendid behaviour of his company B 2/24th; Surgeon Reynolds A.M.D, in his constant attention to the wounded under fire where they fell. Acting Commissariat Officer Dalton, to whose energy much of our defences were due, and who was severely wounded while gallantly assisting in the defence. Assistant Commissary Dunne; Acting Storekeeper Byrne (killed); Colour Sergeant Bourne 2/24th; Sergeant Williams 2/24th (wounded dangerously); Sergeant Windridge 2/24th; Corporal Schiess 2/3 Natal Native Contingent (wounded); 1395 Private Williams 2/24th; 593 Private Jones 2/24th; Private McMahon A.H.C; Private Beckett 1/24th Regiment. A total killed of 17.

Towards the end of 1879, Annie Elizabeth Foster, the secretary of
the Salvation Army in Eccles near Manchester decided to establish
The Ladies' Rorke's Drift Testimonial Fund, to raise money to buy
commemorative bibles to be presented to all the surviving
defenders–'As a small mark of our high appreciation of the splendid
defence of Rorke's Drift.'

Men of B Company who took part in the defence of Rorke's Drift
received an illuminated address from the Mayor of Durban, Mr H.
W. Currie, just before they sailed from Durban to Gibraltar in
January 1880. It stated:

To the Officers, Non-Commissioned Officers and
Men of the 2nd Battalion of HM 24th Regiment.

As the time has now arrived when you must take your
departure from this Colony, We, the Mayor, and Town
Council, as representing the Burgesses of Durban, Natal,
cannot allow you to leave the land whose frontier your heroism
has kept inviolate, without delaying your footsteps for a
moment upon the shore, while we place upon enduring record
this expression of our admiration of your deeds and of our
lasting gratitude to you, for the heroic services performed by
you in the defence of this Colony when menaced by an
invasion of overwhelming numbers of Zulus on the night of
22nd January 1879.

It is not yet a year since, in the shadows of the evening, a
Company of your Regiment saw approaching from the slopes
of the Buffalo River the darkest cloud of invasion that had ever
lowered over the wide frontier of British Dominion in Africa.

The storm which then gathered around you, held in it all the
fierce power caught from a recent victory gained over your
brethren who had fallen fighting at a vast disadvantage, on the
sad and fatal field of Isandhlwana.

Reckless of loss, confident in its numbers and strength, that
wild wave of savage invasion burst upon your hastily
improvised defences, and surged against the scanty defenders
as the sun went down; all through the night, the savage but
doubtless foe renewed again and again its attempts to break
your line, a line which was weak to all save courage, loyalty and

duty. No need for us now to repeat now the story of Rorke's Drift.

As the daylight faded away above the heights of Helpmekaar it left you simple and untried soldiers, holders of an unknown post; when daylight broke again over the Zulu hills, Rorke's Drift had become a name of pride to those who speak the English tongue over the earth, and each and all of that little garrison had become Heroes.

Out of the gloom of a great disaster the star of your victory shone resplendent and Natal, saved by your heroism, dried the tears of her anguish in the glory of your victory.

Take then, Officers, Non-Commissioned Officers and Soldiers of the 2nd 24th Regiment the thanks which we Burgesses of Durban, and Colonists of Natal heartily offer you.

Wherever your future fortunes and destinies of the Empire you serve may call you, be assured you will carry with you the honour, the admiration and the gratitude of those who now bid you FAREWELL!

Who were the men who fought for their lives with such unwavering courage on that day?

This work has been compiled over the course of five decades, the main sources being the J. W. B. Historical Archive; the body of the original work which appeared as *The Rorke's Drift Men* in 2010; and in addition I have spent many hours over the years researching official documentation at the Public Records Office in Kew, and at the National Army Museum in west London. These papers included WO 16–Regimental musters; WO76–Officers' services; WO97–Soldiers' services, and WO100/46–Medals for South Africa, 1877-1879 (see the Bibliography for the full list).

Where possible I have checked Census Returns for all the defenders and their family from 1841 to 1921, and consulted such works of reference as ancestry.com and FamilySearch, and the British Newspaper Library at Colindale. At the end of most tributes I have noted particular research material and official documentation I consulted for that defender in addition to those listed in the Bibliography. I have given a great deal of attention to check the correct spelling of the names of people and locations, burial places and new memorials, and dates of awards and promotions. I made every effort to contact museums and other establishments to get up-to-date information on the whereabouts of medals and their accessibility. Prominent researchers on the subject have graciously offered their help over 50 years, most of whom are no longer with us, and I am grateful to all of them.

I have always been of the opinion that a man who can be considered to have been a defender of Rorke's Drift remains so until proven without doubt that he was not, and it must be confirmed where he was if he was not at Rorke's Drift during the defence on 22/23 January 1879. I take the view that it is not appropriate to dismiss any of them without such proof; and I could be doing them an injustice if I did so. Absence of evidence is not evidence of absence. This was the case in my 1988 book entitled *Rorke's Drift: The Zulu War, 1879*, which was the first publication to state without doubt that Lieutenant Adendorff took part in the defence of Rorke's Drift, when there had been doubts raised many times previously; and it has been the case with some other men who have received tributes in this work.

It will never be established for certain how many men were present at Rorke's Drift during the fighting on 22/23 January 1879. However, it is my opinion that there were about 160 defenders, who were attacked by approximately 3,000 Zulu warriors.

Note: spellings of places or names within quotations may vary, where these have been left as they appeared in the source.

THE DEFENDERS OF RORKE'S DRIFT

A

Robert Adams was killed in action while a patient in the hospital.

He had served in the East Middlesex Militia when he attested for the army on 21 December 1876; and as 987 Private Adams he was posted to D Company, 2nd Battalion, 24th Regiment. He received orders for active service in South Africa and sailed to the Cape with his battalion in February 1878. He took part in the Cape Frontier War, and was sent to the General Depot on 1 November 1878, returning to the service companies on 21 December 1878. During the Zulu War he was killed in action as a defender of Rorke's Drift, having been a patient in the hospital.

During his escape from the hospital Gunner Evans stated: 'I was then standing in the doorway of the hospital, and witnessed five Zulus come in front of the doorway, jumping in their mad frenzy and flushed with their late victory. Just at this moment my newest mates were Adams and Jenkins of the 24th Regiment. What became of these men I can't say, I never saw them again after...'

Robert Adams was buried in the cemetery at Rorke's Drift and his name is inscribed on the monument. His effects were recorded for claim by his next-of-kin. For his service he was entitled to the South Africa Medal with 1877-8-9 clasp, which was sold at auction in 2022.

Gert Wilhelm Adendorff escaped from the disaster at iSandlwana and was a survivor of the defence.

He was born at Graaff Reinet in Cape Province, South Africa, on 10 July 1848. Little is known about his early life, but he is known to have served with the Diamond Fields Horse during the Ninth Cape Frontier War.

He was a lieutenant in Captain Robert Krohn's No. 6 Company of the 1st Battalion, 3rd Regiment, Natal Native Contingent, when the Zulu War began, and escaped from the camp at iSandlwana. Lieutenant Chard reported:

At 3:15pm that day I was watching at the ponts when two men came towards us from Zululand at the gallop. They shouted out and were taken across the river; and I was then informed by one of them—Lieutenant Adendorff of Commandant Lonsdale's regiment, who afterwards remained to assist in the defence—of the disaster befallen at the iSandlwana camp, and that the Zulus were advancing upon Rorke's Drift.

On 2 October 1899, in Pretoria, South Africa, he married Hester Catharia Grobler (born in 1856), and they lived at Elandsfontein, before moving to Pretoria. He worked as a gold commissioner, and became employed as a 'responsible clerk' at the charge office in Elandsfontein during the Anglo-Boer War of 1899-1902. In 1903, while living in Pretoria, he sought compensation from the British for the loss of a mule, which had been commandeered by the Boers, and a scotch cart, which had been commandeered by the British.

By 1917 he was working as a diamond digger in Kameel Kuil near Bloemhof, South Africa. He died there on 30 July 1917, aged 69, and is buried in the town cemetery of Schweitzer-Reneke near Bloemhof.

Anglo-Zulu War Historical Society
Natal Witness for 18 February 1879

William Wilson Allan was wounded in action, and awarded the Victoria Cross for valour at Rorke's Drift.

The exact date of his birth is not certain, though it has been recorded to have been some time in February 1844. His name is sometimes spelt 'Allen' but it is 'Allan' on all the census returns, with no suggestion of the middle name of 'Wilson'—his mother's maiden name—however, he seems to have added the middle name towards the end of his life, and his grave records his name as W. W. Allan.

According to the 1851 census he was born at Kyloe near Berwick-upon-Tweed in Northumberland, and he was then aged six, being the first born of the family. According to local council researchers at Kyloe, who believe they have located his birth certificate, he was born at Beal in Kyloe Parish, Islandshire, which was then the area known as North Durham.

His father, Thomas (born at Coldstream in Berwickshire on 22

September 1816), was an itinerant agricultural labourer, and his family of four boys and four girls were born in different towns on the Northumberland coast. His mother's name was Eleanor (known as Ellen, formerly Weatherston, born at Berwickshire in 1822). In 1851 the family were living at Belford Moor near Berwick-upon-Tweed.

William was aged 15 when he enlisted at York on 27 October 1859, and as 1240 Private Allan he was posted to the 2nd Battalion, 24th (2nd Warwickshire) Regiment of Foot, at Aldershot. He was slightly built, at five feet four inches tall, but he was a tough Geordie character, and was confined in cells on several occasions in the early 1860's before he settled into army life. He served in Mauritius and following 13 years' service in the East, he returned to the depot at Brecon on 21 April 1874. His father died at Bedlington in Northumberland on 17 January 1872, unaware that his son would gain the Victoria Cross.

He married Sarah Ann Reeves at the Brecon Registry Office, on 16 August 1876, his new wife being 12 years younger than him. Her father, Richard, had been a staff-sergeant in the Monmouthshire Militia. Their first two daughters, Helena Letitia and Elizabeth Alice, were born in Brecon in April 1877 and on 11 July 1878 respectively.

William was promoted to lance corporal on 18 May 1876, corporal on 6 July 1877, and having gained a 2nd Class Certificate of Education, he became an assistant-schoolmaster. In 1878 he was awarded a prize for 'Good shooting and judgement of distance.' Corporal Allan (as Allen) was posted to his battalion on 26 January 1878, and on 2 February he sailed with his unit from Portsmouth on the troopship *Himalaya* for active service in South Africa. He took part in the Cape Frontier War of 1878, being promoted lance sergeant on 22 May 1878, and being reduced to corporal at Pietermaritzburg, on 21 October 1878.

His award of Victoria Cross was announced in the *London Gazette* for 2 May 1879, which stated:

It was chiefly due to the courageous conduct of these men [Corporal William Allan and Private Frederick Hitch] that communication with the hospital was kept up at all. Holding together a most dangerous post, raked in reverse by the enemy's fore from the hill, they were both severely wounded, but their determined conduct enabled the patients to be withdrawn from the hospital, and when incapacitated by their wounds from fighting, they continued, as soon as their wounds had been dressed, to serve out ammunition to their comrades during the night.

Disabled by the injuries he received during the defence of Rorke's Drift, he was taken to Helpmekaar, and on 4 February he wrote a letter informing his wife, 'I am getting the better of my wound more rapidly than could be expected... My arm is mending quickly'. He was transported back to England on HMS *Tamar* and taken to Netley Military Hospital. The Zulu slug had left William's arm partly disabled, but with such a strong constitution he was well enough to attend a victory celebration banquet at Portland Hall in Portsea, on 25 October 1879, organised by the people of Portsmouth for the servicemen who had fought in the Zulu campaign.

By 8 November he was serving as provisional staff sergeant with the 3rd/24th Regiment Militia. His award of Victoria Cross had been announced in the *London Gazette* of 2 May 1879, and on 9 December 1879, he went to Windsor Castle to receive the Victoria Cross from Queen Victoria. He also received the South Africa Medal with 1877-8-9 clasp. On 11 June 1880, William was appointed sergeant at the Colchester depot.

He visited the north-east in January 1880, and he returned to Brecon for the birth of his first son, Llewellyn Glendower, in July 1880. Grace was born in July 1883, Margaret Mary was born in April 1882, but she died an infant at Colchester in January 1883, and Gwlydo Annie was born in 1885.

On 13 November 1880, one of Sergeant Allan's fellow defenders of Rorke's Drift, William Partridge, 24th Regiment, married his wife's sister, Mary Letitia, known as 'Polly', at the Brecon Registry Office, and Sarah's brother, Richard Reeves, was also serving with the 24th Regiment in 1881. In 1886 William became sergeant instructor of musketry, to C Company, 4th Volunteer Battalion of the South Wales Borderers, stationed at Monmouth, where he made the family home at 85 Monnow Road, St Mary's Parish, and became a well-known and respected member of the community. Sarah opened a grocery shop next door at number 87. A child named Jessie was born in 1886, but she died less than two years later. Olive was born in April 1888.

Sarah gave birth to Sybil Jean in January 1890, but a serious influenza epidemic hit the town, and it was thought that William was a victim. However, he was seriously ill with dropsy for seven days, and when further complications developed he deteriorated and died of: 'aortic valvular disease of the heart' at his home on 12 March 1890, aged 46. He was buried with his baby daughter at Monmouth Cemetery, with military honours provided by the South Wales Borderers, and a stone cross was erected at his grave by the 4th Volunteer Battalion.

Sergeant Allan's sudden death left his wife and children in difficult circumstances, so the Mayor of Monmouth set up a benefit appeal to help them. Among the subscribers were pupils from the Whittington School on Highgate Hill in north London, and two of the eight-year-olds wrote moving and sympathetic letters to the Allan family.

His Victoria Cross is with the South Wales Borderers Museum at Brecon, with an inscribed pocket-watch which was given to the museum by his grandson. It had been presented to Sergeant Allan by the Mayor of Brecon while he was serving at the barracks as an instructor. Sarah died at 50 Cinderhill Road in Monmouth in January 1906.

His grave was renovated and a re-dedication service was held there in 2018, during which the regiment displayed his Victoria Cross.

Alnwick Mercury for 31 January 1880
Brecon County Times for 29 March 1879
Monmouthshire Beacon and South Wales Advertiser for 15 March and 19 April 1890

William Anderson was killed at Rorke's Drift.

He is believed to have been born in England. He was a corporal serving with the 2nd Battalion, 3rd Regiment, Natal Native Contingent, and was a patient in the hospital suffering with fever. However, it seems that he had taken his place at the ramparts when he lost his nerve and was in the act of leaving the scene when he was shot dead from behind. In his account dated 3 February 1879, Reverend Smith recorded:

The garden must have been occupied, for one unfortunate Contingent corporal, whose heart must have failed him when he saw the enemy and heard the firing, got over the parapet and tried to make his escape on foot, but a bullet from the garden struck him, and he fell dead within a hundred and fifty yards of our front wall.

He was buried in the cemetery at Rorke's Drift, and his name is inscribed on the memorial.

James Ashton was a survivor of the defence.

Born as Anthony McHale, probably in Ireland, although his WO97 papers state he was born at St Mary's Parish in Liverpool, during June 1841. His enlistment papers record him as Church of England, but he was actually Church of Ireland (Protestant). Colour Sergeant Bourne stated: '1939 Ashton was a lusty Irishman…', but as a point of interest, the 1841 census for Liverpool records a James Ashton, aged nine months, who was the son of John and Alice Ashton, living at Cavendish Street, St Mary's, and the parish register of St Peter's C of E Church at St Mary's records the baptism of a James Ashton on 17 January 1842, to John and Alice Ashton, a carter, living in Cavendish Street.

He left his job as a domestic groom to enlist into the army at York, on 2 March 1859, and as 1939 Private James (John) Ashton he was posted to the 2nd Battalion, 24th Regiment. He was five feet five and a half inches tall, with a fresh complexion, hazel eyes and dark brown hair. He gave his age as 17 years. He was posted to the sugar island of Mauritius on 23 May 1860, spending a week in prison there in 1862, before being posted to India on 6 October 1865. His conduct pay was increased to two pence a day on 16 February 1868, and he re-engaged at Secunderabad on 13 April 1869, to complete 21 years' service. He forfeited his good conduct pay and he was deprived of two days' pay for being absent on 8 March 1872, but one penny a day good conduct pay was restored two days later. He returned from India and home service began on 4 January 1873. His good conduct pay was forfeited and restored several times, and he was imprisoned by his commanding officer for seven days in April 1874, for fraudulent enlistment, when he admitted his true name and place of birth.

He received orders for active service in South Africa, and sailed to

the Cape in February 1878. He fought in the Cape Frontier War, and during the Zulu War he was one of the oldest soldiers to take part in the defence of Rorke's Drift. On 23 January 1879, when the Zulus had withdrawn, Private Ashton reported to Lieutenant Bromhead with a Zulu prisoner and was told to 'get the hell out of here—and I did.' Lieutenant Smith-Dorrien had erected a gallows at Rorke's Drift for making reims, and stated, 'On returning to Rorke's Drift after the battle, I saw two Zulus hanging from my gallows.' For his service he received the South Africa Medal with 1877-8-9 clasp. He was on colonial leave from 6 March 1879, so his copy of the Commemorative Address was forwarded to 25 Brigade Depot at Brecon.

His good conduct pay was restored to two pence on 24 November 1880, and he returned for home service on 6 March 1881. He was discharged from the army at Brecon on 12 April 1881, his conduct being very good, he was in possession of two good conduct badges, and he was awarded a pension of ten pence a day. His intended place of residence was Knockmore, County Mayo, Ireland, where he died and is buried.

Francis Attwood was awarded the Distinguished Conduct Medal for gallantry during the defence.

He was born on 29 September 1844, at 20 Norman Street, off the City Road, in the St Luke's district of London, the son of Francis Attwood, a shoemaker, and his wife, Mary Ann (formerly Boost).

He enlisted into the Army Service Corps, being given the service number C/2469. In 1878 he received orders for active service in South Africa, and arrived at Cape Town on 25 October of that year. He had been working as a clerk in Pietermaritzburg, when he was sent to the mission station at Rorke's Drift in January 1879, 'as a punishment' for his tendency to be argumentative. He wrote six letters to an aunt and uncle while he was in South Africa, and the second one, written in Helpmekaar on 2 January 1879 states:

The Sergeant-Major I am with and I do not agree very well. We are continually quarrelling, and he takes every advantage he can of me, but I will try that he does me no injury if I can help it.

Although he was considered to be a stubborn man by nature, he had been promoted to corporal by the time he arrived at Rorke's Drift. After helping to remove the bags and boxes from the store to be used at the barricade, he took his place at one of the upper windows of the building to shoot at Zulus who were rushing forward trying to throw lighted spears on the roof to set it on fire.

Some newspapers noted:

One Lucky Bullet Saves Hundreds of Lives—In the middle of the fight at Rorke's Drift, when the Zulus had fired the hospital, a rush was made by a band of the enemy to fire the storehouse, the other building which outlasted the defence. As fast as these Zulus came on with firebrands they were shot down, but one managed to escape the fire, and got in close to the wall of the storehouse. The defenders, with their rifles through the loopholes, could not slope their weapons to kill him, and it seemed as if his purpose of firing the thatch on the roof of the house should succeed.

Fortunately, a young corporal of the Army Service Corps named Attwood bethought himself of a plan to rid the camp of the Zulu. As luck would have it, there was a small square hole in the wall which had been used as a window and the Zulu happened to get below this. Attwood, with his carbine, made his way to this hole, and, pushing out his weapon, let it hang pointing to the ground. It was impossible to take aim in this awkward position, so he trusted to fate.

The Zulu had by this time stuck a firebrand on the end of his assegai, and was in the act of rising up to set fire to the thatch, when Attwood, not seeing the Zulu at all, but knowing about his position, fired the carbine with his thumb. The shot probably, in fact, saved Natal from an invasion of the Zulus.

The Zulu, at daylight, was found at the spot with his skull smashed in, and the assegai with the firebrand stuck on the end of it, held tightly in his dead hand.

Francis was promoted sergeant dated from the day of the defence, and for his gallant conduct he was awarded the Distinguished Conduct Medal, which was announced on 29 July 1879, and presented to him in the town square at Pietermaritzburg, on 13

September 1879. He also received the South Africa Medal with 1878-9 clasp.

By 1880, Francis had returned to England and was stationed at Aldershot. On being posted to Plymouth he took accommodation for himself and his partner, Amy Jane Burgess (originally Wood), a widow with a son named Ross William, at 5 Cremyll Street, East Stonehouse, Plymouth, where Amy Mary was born in 1883. They then decided to get married. However, circumstances dictated that they could not do so in East Stonehouse. They married at the parish church of St John the Evangelist in Westminster, London, on 25 September 1883, giving their address as 28 Horseferry Road in south-west London, and Francis was described as a baker. They returned to East Stonehouse, but only five months after their marriage, Francis died after an epileptic convulsion at their home in Cremyll Street on 20 February 1884. He was buried with full military honours at Milehouse Cemetery, Plymouth.

The headstone at Sergeant Attwood's grave was badly damaged during a bombing raid in 1941, and a quarter of a century later Milehouse Cemetery was cleared and the remains of Sergeant Attwood were re-interred in communal ground at Efford Cemetery in Plymouth. A memorial plaque was placed in Stoke Damarel Church, and in 2009 a new headstone was unveiled at his grave.

Birth certificate–St Luke's, Middlesex Y576643
Death certificate–East Stonehouse FC721725
Marriage certificate–Westminster W177058
Marriage certificate of his parents–St Giles, East London PAS6036384
Corporal Francis Attwood: Six letters written while he was on active service in South Africa, from November 1878 to December 1879, including one dated 25 January 1879, giving his account of the action at Rorke's Drift.
Tralee Chronicle, Ireland for 15 July 1879

B

Thomas Barry was a survivor of the defence.

He enlisted at Newport in Monmouthshire, on 5 April 1877, and as 1381 Private Barry he was posted to the 2nd Battalion, 24th Regiment on 11 May 1877. He sailed for active service in South Africa on 1 February 1878, taking part in the Cape Frontier War of 1878 and in the Zulu War, being present at the defence of Rorke's Drift.

He transferred to A Company on 1 March 1879. His name appears on the Company list at Rorke's Drift on 8 March 1879, when he was confined for ten days for making replies when ordered for duty. For his service in South Africa he received the South Africa Medal with 1877-8-9 clasp.

He sailed with the unit to Gibraltar, where he served from 12 February to 10 August 1880, during which time he was fined for drunkenness on 28 May, 2 July and 7 July 1880. He was posted to India on 11 August 1880, and returned to England on 26 April 1883. He received his pay at Gosport in Hampshire, until 20 June 1883, and he was discharged to the army reserve on 21 June 1883. A travel warrant with the destination of Newport was issued to him, and his intended place of residence was care of the Post Office in Merthyr Tydfil.

William Beckett was a patient in the hospital, and was mortally wounded.

He was born at 15 Duncan Street in the Higher Broughton district of Salford, on 27 January 1856, the son of an engraver named John Beckett, and his wife Sarah (formerly McGlocklin)

He enlisted at Cross Lane Barracks in Salford on 14 April 1874. He served at the 24th Regiment depot in Brecon from 22 April to 16 June 1874, before joining the 2nd Battalion at Aldershot, as 135 Private Beckett. He remained at Aldershot from June to November 1874.

He transferred to A Company of the 1st Battalion on 25 November 1874, and sailed to Gibraltar as part of the draft for service at the Cape of Good Hope. He served at Cape Town from

March 1875 to September 1877, when he was sent with a draft of the battalion on 2 August 1877, being stationed at Komgha in the Eastern Cape. He was stationed at King William's Town, where he forfeited one penny of his good conduct pay on 11 October 1878.

He was a patient in the hospital at Rorke's Drift, and Private Waters stated: 'He [Beckett] was assegaied right through his stomach, and went into laager next morning. Doctor Reynolds did all he could to save him...' However, Private Beckett had been lying out all night dangerously wounded and exposed to the elements and the doctor: 'did not succeed'.

Private Beckett died of his wounds on 23 January 1879. He was 23-years-old. He was buried in the cemetery at Rorke's Drift and his name is inscribed on the monument. For his service he was awarded the South Africa Medal with 1877-8-9 clasp, and his effects were recorded for claim by his next-of-kin. His South Africa Medal was sold at auction in 1998, which had been the property of a descendant of the family. His field sewing kit, known as a 'housewife', was on display during the *Clash of Empires: The 1879 Anglo-Zulu War* exhibition held at the Royal Philatelic Society in London in 2023.

William Bennett was a survivor of the defence.

He was a native of Fylde in Lancashire, and in 1879 his mother was living at Wesham near Kirkham in that county.

He enlisted at Brecon on 21 November 1876, and as 918 Private Bennett he was posted to the 2nd Battalion, 24th Regiment. He received orders for active service in South Africa, and sailed to the Cape in February 1878. He took part in the Cape Frontier War, later being confined cells for eight days, and during the Zulu War he was present at the defence of Rorke's Drift. He deserted at Pinetown on 21 December 1879. For his service he was entitled to the South Africa Medal with 1877-8-9 clasp, but due to his desertion the medal was never issued and was returned to the mint.

A death notice for a Trooper W. E. Bennett, 4th South African Horse, appeared in a Great War Roll of Honour published in the Natal Mercury Pictorial of 30 June 1916, which is almost certainly the Rorke's Drift man, who had succumbed to an attack of enteric fever while serving in East Africa. He had previously served in the Natal Mounted Rifles under Colonel Sparks. Trooper Bennett succumbed to an attack of enteric fever in East Africa. He was the son of Meyrick Bennett of Messrs Randles Brothers and Hudson, of Durban, who was the firm's managing partner in Johannesburg. The article stated that William played football for Berea Park Football Club of Pretoria, and included a picture.

Natal Mercury Pictorial of 30 June 1916
Preston Pilot for 26 March 1879

William Henry Bessell was a survivor of the defence.

He was born on 12 April 1856, at 1 Edgar Place in Stepney, London. He was the third child of five to a bricklayer named James Bessell, and his wife Caroline Anna (formerly Slow), who had married at St Peter's Church in Stepney on 31 May 1847. William was baptised with his two older siblings at the same church in Stepney on 6 May 1858.

By 1860 they had moved to 4 Chester Street in Bethnal Green, London, and several family losses followed. The 1861 census shows that William's eldest brother, James, was 'a convicted boy under sentence of detention' aboard the notorious prison vessel HMS *Cornwall*. By 1864 they had moved to 55 Lessada Street in Bethnal Green, where his eldest sister died of fever aged 11, and his father died of bronchitis on 12 May 1867, after the family had moved to 1 Green Street in Bethnal Green. They moved to 4 Punderson Gardens in Bethnal Green, where his mother gave birth to a step-sister, and on re-marrying she gave birth to a step-brother.

The 1871 census shows that William was in the Staines Industrial School for Juvenile Offenders, and probably in consequence of being on the wrong side of the law again, he enlisted at Bow Street Police Court in London on 27 February 1877. His trade was recorded as a porter and his description was given as five feet five and a quarter inches tall, with a fresh complexion, brown hair and hazel eyes. He had a brown patch on his left arm. As 1287 Private Bessell he was posted to the 2nd Battalion, 24th Regiment, at Brecon, and he was posted to Dover and Chatham, where he was admitted to hospital from 15 to 30 January 1878, suffering from gonorrhoea.

He received orders for active service in South Africa and sailed to the Cape in February 1878, taking part in the Cape Frontier War, and during the Zulu War he was present at the defence of Rorke's Drift.

Private Caleb Wood stated that during the defence:

The firing got very slack—just now and again from their 'Brown Bess's'. They were evidently getting tired of their job. 'Now chaps,' said Corporal Bissell, 'What do you say we fill a pipe and have a smoke?' 'Right ho', we replied. 'Keep a sharp look out and we can have a few draws each.' The pipe was filled and Oh how nice it was.

Following the arrival of the relief column on the morning of 23 January, William Bessell was promoted to corporal to replace some of the men who had been killed in action.

He had been making a monthly remittance of one pound to his Aunt Mary (Porter), of 252 Green Street in Bethnal Green, and in March 1879, the remittance was changed to two pounds per month and was then paid to his mother, who had become Mrs Thomas Stoneham at Polar Parish Church on 12 September 1875. He was in receipt of good conduct pay from 11 September 1879. However, he was tried and imprisoned on 25 November 1879, reduced to the rank of private and forfeited his good conduct pay. He was confined until 16 February 1880, when he was posted with the regiment to Gibraltar, before being posted to India in August 1880, and arrived in Secunderabad on 17 September. On 14 December 1880, William was hospitalised several times in Secunderabad with various ailments, and on 17 February 1881, his good conduct pay was restored. Having reached his expiry date for army service on 1 May 1883, he embarked on the SS *Armenia* with the other 'time served men' for the return journey to England, and was discharged to the first class reserves.

He gave his intended place of residence as 252 Green Street in Bethnal Green, the home of his aunt Mary. He received his final discharge from the first class army reserve on 26 February 1889. His mother died in 1891, at a time when William began to descend into alcoholism. He was living at Grays Inn Buildings in Holborn in 1901, with Jane F. Bessell, stated on the census to be his wife, along with two young boys named William and Albert, although there is no record of a marriage on the registers in Great Britain, so she was probably his common-law wife.

William had been employed as a bricklayer, but his depression deepened and the drinking bouts became more frequent. The family moved to 27 Sonning Buildings in Mount Street, Bethnal Green, and he took employment as a bar and cellar man at the King's Arms on High Street in Shoreditch, which would do nothing to lessen or discourage his drinking habit. He was stated to have imagined he could see things crawling about. He was admitted to the Bethnal Green Workhouse on 17 July 1903, and on the following day he was transferred to 'Justice Ward' of the Bethnal Green Infirmary, where he died at the age 46. The cause of death was recorded as 'delirium tremens and pneumonia.' The area where he was buried at Manor Park Cemetery has been reused.

The bible presented to him by The Ladies' Rorke's Drift Testimonial Fund is held at the Brecon Museum, along with the bibles of David Jenkins and Charles Mason (Frederick Herbert Brown).

Birth certificate—Mile End Old Town FC697536
Baptismal records—St Peter's Church, Stepney
Parents' marriage certificate—Stepney AB109535
Father's death certificate—Bethnal Green FC894871
Mother's second marriage certificate—Poplar AB109536
Death certificate—Bethnal Green FC894872
London Evening Telegraph for 22 July 1903

John Bly was a survivor of the defence.

He attested for the British Army in about November 1872, and as 2427 Private Bly he was posted to the 2nd Battalion, 24th Regiment, on 1 January 1873. He sailed with the regiment for active service in South Africa in February 1878, where he took part in the Ninth Cape Frontier War, and in the Zulu War, being present at the defence of Rorke's Drift. For his service he received the South Africa Medal with 1877-8-9 clasp.

He was sent to Netley Military Hospital on 1 February 1880, and was transferred to the Army Reserve.

John Bly died in Liverpool in June 1910 and he was buried in an unmarked grave at Walton Cemetery.

Frank Bourne was awarded the Distinguished Conduct Medal for gallantry during the defence.

He was born on 27 April 1855, at 2 The Brook, Balcombe, near Crawley in Sussex; the youngest of eight children to James Bourn (recorded without the 'e'), an agricultural labourer, and his wife Harriett (formerly Galton). It may have been due to working out in the wet and frosty fields in the winter of 1872 that prompted him to travel to Reigate on 18 December, to enlist into the army, and as 2459 Private Bourne he was posted to the 2nd Battalion, 24th Regiment. His father attempted to prevent him, but he was persuaded not to do so. He had a dark complexion, grey eyes and brown hair. He stated:

> Now the 'A' Company of any regiment in those days was always called the Grenadiers' Company and was supposed to have the biggest men. I think the Sergeant-Major must have been a wee bit humorous for he posted me to our 'A' Company, although I stood only five feet six inches and was painfully thin.

He settled into army life very well, and was promoted corporal on 11 April 1874.

He received orders for active service in South Africa, and sailed to the Cape with his unit in February 1878, where he was promoted three times within as many weeks; Lance Sergeant on 7 April 1878, Sergeant on 15 April 1878, and Colour Sergeant in B Company on 27 April 1878, while serving in the Cape Frontier War.

Colour Sergeant Frank Bourne was the senior NCO of a line regiment who took part in the defence of Rorke's Drift. A recommendation that he should be awarded the Distinguished Conduct Medal was submitted to Queen Victoria, and her approval was announced on 28 July 1879. He stated:

> Now, for the men who fought that night. I was moving about amongst them all the time and not for one moment did they flinch, their courage and their bravery cannot be expressed in words; for me they were an example all my soldiering days.

In a letter from Rorke's Drift dated 21 February 1879, to the parents of a soldier killed in action at iSandlwana, he stated: 'Thank God I escaped with only a small scratch from a spent bullet rendering my arm useless for a time.'

For his service he received the South Africa Medal with 1877-8-9 clasp. He served at Gibraltar in 1880, and in India and Burma. Men of B Company who took part in the defence of Rorke's Drift received an illuminated address from the Mayor of Durban just before they sailed to Gibraltar in January 1880.

He married Eliza Mary Fincham, the daughter of a mariner, at St Thomas's Cathedral in Bombay, on 27 September 1882, and they had five children. Percy was born in 1883, Sydney was born in 1887; Beatrice Maud Mary was born in 1889, while Mary and Constance were born during his service in Kent. Percy attended the Blue Coat School in Liverpool, and became a commander in the Royal Navy.

He became quartermaster and honorary lieutenant on 21 May 1890, and on 1 May 1893, he was appointed acting lieutenant and quartermaster at the Hythe School of Musketry in Kent. He retired on 18 December 1907.

Soon after the outbreak of the Great War he was re-employed as quartermaster and honorary major, 1915, serving as quartermaster and acting adjutant at the Irish Command School of Musketry in Dublin from 24 January 1916. He retired as honorary lieutenant colonel on 3 June 1918, being awarded the Order of the British Empire (OBE) in recognition of his services. For many years he was active in assisting Lord Roberts VC in promoting marksmanship within the Society of Miniature Rifle Clubs in London.

On 4 July 1910, at Beckenham in Kent, he completed a roll of defenders. Lieutenant Chard had himself compiled a Roll of Defenders on 3 February 1879, and when this was published in 1937, Colonel Bourne was prompted to produce an amended Roll. He kept in touch with many of the survivors, who came to be known as 'Rorke's Drift Men.' He wrote a letter to the *Daily Mail* on 24 August 1932, naming the survivors of the defence. At that time he was living in South Street, Dorking, and on 29 July 1932, the *Epsom District Times* reported that he had told his story of the defence to the Dorking Rotary Club.

He attended the laying up of the colours of the 1st Battalion, South Wales Borderers in Brecon Cathedral on Easter Sunday, 1 April 1934, and from 7 to 14 July 1934, he attended the Northern

Command Tattoo at Ravensworth Castle in Gateshead, when the South Wales Borderers re-created the action at Rorke's Drift, and he appeared in the arena with four surviving comrades from the garrison.

On 20 December 1936, he broadcast his reminiscences on the BBC Radio programme *I Was There!*, and as a result of this he received over 350 letters, to which he replied personally to everyone. Unfortunately, the programme was not recorded, but on 30 December 1936, the BBC publication *The Listener* carried an article based on the radio broadcast, a transcript of which has survived.

There are two things which I think have made Rorke's Drift stand out so vividly all these years. The first, that it took place on the same day as the terrible massacre at iSandlwana, and the second, that Natal was saved from being overrun by a savage and victorious foe. If there are any service, or ex-servicemen listening, may I say this to you; that if your company had found itself in the same position as we were, you would have done the same as we did, fought it out and won!

Frank Bourne was a very modest man, who considered himself lucky to have been present at Rorke's Drift, and the anniversary of the battle was commemorated by a dinner held in his home at 16 King's Hall Road in Beckenham. His wife had died in 1931, and Colonel Bourne died of uracemia, enlarged prostate, and senility, at 'Stoneroof', 68 South Street in Dorking, on the day after VE Day, 9 May 1945, aged 90. He died at the home of his oldest child, Beatrice, and her husband registered his death.

He was buried with military honours at Elmer's End Cemetery in Beckenham. A bearer party of six sergeants with an officer from the 1st Battalion, South Wales Borderers, and the regimental sergeant major of the Infantry Training Centre attended with wreaths from the regimental association. The colonel of the regiment, his two sons and two sons-in-law were also present. At the end of the service the organist played *Men of Harlech*. A commemorative blue plaque was placed at one of his former homes at 16 King's Hall Road in Beckenham in 2001, and his medals are with the South Wales Borderers Museum.

Birth certificate–Lindsfield, Cuckfield CN414153
Marriage certificate–Secunderabad F2007/6454/X
Death certificate–Dorking, Surrey South-Eastern HD036194
Epsom District Times for 29 July 1932
Daily Mail for 24 August 1932
Dorking County Post for 10 May 1945 (death notice)
The Listener dated 30 December 1936 taken from the BBC Radio
programme *I Was There!* recorded by Colonel Frank Bourne on 20
December 1936
Sunday Express for 22 January 1938

Gonville Bromhead was awarded the Victoria Cross for valour as
the commanding officer of the 24th Regiment at Rorke's Drift.

He became the most famous Bromhead, but several members of
his distinguished family gave great service to the Church, and the
heritage of their military prowess dates back to the Jacobite
Rebellion, Wolfe's campaign at Quebec, the American War of
Independence, the Peninsula and the battle of Waterloo, the Crimea,
several of Britain's colonial campaigns during the reign of Queen
Victoria and the two World Wars. Members of the family are serving
with the armed forces to this day.

Gonville was born on 29 August 1845, at Versailles in the
Yvelines department of Paris, the youngest of four sons in a family of
ten children to Edmund de Gonville Bromhead, who lived at Thurlby
Hall near Lincoln, a country house built in the early eighteenth
century, and Judith Christine Cahill, the youngest daughter of the
pioneering archaeologist, Captain James Wood, of Woodville House
in County Sligo, Ireland. On their marriage Edmund built a house
named 'Cairnsfoot' at St John's Parish in Sligo, where they made their
home. However, on the outbreak of the terrible Irish potato famine
in the mid-1840s, they spent some time at Versailles near Paris, and
then they returned permanently to Thurlby Hall. Gonville was deaf to
some degree.

Close by Thurlby Hall, among trees just off the beaten track, is the
medieval Norman church of St Germain. The Bromhead family
worshipped at the church, and Edmund donated one thousand
pounds of his own money for restoration in 1842. Gonville's parents
are commemorated with a stone in the church and they are buried in

the churchyard.

A letter I received from one of Gonville Bromhead's descendants states: '...you refer to Lieutenant Bromhead as 'Gonny' taken presumably from Gonville, his first name. He himself pronounced his first and surname as if the 'O' was replaced by 'U'–Gunville Brumhead–as it were. As told to me by my Grannie.'

Gonville's older brothers, Edward, Benjamin Parnell and Charles James, were educated at St John's Diocesan School in Lincoln, and he began his education at the Thomas Magnus Grammar School in Newark-on-Trent in 1860. He excelled at various activities, including combat sports such as boxing and singlestick, and he excelled at cricket. The team was coached by county professionals, and was apparently taken to away matches by 'a coach and four spanking greys.' The Newark Magnus publication described him as a member of the cricket eleven:

> Gonville Bromhead, afterwards famous as in command at Rorke's Drift, a left-hand medium bowler. Mention of it (Rorke's Drift) could still bring cheers at Magnus gatherings many years afterwards. Bromhead became the fourth old boy to give his name to a House.

At the time of the 1861 census Gonville was the only boy left at home in Thurlby Hall. He left the school in 1864, and followed his brothers into the military by entering the 24th Regiment as ensign by purchase three years later.

On 20 April 1867 he entered the 24th (2nd Warwickshire) Regiment of Foot, as ensign by purchase, and was trained at Croydon, where he gained popularity among his fellow officers as one who was a helpful senior to new recruits. At nearly six feet tall and with a powerful frame, he became a champion at any sport he cared to put his hand to. He made a good impression, and an article about him published in *The Hartlepool Mail* of 26 February 1879, stated:

> I was with him for some time at the army tutors at Croydon some twelve years ago, and it is interesting to look back upon him as he appeared to us at the time. About five feet ten inches in height, so well-built that he did not look as tall, he seemed to

me to be quite the bean ideal of an English officer. It was our custom of an evening, as soon as 'study' was over, to indulge in bouts of wrestling, boxing and singlestick in the gymnasium outside, and Bromhead was so expert in all of these that he invariably beat everyone opposed to him. With all this he was so kind and genial that the youngsters among us could chaff him and play tricks on him with impunity, and without fear of retaliation. Quiet and most unassuming in his demeanour, he nevertheless often showed friendliness to those who happened to be unpopular. By kindness to newcomers, and in a thousand other ways, the thorough worth and goodness were with him.

He was promoted by selection to the rank of lieutenant on 28 October 1871. Unfortunately he was developing a hearing problem which threatened the progress of his military career. However, in 1878 he was the officer in command of B Company, 2nd Battalion, 24th Regiment, when the unit received orders for active service in South Africa, and they embarked aboard the troopship Himalaya at Portsmouth on 1 February 1878, to set sail for the Cape of Good Hope, where he took part in the Ninth Cape Frontier War, and the Zulu War.

For his gallant conduct at the defence of Rorke's Drift, Lieutenant Gonville Bromhead was mentioned in dispatches and was awarded the Victoria Cross, which was announced in the *London Gazette* on 2 May 1879. He received the medal from Sir Garnet Wolseley, while he was still on active service at Pine Tree Camp, Utrecht, Transvaal, on 22 August 1879.

The official citation for the Victoria Cross stated:

The Lieutenant-General commanding the troops reports that, had it not been for the fine example and excellent behaviour of these two Officers (Lieutenants Chard and Bromhead) under the most trying circumstances, the defence of Rorke's Drift post would not have been conducted with that intelligence and tenacity which so essentially characterised it. The Lieutenant-General adds that its success must, in a great degree, be attributable to the two young Officers who exercised the Chief Command on the occasion in question.

He remained stationed at Rorke's Drift for a while after the battle, where his 'quiet and unassuming demeanour' had not faded with the fame he was beginning to have thrust upon him, and which he found difficult to accept. A contribution to this would almost certainly have been because he, like Major Chard, had already begun to suffer the effects of the jealousy their unwanted hero status would also create. Major Francis Clery of the 32nd (Cornwall) Light Infantry, observed:

> ...the height of his enjoyment seemed to be to sit all day on a stone on the ground smoking a most uninviting-looking pipe. The only thing that seemed equal to moving him in any way was an allusion to the defence of Rorke's Drift. This used to have a sort of electrical effect upon him, for he would jump up and off he would go, not a word could be got out of him. When I told him he should send me an official report on the affair it seemed to have a most distressing effect on him.

Although his younger brother Charles had become a favourite of Sir Garnet Wolseley, it did not stop the general from remarking in his journal of 11 September 1879:

> I have now given away these decorations (the Victoria Cross) to both the officers who took part in the defence of Rorke's Drift, and two duller, more stupid, more uninteresting men or less like gentlemen it has not been my luck to meet for a long time.

He also received the South Africa Medal with 1877-8-9 clasp. He was promoted captain and brevet major, dated back to 23 January 1879, and he was twice mentioned in dispatches, on 1 March and 15 March 1879. He and Major Chard had the rare distinction of being thanked by the British Parliament.

He served at Gibraltar in 1880, and while home on leave in June that year he was invited to Windsor Castle for an audience with Queen Victoria, who gave him a signed photograph. He was guest of honour at several functions, and on 25 June he was invited to Lincoln Masonic Hall, where the Mayor presented him with a jewelled sword and an illuminated address. In his acceptance speech at the Masonic Hall, which was sometimes interrupted by loud cheers, he stated:

Mr Mayor and citizens of this ancient city of Lincoln, I beg to thank you very much for the very kind and flattering address with which you have presented me this day, and also for this magnificent sword, which I assure you will always remain in my family as an heirloom forever. I feel great difficulty in adequately expressing to you my deep sense of the sympathy and kindness with which I have been received since my return to England, but I assure you nothing had given me greater gratification than the splendid reception I have met with this day, especially, as since my boyhood, when I left Thurlby, I have been personally almost a stranger in these parts. I am not vain enough to take this great reception all to myself, and I beg to thank you on behalf of Major Chard, Surgeon-Major Reynolds, Mr Dalton, Mr Dunne and the Reverend Mr Smith, all brave and stalwart men, who were with us on 22 January 1879, and the greater part of whom I am proud to say I still retain in the company which I have the honour to command. I beg to thank you again for the very kind reception which you have given me.

The tenants of Thurlby Hall presented him with a commemorative revolver, and the address which accompanied it stated:

We the undersigned living in Thurlby, justly proud of the part which you took in the heroic defence of Rorke's Drift, beg your acceptance of the accompanying revolver as a token of our esteem and admiration of your gallant conduct which has brought honour to the name of England and especially to Thurlby, your native place. We would, at the same time, take this opportunity of offering to you our congratulations on you obtaining the rank of Captain and Brevet Major; and of your receiving the Victoria Cross.

We trust that you may be spared to a long life of usefulness in the service of our country and that we may see you amongst us again in Thurlby.

We hope that you may never find yourself face to face with such numbers as you successfully met at Rorke's Drift, but should this occur, we trust that our revolver may not fail you in the hour of need and we are certain that it could not be held by a worthier hand.

The revolver is at the museum in Brecon, along with a broken shield shaft that Gonville had picked up at Rorke's Drift; and two heads of spears which were recovered at Rorke's Drift by Lieutenant Colonel J. Audley-Lloyd.

In August 1880 he was posted to Secunderabad in India, and returned to England later that year. On 1 July 1881 the 24th Regiment were re-designated the South Wales Borderers. From 1 October to 5 December 1882, he attended the Hythe School of Musketry, where he gained a first Class Extra Certificate. On 2 January 1883 he sailed from Portsmouth on the *Serapis*, to join the 2nd Battalion, South Wales Borderers, at Secunderabad. He was promoted major on 4 April 1883. He took part in the expedition to Upper Burma from 27 October 1886 to 24 May 1888, taking part in the Third Burmese War in November 1885, for which he received the Burma Medal with 1885-9 and 1887-9 clasps.

Major Bromhead never married, and according to Brigadier David Bromhead his main passion was for salmon fishing. He died of enteric fever, at Camp Dabhaura in Allahabad, India, on 9 February 1891, aged 46, and he was buried at the New Cantonment Cemetery in Allahabad. He left his medals to his brother, Charles, and they are with the Regimental Museum in Brecon. His name is inscribed on the colour pole of the 24th Regiment, and there is a stained glass memorial window dedicated to him at the church of St Germain. His great-great-nephew, Brigadier David Bromhead, was appointed colonel of the Royal Regiment of Wales in 1994.

Bancroft, James W.: *The Rorke's Drift Commanders: Gonville Bromhead and John Chard*, 2022
Biographical History of Gonville and Caius College, 1349-1897 (Four Volumes), 1897
Bromhead, David de Gonville
Bromhead, Lieutenant Colonel, Sir Benjamin Denis, 5th Baronet (Letters)
Burke's Peerage
Daily Express for 16 October 1984—Brigadier's blood line to Rorke's Drift
Illustrated London News for 21 February 1891

Lincolnshire Chronicle for 23 March 1855
Lincolnshire Family History Society
Lincolnshire Local Studies at Lincoln Central Library
London Gazette for 19 February 1806 and 2 May 1879
Magnus Church of England Academy History
Newark Advertiser for 12 March 1879 and 18 February 1891
Record of Service Ledger for the 2nd/24th Regiment
Regimental Museum of the Royal Welsh at Brecon
St Germain Church in Thurlby—monumental inscriptions
Truth periodical for 1891
World periodical for 18 February 1891

Charles Bromwich was an older brother of Joseph Bromwich, and a survivor of the defence.

He was born on 7 June 1840, at Milverton near Leamington Spa in Warwickshire, the first child of Joseph Bromwich, a journeyman painter, and his second wife.

Joseph had married Mary Kimberley at Milverton on 18 October 1835, and a son named William was born on 18 October 1835; but Mary died soon after the birth.

On 16 March 1840, in Milverton, Joseph married Maria Keyte (1820-1896) of Lee Wooton in Warwickshire, and they settled in Milverton.

Three girls were also born at Milverton between 1841 and 1846, and when they moved to Saltisford Rock, Joseph and three other boys were born between 1852 and 1858. By 1861 the family had moved to Hadley's Yard in the parish of St Mary's, Warwick, where four boys and a girl were born. Joseph senior died in 1875.

Charles had served in the 2nd Warwickshire Militia from 11 October 1858, before enlisting into the regular army at Plymouth, on 22 March 1859, and as 981 Private C. Bromwich he was posted to the 2nd Battalion, 24th Regiment. He served at Mauritius, and re-engaged at Fulwood Barracks in Preston on 20 August 1869, to serve 21 years, before serving in the East Indies.

He received orders for active service in South Africa and sailed to the Cape in February 1878. He took part in the Cape Frontier War, being sent to the general depot at Pietermaritzburg on 31 October 1878. During the Zulu War he and his brother, Joseph, were present at the defence of Rorke's Drift. For his service he received the South Africa Medal with 1877-8-9 clasp.

He transferred to the 91st Highlanders at Cape Town on 30 November 1879. He became attached to the Royal Welch Fusiliers on 19 May 1880, for the purpose of discharge, which occurred on 9 June 1880. His intended place of residence was the home of his widowed mother, Maria, at 12 Brook Street in Saltisford, Warwick.

He married Emma, who was from Brixton, and the 1881 census records that they lived in the Old Grammar School Butts at Warwick St Mary.

Charles died in Warwick on 27 May 1893, aged 52, and he is buried in Warwick Cemetery.

Birth notice, IGI Individual records

Joseph Bromwich was a younger brother of Charles Bromwich, and a survivor of the defence.

He was born on 18 November 1856, at Saltisford Rock in St Mary's Parish, Warwick. He was the fifth son of six in the family of nine children born to Joseph Bromwich, a journeyman painter, and his second wife.

Joseph had married Mary Kimberley at Milverton on 18 October 1835, and a son named William was born on 18 October 1835, but Mary died soon after the birth.

On 16 March 1840, in Milverton, Joseph married Maria Keyte (1820-1896) of Lee Wooton in Warwickshire, and they settled in Milverton.

Charles was born in 1840, followed by the birth of three girls between 1841 and 1846, and when they moved to Saltisford Rock, Joseph and three other boys were born between 1852 and 1858. Charles joined the 24th Regiment in 1859, which at that time had its depot at Warley in Birmingham, and by 1861 the family had moved to Hadley's Yard in the parish of St Mary's, Warwick, where a girl were born.

Joseph senior died in the spring of 1875, and Joseph left his job as a porter to join the 28th Infantry Brigade on 29 August 1877. He was described as five feet five and a half inches tall, with a fair complexion, brown eyes and dark brown hair. He had a 33 inch chest measurement, and his religion was Church of England. 1028 Private Bromwich transferred to the 2nd Battalion, 24th Regiment, on 31 January 1878, and was given the new service number 1524.

He received orders for active service in South Africa and sailed to the Cape in February 1878, where he took part in the Cape Frontier War. During the Zulu War he and his brother, Charles, were present at the defence of Rorke's Drift. Joseph was transferred to A company on 29 January 1879, to replace men of that unit who had been wiped out at iSandlwana. For his service he received the South Africa Medal with 1877-8-9 clasp.

He served at Gibraltar, and while serving in India he was granted good conduct pay, gained a fourth class certificate of education, and by 1882 he had earned two good conduct badges. In April 1882 he was admitted to hospital with chronic hepatitis and an abscess on the liver, and in May of that year he was shipped back to Netley hospital where he was found to be suffering from a chronically damaged liver with a liability for it to recur in a hot climate. His condition was judged to be the result of climate and military service, and not to have been aggravated by intemperance or misconduct. The medical board considered the condition to be permanent and would for some 12 months impair Joseph's ability to earn a living. He was declared medically unfit for further service and invalided out of the army on 25 July 1882, with a pension of seven pence a day for 12 months, which was later changed to a permanent pension.

Joseph returned to the home of his widowed mother at 12 Brook Street in Saltisford, Warwick. He met Betsy Fellows Davis of Bilston in Staffordshire, and they married at St Mary's parish church in Warwick on 22 April 1883. Charles' wife Emma was a witness at the wedding. By 1891 Joseph and Betsy had moved to 183 Darwin Street, in the parish of St Albans, Aston, Birmingham, where they established a boot and shoe repairing shop. They eventually moved to 14 Asylum Road in St Stephen's Parish, Selly Oak, Birmingham, where Joseph took employment as a shoe repairer. The 1901 census shows them as having a 15-year-old daughter named Elina, who had been born in Birmingham. They then moved to 5 Duke Street in Bilston, Staffordshire, the place where Betsy had been born, and Joseph continued to work as a boot and shoe repairer.

Betsy died in 1914, and by the end of the year Joseph's health was in decline. He was diagnosed to be suffering with cancer of the tongue. Early in 1916 he was admitted to the workhouse infirmary at Heath Town in Wolverhampton, where he spent his last days awaiting the end. He died on 25 February 1916, aged 60. As the Great War was raging in Europe he was buried with a private family ceremony, in an unmarked grave in Bilston Cemetery in Wolverhampton (section D, plot 55). His South Africa Medal sold at auction in 2016, and from the publicity attention a new headstone memorial was erected at his grave a few months later.

Birth certificate—Warwick FC470770
Death certificate—Willenhall HD021027
Marriage certificate—St Mary's, Warwick Y569854
WO form 457

Thomas Buckley was a survivor of the defence.

He was born on 23 March 1859, probably in Ireland. He attested for the army at Liverpool, on 15 February 1877, and as 1184 Private Buckley he was posted to the 2nd Battalion, 24th Regiment, at Brecon, a week later. He sailed for active service in South Africa in February 1878, and took part in the Cape Frontier War. During the Zulu War he was present at the defence of Rorke's Drift. For his service he received the South Africa Medal with 1877-8-9 clasp.

He made a monthly remittance of one pound to a Mr Buckley, presumably his father, in March 1879. He served at Gibraltar in 1880, and he was promoted corporal in India on 1 August 1883, but he was reduced to private on 6 October 1883. He returned home from Burma on 12 January 1889. He received the Indian General Service Medal with Burma 1885-87 and Burma 1887-89 clasps.

He discharged from the British Army in 1899, when he must have been about 40, and went back to South Africa to fight in the Boer War with the Imperial Light Horse, where he stated that he was 'in the siege of Ladysmith, and he is believed to have served with the Royal Flying Corps in the Great War. Tom presumably lived in straightened circumstances as he resided at the Thomas Lloyd Hostel in Liverpool. He was present at a Brecon reunion in 1926, and at a reunion of the South African War Veterans' Association in Birmingham on 6 March 1931.

In 1924 *The Times* stated that he was 'a London Man', and in 1961, a Captain G. F. Court, late of the Natal Police, stated in the *Natal Witness* that in 1930 he, and a man named Mallleieux, formerly of the Cape Mounted Rifles, had a conversation with 'moustached and bespectacled' Thomas Buckley on a park bench at Brook Green in Hammersmith, West London, which is still a popular public area east of Hammersmith Broadway. He also stated that the man spoke in a 'deep-toned Irish voice.' The conversation centred on two dogs which Buckley said were at the battle of iSandlwana. They were a dalmatian called Flip, which Colonel Degacher of the 24th Regiment had brought out with the regiment, and a greyhound named Kreli, which they adopted after they had found it in South Africa.

The Regimental Association kept in contact with him until 1933, when the letters sent to his last known address were returned; probably because he had moved up to Liverpool. Having lost or sold his medals a set of replacements were issued to him on 5 July 1934; possibly to wear at the Northern Command Tattoo. However, he did not attend, probably due to illness, as he died on New Year's Eve, 31 December 1934, and was buried by the Royal British Legion in an unmarked grave at Anfield Cemetery in Liverpool (section 19 / grave 923).

Natal Witness for 21 January 1961
South Wales Borderers Regimental Journal for March 1932
The Times for 2 February 1934

Thomas Burke was a survivor of the defence.

He was born in Liverpool, on 29 November 1858, the son of Michael and Catherine Burke (formerly Gullery), and was baptised at St Mary's (Roman Catholic) Church, Highfield Street, Liverpool 3, six days later. He was employed as a labourer, and, like Patrick Kears and John Thomas, he had served with the 2nd Royal Lancashire Militia (Duke of Lancaster's Own Rifles), which formed the 3rd and 4th Battalions, King's (Liverpool) Regiment, when he enlisted at Liverpool, on 14 February 1877, aged 18 years and four months. He was five feet four and a half inches tall, with a fair complexion, blue eyes and brown hair. He attested at Brecon on 16 February 1877, and 1220 Private Burke was posted to the 2nd Battalion, 24th Regiment, on 11 May 1877.

He received orders for active service in South Africa, and sailed to the Cape in February 1878. He took part in the Cape Frontier War, and during the Zulu War he was present at the defence of Rorke's Drift. He was granted one penny a day good conduct pay on 6 October, and for his service he received the South Africa Medal with 1877-8-9 clasps. He did not receive the Address from the Mayor of Durban.

He served at Gibraltar in 1880, and in India until 27 May 1883. He reached the rank of corporal on 1 November 1881, and his good conduct pay was increased to two pence a day on 16 February 1883. On returning home he transferred to the army reserve at Warrington, on 21 June 1883, transferring to Brecon on 25 May 1884, and to Liverpool on 15 October 1884. His character was described as very good.

On 19 October 1884, he re-joined as 871 Corporal Burke, in the 1st King's (Liverpool) Regiment. He served in India in 1885, and on 8 July 1885, he was tried for being drunk on duty, being confined for five days and reduced to the ranks. He was also fined one pound and forfeited his good conduct pay. He served in Burma from 1885 to 1887, being promoted lance corporal on 22 March 1886, and having his good conduct pay of two pence a day restored. He returned to India, gaining a 2nd Class Certificate of Education on 14 June 1887, and being promoted corporal on 21 June 1887. He re-engaged at Fyzabad, on 20 August 1888, to complete 21 years' service. He rose to the rank of sergeant on 6 February 1890, and was entitled to three pence a day good conduct pay from 16 June 1890.

He suffered from two forms of venereal disease, for which he received treatment in 1885 and 1886, and he suffered from dyspepsia (severe indigestion) caused by the climate and intemperance (excessive alcohol). He was admitted to hospital several times, the last occasion being on 21 May 1891. He was charged with drunkenness when on duty on 4 June 1891, being sentenced to be reduced to corporal and to forfeit one penny a day good conduct pay. He returned to duty as sergeant on 16 June 1891.

On 27 February 1892, a medical board in Aden declared that he was suffering from debility, and being recommended for a change of climate he returned home on 6 April 1892. For his service he received the Indian General Service Medal with Burma 1885-87 clasp. He was posted to the Regimental Depot at Liverpool on 11 June

1892, but he was admitted to hospital in Warrington on 29 June after suffering an attack of dyspepsia. He became entitled to four pence a day good conduct pay from 16 February 1895. He discharged at his own request on 10 May 1897. His character was described as fair and his habits intemperate. It was recorded in a Liverpool newspaper that a Michael Burke, father of Thomas, died in the workhouse on 16 March 1897, which may have influenced Sergeant Burke's decision to leave the army soon afterwards.

He became the landlord of the Crown Vaults public house on Park Road in Liverpool, and in spite of the nature of his illnesses, he married Honora Lambert, and had three children, making the family home at Wellesley Road in Toxteth, Liverpool 8. Robert was born in 1903, but he died aged only nine months, and Thomas Aloysius, who was born in 1906, and died aged only 39.

Thomas Burke died on 23 April 1925, and he was buried in Ford Roman Catholic Cemetery at Litherland in Liverpool, where his two sons are buried with him, along with his wife, who died in 1950, beneath an impressive stone obelisk topped by a wheel of eternity. His age inscribed on the monument is 64, but this does not tally with his enlistment papers, or some other sources, and he was probably in his sixty-seventh year. He may have lied about his age because his wife was much younger than him. A re-dedication service was held at his graveside in 2002, to honour his name and the part he played in the heroic defence of Rorke's Drift.

James Bushe was wounded in action during the defence.

He was born at St John's Parish in Dublin, in about 1852, and had been employed as a tailor when he enlisted for the 24th Regiment in Dublin on 14 September 1870. He was just over five feet five inches tall, with a fresh complexion, grey eyes and black hair. His religion was Church of England. As 2350 Private Bushe he was posted to the 2nd Battalion, and joined the unit at Chatham on 28 September 1870.

His army life began well, and after serving in India for two years he was promoted to corporal on 20 November 1875, gaining a third class certificate of education, and he was granted two pence a day good conduct pay from 15 September 1876. However, he was confined for drunkenness on 13 May 1877, tried by court martial four days later, and sentenced to be reduced to private and to forfeit a penny a day of his good conduct pay. He was appointed lance corporal on 20 September 1877, but a month later he reverted to private again. He forfeited his good conduct pay, but it was restored on the same day.

He received orders for active service in South Africa, and sailed to the Cape with the regiment in February 1878. He took part in the Cape Frontier War, and during the Zulu War he was wounded at the defence of Rorke's Drift. Lieutenant Chard stated:

> I was glad to seize an opportunity to wash my face in a muddy puddle, in company with Private Bush 24th, whose face was covered with blood from a wound on the nose caused by a bullet which had passed through and killed Private Cole 24th. With the politeness of a soldier, he lent me his towel, or, rather, a very dirty half of one, before using it himself, and I was very glad to accept it.

James was promoted to lance corporal soon after the defence, and to corporal on 28 November 1879. For his service he received the South Africa Medal with 1877-8-9 clasp.

He served at Gibraltar in 1880, and having been appointed lance sergeant on 24 November 1880, he re-engaged to complete 21 years' service at Secunderabad in India in the following month. His service continued in the South Wales Borderers with the new regimental number 2360, and he reverted to private at his own request on 30 October 1881. He was granted three pence a day good conduct pay on 16 September 1882. He served in Burma, during which time he reached the rank of corporal again on 27 April 1887, being granted a fourth good conduct badge and he achieved a second class certificate of education.

Having returned home, he discharged from the army as time-served on 10 October 1891. His character and conduct were described as good, and his habits were regular. He received the India General Service Medal with Burma 1887-9 clasp. His South Africa Medal was sold at auction in 2010.

Louis Alexander Byrne was killed in action during the defence.

He was born in Ireland in about 1857, the seventh child of

Richard and Maria Byrne, who moved to Cardiff when Richard became a prominent shipowner, introducing the first steamship to that port. Louis and his elder brother, Alfred, had travelled to South Africa, and Louis was employed in a government appointment when the Zulu War began. The Commissary General was given authority to employ local men who knew the country and could be quickly trained in commissary work, and being accepted as an assistant storekeeper, Louis had ridden up to the border with James Dalton in torrential rain on New Year's Day, 1879. He was killed in action during the defence of Rorke's Drift, and although his body was for some reason buried outside the little cemetery, his name is inscribed on the monument.

Lieutenant Chard said that Byrne: 'was greatly instrumental in forming the entrenchment of biscuit boxes, which was in all probability the means of our successful defence.' In his report he stated: 'Mr Byrne, who had behaved with great coolness and gallantry, was killed instantaneously by a bullet through the head, just after he had given a drink of water to a wounded man of the NNC (Corporal Scammel).' The *Illustrated London News* for 29 March 1879 reports of him 'behaving nobly.'

Illustrated London News for 29 March 1879

C

William Henry Camp was a survivor of the defence.

He was born at Camberwell in Surrey, in about 1854. He left his job as a clerk to enter 25 Brigade at Liverpool on 8 February 1877, and as 1181 Private Camp he was posted to the 2nd Battalion, 24th Regiment at Brecon. He was described as being just over five feet eight inches tall, with a sallow complexion, hazel eyes and dark brown hair. He gained a second class certificate of education and was granted a penny a day good conduct pay.

He received orders for active service in South Africa, and sailed to the Cape on 2 February 1878. He took part in the Ninth Cape Frontier War, 1878, and in the Zulu War, being present at the defence of Rorke's Drift. For his service he received the South Africa

Medal with 1877-8-9 clasp. A metal bedcard with his name and number on it was picked up from the iSandlwana battlefield in 1884.

He served at Gibraltar in 1880, and he was admitted to hospital at Secunderabad in India on 17 September 1880, suffering with rheumatism, dyspepsia and melancholia. He returned to England, and a medical examination at Netley on 25 November 1881, found that he was suffering from melancholia caused by a hereditary predisposition and aggravated by masturbation. The condition was considered to be of a permanent nature rendering him unable to contribute to his own support. He was declared insane and was discharged on 27 December 1881, as unfit for further service. His character was described as very good, and he was in possession of one good conduct badge. An Injury Assessment Board meeting held at the Royal Hospital in Chelsea on 27 February 1882 confirmed all the previous findings and William was awarded a pension of 17 pence a day for 15 months. His intended place of residence was the Union Workhouse at Camberwell.

He was admitted to Brookwood Asylum on 22 February 1883, with melancholia caused by sunstroke; and he is recorded on the 1891 census as still being at Brookwood. Described as 'weakly and thin' he was discharged with no improvement on 30 September 1893, and was admitted to the London County Asylum at Claybury.

A William Henry Camp died at the Leavesden Mental Hospital at Watford in Hertfordshire during the April/May/June quarter of 1900, being about the right age, and his body was unclaimed. It is reasonable to suggest that he was buried in the old cemetery at Leavesden Asylum, which was used until about 1906. However, the records for the hospital were stored in damp conditions at the London Metropolitan Archives and are not viewable to date.

John Cantwell was awarded the Distinguished Conduct Medal for gallantry during the defence.

He was born in May 1845, at St James's parish in Dublin, Ireland, the son of John Cantwell. He was employed as a servant before enlisting into the 9th (East Norfolk) Regiment, on 6 November 1868, at the age of 23 years and six months. 1740 Private Cantwell was described as being five feet-eight inches tall, with a fresh complexion, hazel eyes and light-brown hair, and he had: 'marks of cupping over his left scapula.' He gave his next-of-kin as his sister, Mary, of Melbourne, Australia.

He transferred to the Royal Regiment of Artillery with the regimental number 2076 on 1 April 1872, serving at home until 5 July 1872, when he sailed to the island of St Helena in the South Atlantic Ocean. He gained a fourth class certificate of education on 7 July 1875, and on 16 August 1876, he gained leave to marry Caroline Margaret Dickinson, at the Ladder Hill Garrison in Jamestown, St Helena. His new wife was a 22-year-old seamstress, and they had two children. He returned home on 14 September 1876, and joined N Battery, 5th Brigade, as 23182 Gunner Cantwell, on 1 July 1877. He passed a wheelers course on 4 January 1878.

The unit received orders for active service in South Africa and embarked on the troopship *Dublin Castle* on 9 January 1878. Three of his fellow Rorke's Drift defenders travelled with him; Bombardier Thomas Lewis, and Gunners Abraham Evans and Arthur Howard. They arrived at the port of East London, and marched to King Williamstown, arriving there on 11 February 1878, to find that much of the heavy baggage transported by sea had been broken into. From there they moved to various places in the colony, where they saw active service in the Ninth Cape Frontier War.

He was promoted bombardier wheeler on 29 July 1878. Between July and September the Battery marched from the Transkei to Greytown, pausing for a while at Kokstad. By 3 September 1878, they had moved to Natal, and on 2 November 1878, the Battery was given orders to move to Greytown. They arrived at Helpmekaar in December 1878, where they received the order to move up to the Zululand border at Rorke's Drift.

John had reverted back to gunner on 21 January 1879, and he is believed to have been the artillery store man at Rorke's Drift, probably defending the store building during the battle.

He returned to St Helena from South Africa on 15 May 1879, and arrived at the general depot at Woolwich on 4 July that year; which was the day that British troops defeated the Zulu Army at Ulundi and brought the conflict to a close.

On 11 February 1880, he was recommended to receive the Silver Medal for distinguished conduct in the field for his bravery during the defence, and he was presented with the medal by Queen Victoria in the corridor at Windsor Castle on 8 March 1880. He also received the South Africa Medal with 1877-78-79 clasp.

His next postings were to Malta from 15 December 1880 until 2 October 1884, and to India from 3 October 1884 until 18 January 1886. As 3460 Gunner Cantwell, he served with the 10th Brigade, Royal Artillery, and as 3760 Gunner Cantwell, he served with the 9th Brigade. He served at home from 19 January 1886 until 19 July 1887, when he was discharged from the Woolwich depot: 'In consequence of his having been found medically unfit for further service', his character being described as 'very good'.

His intended place of residence was 2 Phillipa Street in Woolwich, and within a month he was appointed by the Secretary of State for War to join the Civil Service, being employed in the engineering department of the Royal Gunpowder Factory at Waltham Abbey, where former-General Noble of the Royal Artillery was the superintendent. He was employed there for over five years.

However, his wife's health began to fail and he was recommended to go to South Africa, so he resigned and sailed to the Cape on 5 November 1892, where he lived at 8 Picciones Buildings in Loop Street, Durban. He was employed as a prison officer at the Central Prison in Addington, Durban, from 6 January 1893 until 6 May 1893, on a salary of ten pounds a month, until Sir Charles Mitchell appointed him warder at the Central Prison in Pietermaritzburg. He had applied for a transfer back to Durban, when, on 10 August 1898, he was assaulted by one of the inmates, a 'lifer' named A. Dubois, which left him suffering with an enlarged spleen, from which he never fully recovered. Having had his pension commuted on 12 December 1895, and no further payments being made to him, he is known to have greatly annoyed his employers for his constant requests for an increase in his pension, which possibly influenced their punishment of Dubois, who received only five days in solitary confinement on half-rations. He then left the prison service and took employment as a lavatory cleaner, but he considered the hours too long, and by 24 March 1900, he had ceased this type of work.

John Cantwell was living at 2nd Avenue in Greyville, Durban, when he was admitted to the Addington Hospital in Durban. He died there on 14 August 1900, aged 55 (the death certificate states his age as 53). Cause of death was 'hypertrophy of the spleen and valvular cease of the heart.' His daughter, Mrs J. F. Webb, is mentioned on the death certificate, and his effects amounted to: 'furniture and one old suit.' He was buried at the Roman Catholic Churchyard in Durban.

In 1935, through the Durham Light Infantry Comrades Association, Caroline Cantwell, then aged about 80, presented copies of a 'Roll of Defenders' compiled by Lieutenant Chard after the defence, to the South Wales Borderers Museum at Brecon. A forensic handwriting expert has since suggested that the roll may have actually been compiled by John Cantwell. The whereabouts of his Distinguished Conduct Medal and his South Africa campaign medal are not known, but his Long Service, Good Conduct Medal was sold to a private collector at auction in 2002.

Death certificate (Durban)
Natal Mercury for 15 August 1900
Service records (WO97)
The Times for 8 March 1880
War Office papers and muster rolls for N Battery (WO10/ 2530 and WO16/282, 283, 287 and 291)
Zululand Times for 27 December 1934

John Rouse Merriott Chard was awarded the Victoria Cross for valour as the commanding officer at Rorke's Drift.

He was born at Boxhill House in the Plymouth district of Pennycross, on 21 December 1847. The area was originally known as Weston Peverell, but most locals referred to it as Pennycross by the end of the nineteenth century. The house in which he was born was on what is now known as Honicknowle Lane, in the area taken over by the Plymouth YMCA building. There is a plaque commemorating his birthplace high up on the wall of the building just left of the entrance. He came from a large family, being the middle son of three in the family of eight children to Doctor William Wheaton Chard, and his wife Jane.

At the time of the 1841 census they and their first child, Charlotte, were living with Jane's parents at Stoke Climsland in Cornwall. The 1851 census records the family as living at Plympton St Mary in Yealhampton, Devon, and gives John's place of birth as Weston Peverell. The 1861 census gives much the same information except his place of birth as Pennycross, and he was now the oldest of six children still at home.

John was educated at the Plymouth New Grammar School, and attended the Royal Military Academy at Woolwich, where he was remembered for always being late for breakfast. He passed-out in 1868, and was commissioned as lieutenant in the Corps of Royal Engineers on 15 July 1868. After two years at Chatham he sailed to Bermuda in October 1870, being employed in the building of fortifications at the Hamilton Dockyard. His father died in 1873, and he returned to England in January 1874. In the following month he was posted to Malta, where he was again employed in the construction of defences. He returned to England in April 1876, and after a short stay at Chatham, he was appointed to the Western District at Exeter.

As the situation in South Africa worsened he was ordered to report to Aldershot to join the 5th Company, Corps of Royal Engineers for active service at the Cape. The unit set sail from Gravesend on 2 December 1878, arriving at Durban on 5 January 1879. His vaccination injection had become inflamed and his right shoulder was very sore, but British troops were already assembling on the Natal-Zululand border, so with no time to recover he was ordered to take a small party of engineers to join the 3rd Column at Rorke's Drift. For almost the entire journey the tracks were bad, and by the time he arrived at his destination on 19 January the column had already invaded enemy territory. One of the ponts which was used to ferry the troops across the Buffalo River had broken down, so Chard and his men set-up camp on the Natal bank to work on repairing it.

The citation for the award of Victoria Cross to Lieutenant John Chard published in the *London Gazette* of 2 May 1879, states:

> The Lieutenant-General commanding the troops reports that, had it not been for the fine example and excellent behaviour of these two Officers under the most trying circumstances, the defence of Rorke's Drift post would not have been conducted with that intelligence and tenacity which so essentially characterised it. The Lieutenant-General adds that its success must, in a great degree, be attributable to the two young Officers who exercised the Chief Command on the occasion in question.

A Colonial trooper stated: 'The men spoke highly of Chard', and his cool leadership proved invaluable that day. He was appointed captain and brevet major dated from the 23 January 1879, thus becoming the first man in history to move from a lieutenancy to a majority in the army in a single day. He and his fellow defenders received the thanks of the Government.

Major Chard remained at Rorke's Drift to supervise the burial of hundreds of dead Zulus in mass graves, and to work on a more permanent stone perimeter. Suffering the hardships of atrocious conditions, he was struck down with fever, and on 17 February he was taken by ambulance wagon to Ladysmith, where he was looked after by a Doctor Park and his wife. After showing signs of improvement he suffered a relapse, and just after the announcement of his Victoria Cross award it was reported in local newspapers that he had died. However, he was nursed back to health, and was able to report back to duty in time for the re-invasion of Zululand.

He joined Colonel Wood's column at Khambula to inspect the fortifications, and he was involved in all the engineering activities during the Flying Column's advance on the Zulu capital at Ulundi. His unit followed up Colonel Buller's scouting activities, building bridges and repairing roads. While the Second Division was halted at Fort Newdigate to await supplies, Chard was out on picquet duty when he was caught up in a false alarm which caused the British to open fire. Several men were wounded and some horses were killed, and he and his men spent an uncomfortable time sheltering in a muddy trench with British bullets whizzing about above them. He survived the ordeal, and he was in the British square at Ulundi on 4 July 1879, to witness the final crushing defeat of the Zulu Army. He was decorated by General, Sir Garnet Wolseley during a parade of the troops at St Paul's Camp in Zululand, on 16 July 1879. For his service at the Cape he also received the South Africa Medal with 1879 clasp.

Unfortunately, the awards caused bad feeling among his superior officers, who recorded detrimental remarks towards him. However, the expressions of great admiration for John Chard shown by the people of Devon and Somerset for the rest of his life, outshone any jealous criticisms he had to suffer.

Major Chard arrived at Spithead aboard the *Eagle* on 2 October 1879, where the Duke of Cambridge welcomed him and delivered a message from Queen Victoria inviting him to an audience with her at Balmoral Castle. He was invited to a second audience with the Queen on 21 February 1880, when he presented the sovereign with a more detailed account of the action at Rorke's Drift than his official version. He was received at Plymouth as a local hero, being presented with a gold chronometer and a superb sword of honour which had been specially manufactured and richly carved. He was presented with an illuminated address by freemasons in Exeter, and he was guest of honour at dinner receptions in Taunton, and at the Wanderers Club in Chatham. He was held in the highest regard in the West Country for the rest of his life. Queen Victoria was appreciative of his unassuming manner and the modest way in which he told of the events at Rorke's Drift, and it was said at the time when he submitted his official report, which was modest and to the point, that 'He has spoken of everybody but himself.'

In January 1880 he began service at Devonport, and the 1881 census records him as living with his mother and sister Margaret at 19 Portland Villas, in the district of Charles the Martyr in Plymouth.

He went to Cyprus in December 1881, where he was appointed regimental major on 17 July 1886, and during which time his mother died in 1885. He returned home in March 1887. He was posted to Fulwood Barracks in Preston in May 1887. The 1891 census records that he lived in a house close to the barracks at 80 Victoria Road in Fulwood (which still exists), and had a 25-year-old Cypriot servant, named George Theodoulie, working for him.

He remained in Preston until being posted to Singapore on 14 December 1892, where he was Commanding Royal Engineer for three years, and was promoted lieutenant colonel on 18 January 1893. On his return to Britain in January 1896, he took up his final post as Commanding Royal Engineer at the Perth District. In May that year he presented Queen Victoria with Japanese mementoes he had brought back from the East especially for her. He was promoted to colonel on 8 January 1897.

John Chard never married, but he is said to have had a relationship with a woman called Emily Rowe, who bore a daughter to him at Exeter, believed to have been on 16 February 1882, who was named Violet Mary. Emily Rowe, married Lawson Durant, and had a second daughter, named Irene, born on 6 January 1884. Emily Durant died in 1939. Violet's birth would have been kept secret because of the stigma of illegitimacy at the time, and because of Chard's fame and association with the Queen. He left an annuity to Emily and Violet for the duration of her lifetime, and the family have preserved two letters written by Chard and addressed to Emily telling her about his trip to Japan. At his funeral it was recorded that an anonymous wreath bearing the inscription 'That day he did his duty' took pride of place beside a tribute from Queen Victoria on the coffin. It is interesting to wonder who might have sent this wreath?

While in Scotland he was diagnosed to have cancer of the mouth. In November 1896, he was too ill to visit Balmoral at the request of Queen Victoria, and he underwent an operation in Edinburgh. In March 1897 surgeons had to remove his tongue. He was still able to converse quite well, but his condition became critical, and in August 1897 doctors diagnosed that the cancer was terminal. He was placed on sick leave from 8 August 1897. He spent the last days of his life with his brother in the rectory at Hatch Beauchamp, where many friends, including Queen Victoria, expressed their concern about his condition. On 11 July 1897, he had received the Diamond Jubilee Medal and a book containing a signed portrait of his sovereign.

After suffering terrible distress towards the end, he died peacefully in his sleep at Hatch Beauchamp Rectory on 1 November 1897, aged 50. He was buried in the churchyard at Hatch Beauchamp, where a rose-coloured marble cross headstone marks the spot. Queen Victoria sent a wreath bearing an inscription written in her own hand, 'A mark of admiration and regard for a brave soldier from his sovereign.' There was a wreath from Colonel Bourne, and the officers of the South Wales Borderers, and there were tributes from all over the world. For many years the Queen's wreath lay beneath a memorial window which was placed in Hatch Beauchamp Church.

There is a bust of him, and he is named on the 'For Valour' board at the Royal Engineers Museum in Chatham, where there is an officer's sword and a water bottle, and a Zulu shield, assegai and knobkerrie, taken by Chard at Ulundi. There is a plaque at the YMCA Sports Centre at Pennycross in Plymouth; the Territorial Army Centre in Swansea has a 'John Chard VC House'; and Chard Street in Nottingham and Chard Road in Plymouth were named after him.

A memorial plaque has been placed in Jesus Chapel at Rochester Cathedral, there is a bronze bust of him in Taunton Shire Hall, and a brass plaque mounted on wood memorial on the south wall of St

Michael's Church in Ottery states:

> In loving memory of the three sons of William Wheaton CHARD, of Pathe House, Somerset , and Mount Tamar, Devon: Colonel William Wheaton Chard; he served for 30 years abroad in the Royal Fusiliers and commanded the 1st Batt: in Egypt and in India, Born 24 Dec 1841, died 12th Sept 1890, buried at St Budeaux, Devon. Colonel John Rouse Merriott Chard, V.C., R.E. The hero of Rorke's Drift; born 21st Dec 1847, died 1st Nov. 1897, buried at Hatch Beauchamp. The Rev Charles Edward Chard, B.A. Rector of Hatch Beauchamp, Somerset, for 25 years; born 4th Dec 1856, died 12th Sept 1910, buried at Hatch Beauchamp.

The John Chard-Dekarasie Medal in silver was awarded to all ranks of the South African Union Defence Forces from 1952 to 2003 for 20 years long and efficient service, with the John Chard-Medalje in bronze being awarded for 12 years of service.

The location of Chard's Victoria Cross had remained a mystery for many years, until 1972, when, what was described as his South Africa Medal and a 'cast copy' of his VC was offered for auction in London. Sir Stanley Baker, who had portrayed Chard in the film *Zulu!*, purchased the set for £2,700. It was offered auction again in 1996, and one of the most extraordinary stories in the history of the medal began to unfold.

Prompted by the mystery surrounding the whereabouts of the original Victoria Cross, the auctioneers decided to send it to the Royal Armouries at Leeds to be examined. The test revealed it to be identical to all authentic VCs cast from the cascobels of cannon captured by British forces in the East, and consequently proved to be the original medal and not a copy at all.

The Victoria Cross awarded to John Chard is now part of Lord Ashcroft's collection.

Bancroft, James W., *The Rorke's Drift Commanders: Gonville Bromhead and John Chard*, 2022
Birth Certificate (Plymouth)
Cartlidge, Mrs Jill: Private letters concerning her ancestor John Chard dated 2 October 1999 and 26 January 2000

Civil and Military Gazette of Lahore for 29 December 1897
Death certificate (Somerset)
Devon Archives and Local Studies Service
Devon and Somerset census 1841 to 1891
Dunning, Robert: *A History of the County of Somerset*, 2004
Freemasonry, Museum of
Guide to the Church of St Michael in Othery
Natal Colonist for 17 May 1879 and 22 May 1879
Plymouth Historical Society
Plymouth and West Devon Record Office
Plymouth Register Office
Singapore Free Press for 25 March 1893; 18 September 1894; 10 November 1897
Singapore Mid-Day Herald for 18 November 1897
Somerset County Gazette for 6 November 1879
Somerset Archives and Local Studies
St Budeaux Church in Plymouth—monumental inscriptions
St Michael's Church in Othery—monumental inscriptions
St Peter and St Paul Church in North Curry—monumental inscriptions
Tiverton Gazette and East Devon Herald for 7 October 1879
WO32/7737—Lieutenant Chard's report on Rorke's Drift

Thomas Chester was a survivor of the defence.

He was born at Knowle near Warwick, on 3 August 1851, and he was christened in Knowle on 7 December 1851. He was the first child of Thomas Chester and his wife, Charlotte (formerly Chilwell), and his father was living at the Leek Wooton Vicarage near Warwick, where he worked as a groom and coachman. In 1882 they moved to the village of Catthorpe in Leicestershire, the place of Thomas senior's birth, where Charlotte gave birth to three children. The family then moved to 14 Hermitage Street in Cheltenham, where four more children were born, including twin boys. By 1871 they had moved to 2 Harmony Cottages, Leckhampton, Gloucestershire, and Thomas had taken lodgings at 9, Shottery, Old Stratford, and was earning a living as a gardener.

Thomas enlisted for the army at Bow Street Police Courts on 20 February 1877, being described as five feet ten and a quarter inches tall, with a fair complexion, blue eyes and brown hair, and he had good muscular development. He gave his next-of-kin as T. Chester (father), c/o The Conservative Club, Albion Hill, Cheltenham, Gloucester. His religion was stated as Church of England. As 1241 Private Chester he was posted to the 2nd Battalion, 24th Regiment at Brecon, where he attained a fourth class certificate of education.

He received orders for active service in South Africa and sailed to the Cape in February 1878, taking part in the Cape Frontier War, and during the Zulu War he was present at the defence of Rorke's Drift. For his service he received the South Africa Medal with 1877-8-9 clasp.

He served at Gibraltar in 1880, and on 8 May 1881 he was hospitalised at Secunderabad in India, suffering with 'glands', which was the only occasion on which Thomas suffered any kind of illness. He was awarded two pence a day good conduct pay on 20 February 1883. He left India on 1 May 1883 aboard the SS Armenia with the rest of the time served men, and returned to England, where, on 21 June he was discharged to the first class reserve, Bristol District, 28th Gloucestershire Regiment. His conduct on discharge was described as very good and temperate.

He gave his intended place of residence as St Mark's in Cheltenham, and he found accommodation at 16 Grosvenor Terrace, a lodging house in Cheltenham, gaining employment as a porter. He lived next door to a machinist named Ellen Cave (at number 18), and they became a couple and married at All Saints Church in Cheltenham, on 9 December 1883. On 14 May 1884, just five months after the wedding, Thomas was transferred out of the Gloucestershire area at his own request and moved to the Brecon district reserves (South Wales Borderers), leaving Ellen alone and pregnant at 2 Sherborne Place in Cheltenham, and it would appear that the couple separated. Ellen died of phthisis (pulmonary tuberculosis) in the Union Workhouse at Cheltenham on 17 November 1888.

Thomas was discharged from the first class reserve in Brecon on 19 February 1889, having served a total of six years with the colours, and six years with the reserve. He moved to 10 Wood Street in Tylorstown-with-Ferndale, Ystradyfodwg, Glamorgan, where he took lodgings and obtained employment as a coal trimmer underground at the no. 5 pit at the Ferndale Colliery. By 1901 he was living at 7 Long

Row in Ystradyfodwg.

Tragically, Thomas was killed in a pit accident at Ferndale on 12 February 1908, and an inquest found that:

> Thomas Chester was killed on 12 February 1908. He was a coal trimmer aged 55. Deceased was breaking up a lump of coal which had fallen on the empty road leading to No. 1 pit screens, when he 'was knocked down by a wagon which was being lowered towards the screens. Deceased had stood to one side to allow two wagons to pass, but was not aware that others were to follow.

Thomas was buried at St Gwynnos Anglican Churchyard at Llanwonno, attended by friends, neighbours and fellow miners. His grave remains unmarked. His South Africa Medal was donated to the Regimental Museum at Brecon by a relative.

Birth certificate–Knowle, Solihull, Warwick–CN372303
Marriage certificate–All Saints, Cheltenham
Wife's death certificate–Cheltenham HD098792
Death certificate–Llanwono, Pontypridd WHD003282

James Chick had been a patient in the hospital and was killed in action.

He may have been a native of Northampton. He enlisted for 25 Brigade on 3 March 1877, attested on 8 March 1877, and as 1335 Private Chick he was posted to D Company, 2nd Battalion, 24th Regiment, and he was at the Brecon depot from 3 March to 11 May 1877. He acted as assistant schoolmaster during 1877. He received orders for active service in South Africa and sailed to the Cape with his battalion in February 1878. He took part in the Cape Frontier War, and during the Zulu War he was killed in action as a defender of Rorke's Drift. He had been a patient in the hospital and was killed at the barricades by a Zulu slug. He was buried in the cemetery at Rorke's Drift and his name is inscribed on the monument. For his service he was entitled to receive the South Africa Medal with 1877-8-9 clasp. There is no trace of a claim for his effects.

WO16-1579

Thomas Clayton was a survivor of the defence but not of the Zulu War.

He was born on 16 May 1855, at Draper's Lane in Leominster, the first child of ten born to Thomas Clayton, a railway worker, and his wife, Emily (formerly Davenport). Thomas and his sister Sarah were baptised together on 26 February 1860. By 1861 they had moved to the railway house at Kingsland Crossing, where Emily became the gate keeper for the railway crossing, and Thomas senior was working as a railway plate-layer. The family moved into the village of Kingsland, and Thomas junior obtained lodgings at 'Thornlands' in Kingsland, gaining employment as a general servant.

Thomas enlisted into the Monmouthshire Militia in 1873, and then into the regular army via the Militia Returns for 8 February 1876. As 735 Private Clayton he was posted to the 2nd Battalion, 24th Regiment, stationed in Dover. He received orders for active service in South Africa and sailed to the Cape with his unit in February 1878. He took part in the Cape Frontier War, and during the Zulu War he was present at the defence of Rorke's Drift.

Sadly, Private Clayton was amongst the number of men afflicted by various ailments caused by bad conditions and he was transferred to the hospital at Helpmekaar, where he died on 5 April 1879, just one month from his 24th birthday. He was buried in the Military Cemetery at Helpmekaar, the cause of death being given as fever. His name appeared on the casualty lists published in the *London Gazette* on 23 May 1879.

Robert Edward Cole was a survivor of the defence.

He was born on 28 November 1858, at Brompton Barracks in Chatham, Kent, where his father George Cole was serving with the 24th Regiment. His mother was Eliza (formerly Roche). Although the register of births was first introduced in 1837, it did not become compulsory until 1871. When Eliza and George registered their youngest son in 1858, they chose to do so with the regiment and not the civil authorities. His birth certificate is therefore held by the General Register Office in their 'foreign births' section, even though

Robert was born in England. His father was medically discharged from the army in 1864, having served his country for most of his adult life. George and his family moved into a temporary home at 12 Nova Scotia Street, Birmingham, gaining employment as a day labourer, and by 1871 they had moved to their permanent home at 7 Lench Street in Aston, Birmingham. Robert had two siblings and all three children obtained employment with the British Small Arms Company (BSA) in Aston.

Robert attested for the army on 29 October 1877, and as 1459 Private R. Cole he was posted to F Company, 2nd Battalion of his father's old unit, the 24th Regiment, at Brecon. He was five feet six inches tall, with grey eyes and brown hair. His religion was Church of England, his trade a gun maker, and he gave his next-of-kin as his brother, George Cole, of 7 Poplar Place in Sherbourne Road, Birmingham.

He was twice hospitalised in Chatham and received treatment for scabies and 'glands', just prior to receiving orders for active service in South Africa, and he sailed to the Cape in February 1878, taking part in the Cape Frontier War. Robert did not accompany the rest of the men of F company when they invaded Zululand, as he was in hospital suffering from typhoid fever. During the defence he had to be assisted from the hospital, where Michael McMahon saw him having difficulty in reaching the safety of the inner perimeter and ran to his aid, and Private Hitch also assisted in his escape by giving covering fire. For his service he received the South Africa Medal with 1877-8-9 clasp.

He was again hospitalised in Natal for 40 days, being treated for syphilis. He served at Gibraltar in 1880, and in India, where he was admitted to hospital on numerous occasions suffering with a variety of ailments. However, he had put his time to good use by gaining a fourth class certificate of education, and he received one penny a day good conduct pay from 19 June 1882. He arrived back in England on 1 December 1883, and was discharged to the First Class Army Reserve at Brecon. He held one good conduct badge and his character was described as 'good' and his habits were 'temperate'. He was finally discharged in 1893.

He returned to work at BSA, and on 23 August 1884, he married 18 year old Elizabeth Gibelin, at St Bartholomew's Church, and they lived at number 2 court, Lower Tower Street, Birmingham. They had five children; Eliza was born in 1886, Gertrude was born in 1888, Robert was born in 1890 (died aged two), Elizabeth was born in 1893 and Edith was born in 1896. They moved to 7 Floodgate Street, Birmingham, but they moved back to their home area and lived at 11 Court, 3 Lower Tower Street, and Robert became a licensed hawker of fruit and vegetables.

Robert died at his home on 19 August 1898, aged 40, the cause of death being given as 'malignant disease of the lungs, and asthenia', the latter being the same condition as had been suffered by his father. He was buried in an unmarked public grave at Witton Cemetery in Aston, Birmingham (section 164, grave 54737), where fellow defender Samuel Parry was buried at around the same time, and Joseph Windridge was laid to rest four years later. In 2015, memorials to Robert, Sam and Joseph were dedicated at the cemetery.

Kent Life for November 2008–*Local Hero: From Chatham to Fighting Zulus*

Thomas Cole was killed in action during the defence.

He was born in about 1855. He enlisted at Monmouth on 23 March 1876, and as 801 Private Cole he was posted to the 2nd Battalion, 24th Regiment, at Brecon on 20 June 1876. With such a surname it was inevitable that he would be given the nickname 'Old King Cole' by the men of B Company. He received orders for active service in South Africa and sailed to the Cape with the battalion in February 1878. He took part in the Ninth Cape Frontier War, and during the Zulu War he was killed in action at Rorke's Drift, when a Zulu slug went through his head.

He was one of six men who were ordered to barricade themselves in the hospital to defend the patients as best they could. Private Hook stated:

I had charge with a man that we called Old King Cole of a small room with only one patient in it. Cole kept with me for some time after the fight began, then he said he was not going to stay. He went outside and was instantly killed by the Zulus.

Lieutenant Chard stated:

I was glad to seize an opportunity to wash my face in a muddy puddle, in company with Private Bush 24th, whose face was covered with blood from a wound on the nose caused by a bullet which had passed through and killed Private Cole 24th.

Thomas was buried in the cemetery at Rorke's Drift and his name is inscribed on the monument. He was entitled to the South Africa Medal with 1877-8-9 clasp, but there is no record of a claim for his effects.

Thomas Collins was a survivor of the defence.

He was born on 13 September 1861, at Pelcomb in Camrose, near Haverfordwest, Pembrokeshire, and he was christened in that town on 15 January 1862. He was the seventh child of eight born to Thomas Collins, a farm labourer, and his wife, Dorothy (formerly Lewis), who had married on 19 February 1843, in the parish church of St Martin, Haverfordwest. Thomas junior was already working as a farm labourer at the age of 12, and when the family moved to the Tenby area, he remained in Haverfordwest, where he lived in St Martins. His three eldest siblings had died young, his mother died of gastritis at Broom Lane in Begelly, Pembroke, on 24 May 1873, and just over a year later his father died suddenly at the same address on 8 July 1874.

Thomas drifted across to Monmouthshire, where he enlisted in the Monmouthshire Militia, before joining the regular army on 22 May 1877. He was aged 15 years and eight months, but his age on enlistment was stated to be 'apparently 22.' He was described as five feet six-and-a-half inches tall, with grey eyes and light-brown hair. He had a chest measurement of 38 inches, and he had a wart on his back. His religion was Church of England. As 1396 Private Collins he was posted to the 2nd Battalion, 24th Regiment, at Brecon, joining the regiment at Chatham.

He received orders for active service in South Africa, and sailed to the Cape in February 1878. He took part in the Cape Frontier War, and at the age of 17 he was possibly the youngest man to take part in the defence of Rorke's Drift. For his service he received the South Africa Medal with 1877-8-9 clasp.

While serving at Gibraltar on 8 June 1880, he was confined and charged with being drunk on picquet duty, and sentenced to 42 days imprisonment with hard labour. In the meantime most of his surviving siblings moved to Nebraska in the United States. He then saw service in India, and extended his service to 12 years on 27 August 1882. In 1884 he served at Madras, then Wellington, then back to Madras.

He re-engaged at Rhaniket in Bengal, on 19 August 1889, for such term as would complete 21 years' service. Having twice been admitted to hospital with rheumatism the medical officer recommended a change of climate, and Thomas was shipped back to England to be admitted to Netley hospital on 22 April 1891. A medical board found him to be suffering from severe rheumatism attributable to climate, and he was invalided out of the army on 16 June 1891. He gave his intended place of residence as: 'c/o, the Star Inn, Pontypool.' He settled in Newport, where he lived at 19 Arlington Street, and obtained work as a labourer.

The Newport Borough Asylum (now St Cadoc's Hospital) opened in 1906, and Thomas's health had deteriorated so much that he was one of the first patients to be admitted to the Asylum, where he remained for the rest of his life. He died on 17 April 1908, aged 47, the cause of death being recorded as phthisis pulmonalis. There was an obvious hereditary weakness in the constitution of his family because it was the same illness which had struck down two of his siblings. He was buried in the cemetery within the grounds of the Asylum.

Parent's marriage certificate–St Martins, Haverfordwest TWA789731
Birth certificate–Haverfordwest CN002575
Mother's death certificate–Begelly, Pembroke WHD001778
Father's death certificate–Begelly WHD001779
Death certificate–Caerleon, Newport WHD002662

John Connolly was a survivor of the defence.

He stated that he was born at Castletown Berehaven (now Castletownbere) in Munster, County Cork, Ireland, in 1859, the son of a fisherman named John Connolly, although his service papers record that he was born at Trevethin in Pontypool, Monmouthshire.

He had served with the Monmouthshire Militia when he enlisted on 24 November 1876, at Newport, where he had been working as a labourer and as 906 Private Connolly he was posted to G Company, 2nd Battalion, 24th Regiment. He was five feet six and a half inches tall, with a fresh complexion, blue eyes and light-brown hair. He had a cross tattooed on his left forearm, and his religion was Roman Catholic. He gained a fourth class certificate of education.

He received orders for active service in South Africa and sailed to the Cape with the battalion in February 1878, taking part in the Cape Frontier War. He was sentenced to 168 hours imprisonment with hard labour on 27 August 1878. During the Zulu War he was present at the defence of Rorke's Drift. He stated:

Having been injured in the left leg at the knee when [he slipped as he was] loading a wagon at the Tugela River [on 5 January 1879] I was in the hospital at Rorke's Drift under treatment and in bed...

Henry Hook reported:

All this time Williams was getting the sick through the hole into the next room, all except one, a soldier of the 24th named Conley [Connolly] who could not move because of a broken leg. Watching my chance, I dashed from the doorway and, grabbing Conley, I pulled him after me through the hole. His leg got broken again, but there was no help for it. As soon as we left the room the Zulus burst in with furious cries of disappointment and rage. Now there was a repetition of the work... Again I had to drag Conley through, a terrible task because he was a very heavy man.

Surgeon Reynolds reported that Hook and Connolly: '...made their way into the open at the back of the Hospital by breaking a hole in the wall with a pickaxe and then through a small window looking into what may be styled the neutral ground.'

He was admitted to hospital in Natal on 25 February 1879, suffering from synovitis, due to a partial dislocation of the left knee, and being recommended for a change of climate he was invalided home on 11 March 1879. He sailed back to England on HMS *Tamar*, and on 3 May he gave an account of his experience at Rorke's Drift to Captain Liddell, at the request of Lady Frere, in which he records:

I crawled out of the window by placing mealie bags, and made for the bush by sitting down and pushing myself along feet first. After going fifty yards I got into the bush and laid down to keep out of sight. The Zulus kept passing me all night, but either did not see me or thought me dead. About 5am I crawled back into the entrenchment.

For his service he received the South Africa Medal with 1877-8-9 clasp.

He was admitted to Netley Hospital on 10 June 1879, and on being examined on 21 July he was declared unfit for further service and discharged on 4 August 1879. His character was described as fair, and his intended place of residence was Hereford. An injury assessment board held at the Royal Hospital, Chelsea, considered the injury to be permanent, and insofar as employment he could do nothing at the moment, and awarded him a pension of six pence a day for six months. He appeared before an assessment board for a second time on 2 September, and his award was increased to twelve pence a day for 12 months, which was made permanent in 1880.

He is believed to have returned to Castletown and married Catherine Crowley in 1885. They had four sons, John, James, Thomas and Joseph. In 1887 they lived at 13 Seyborfach Street in Pentre, and they eventually made their home at Llangyfelach Street in Dyfatty, Swansea. It was reported in local newspapers that:

Recently, through the efforts of Captain Colquhoun his pension of 1 shilling a day was increased to 1 shilling a 6 pence; a fund was raised for his assistance, and the United Service Brigade attended to some of his needs.

John died in the village of Brynhyfryd near Swansea on 6 November 1906, aged 47, and was buried in an unmarked grave at Danygraig Cemetery in Port Tennant, Swansea. A new headstone was dedicated at the grave in 2019.

Private Connolly's account of the action and how he escaped from the hospital has been described as dubious, based on the fact that it seems to contradict the account of Henry Hook. Although I find it disappointing that Connolly fails to mention Hook, the man who almost certainly saved his life, the events he speaks of could well have happened after Hook dragged him through the second hole.

Cardiff Times for 10 November 1906
Eastern Evening News (Norfolk) for 7 November 1906
Herald of Wales and Monmouthshire Recorder for 26 February 1887

Anthony Connors was a survivor of the defence.

He was born at Westminster in London in 1852. He joined the army in the summer of 1870, and as 2310 Private A. Connors he joined the 2nd Battalion, 24th Regiment, in India, on 28 December 1871. He was five feet six and a half inches tall, with a fresh complexion, grey eyes and brown hair. He was sentenced by civil power to serve 168 days imprisonment with hard labour at Millbank Prison in London. He returned to his regiment and on receiving orders for active service he sailed to South Africa on 17 July 1878. He took part in the Cape Frontier War, and was present at the defence of Rorke's Drift. He remained at Rorke's Drift after the battle, where he was accidentally shot by a comrade while they were on duty slaughtering cattle. For his service he received the South Africa Medal with 1877-8-9 clasp.

He was sent to Netley Hospital from Gibraltar on 18 July 1880, and an injury assessment board held at the Chelsea Hospital on 18 August 1880, confirmed that he had received a gunshot wound in the left thigh which would seriously affect his powers regarding employment. He was awarded a pension of seven pence a day for six months and was discharged from the army on 14 September 1880, his character being described as fair. His intended place of residence was London.

WO116/120

Timothy Connors was a survivor of the defence.

He was born at Killeady in County Cork, Ireland, in about 1842. He left his job as a labourer to enlist at Bandon in County Cork, on

15 March 1860. He was just under five feet five inches tall, with a fair complexion, light-blue eyes and dark-brown hair, and as 1323 Private T. Connors he was posted to the 2nd Battalion, 24th Regiment.

He was admitted to hospital for treatment of a social disease on 6 March 1862, and having re-engaged at Rangoon on 26 July 1867, he was later tried by court martial, but his offence and punishment was not recorded. He was admitted to hospital in Secunderabad for treatment of hepatitis on 11 November 1870, and after being examined by a special invalidity committee he was recommended to be sent to England for a change of climate, being admitted to Netley Hospital. He was admitted to the hospital at the barracks in Warley, Birmingham in March 1873.

He received orders for active service in South Africa and sailed with the battalion to the Cape in February 1878. He took part in the Cape Frontier War, and during the Zulu War he was present at the defence of Rorke's Drift. For his service he received the South Africa Medal with 1877-8-9 clasp.

He received the Long Service and Good Conduct Medal at Gibraltar on 1 April 1880, and he was shipped to England from India, being discharged at the Colchester depot on 19 April 1882. His intended place of residence was Quogh near Bandon in County Cork, and he was registered as an out-pensioner from the Chelsea Hospital.

William Cooper was a survivor of the defence.

He was born on 16 July 1855, at Whybro's Yard in Tottenham, north London. He was the second of three sons born to William Cooper, a horse keeper, and his second wife, Elizabeth (formerly Angel). His father had several children to his first wife. By 1861 they lived at number 3, Factory Yard, Edmonton, but both parents had died by 1865. William went into boarding at 6 Harewood Cottages in Edmonton, north London, and earned a living as a domestic servant. He enlisted into the army on 10 December 1872, and as 2453 Private Cooper he was posted to F Company, 2nd Battalion, 24th Regiment, at Warley in Birmingham, on 1 January 1873.

He received orders for active service in South Africa and sailed to the Cape with the battalion in February 1878. He took part in the Cape Frontier War, and during the Zulu War he and Private Robert Cole were sent to Rorke's Drift with a ration party on 21 January

1879, and he was present at the defence of the post on the following day. He was sent to the general depot at Helpmekaar on 28 March 1879, as time expired, where he appeared before a discharge board at Pietermaritzburg on 4 April 1879, an on 19 May he embarked for England, where he was sent to Netley Hospital and discharged to the 1st class reserve. For his service he received the South Africa Medal with 1877-8-9 clasp.

He married Eliza Rhoades on 30 June 1881, at St James Parish Church in Croydon, and they made their home at 10 Grove Terrace in Cross Road, Croydon. They had two children; Jessie was born in 1882, and William Joseph was born in 1885. William Joseph was killed in action serving with the Royal Artillery in France during the Great War. By 1891, William and Eliza had moved to 48 Borough Hill in Croydon, and in about 1904 he obtained employment as a brewer's drayman at the firm of Crossland and Paulin of Croydon.

William attended the laying up of the colours of the 1st Battalion, South Wales Borderers in Brecon Cathedral on Easter Sunday, 1 April 1934, and from 7 to 14 July 1934, he attended the Northern Command Tattoo at Ravensworth Castle in Gateshead, when the South Wales Borderers re-created the action at Rorke's Drift, and he appeared in the arena with four surviving comrades from the garrison.

William and Eliza moved to a cottage facing the South Downs in the village of Cocking in West Sussex for a while, and when they had both retired in about 1916 they made their home at 6 Cranmer Road in Worthing, which was closer to their daughter. However, the Second World War was raging and William had stated that he was worried about the conflict. He was also having trouble with failing eyesight.

On 19 February 1942, Eliza left him downstairs having his supper and went to bed. The next morning she found him in the kitchen lying dead with his head in the oven. He was aged 86. He had died through gas poisoning, and his funeral took place at the Woodvale Crematorium in Worthing, and his ashes were scattered in the Garden of Remembrance (section 6134). The regiment stressed that they would have provided for a military funeral but by the time they were informed of his death it was too late. A memorial was placed at his home in Cranmere Road in 2008.

Birth certificate–Tottenham CN199833
Marriage certificate–Croydon MXD321806
Death certificate–Worthing, West Sussex HD003072
West Sussex Gazette for 12 April 1934 and 26 February 1942
Worthing Gazette for 25 February 1942

D

James Langley Dalton was wounded in action, and was awarded the Victoria Cross for valour at Rorke's Drift.

For *The Rorke's Drift Men* I took most of the information about Dalton's birth from the census returns. However, further research states that he was actually born on St George's Day, 23 April 1834, and baptised on 8 May 1834, at St Dunstan in Holborn, west London. St Andrews and St Dunstan are both in Holborn.

He was born in 1834, in the parish of St Andrews in Holborn, London. He was the second son of two in the natural family of four children to James Dalton, and his wife, Susan. The family was living on Brick Lane in the parish of St Luke's in London.

Research suggests that his grandparents were Robert Langley and Catherine Byron, both born in 1790 in Ireland. They had a daughter named Susan Langley, who is believed to have been born in 1808, and is probably James Langley's mother. On his VC papers at Kew he gave his next-of-kin as 'Susan Langley'.

Of his siblings, Catherine was born in Dublin in 1827; Robert (Byron) was born in 1832, being baptised on 2 June 1832, at the Church of St John the Evangelist in Lambeth; and Susan was born in London in 1844. A child named Rose was born in London in 1849, and it seems that she was adopted by James and Susan.

James gave up his job as a clerk in a stationers' shop to enlist into the army, at Victoria, London, on 20 November 1849, being just under six feet tall, with a fresh complexion, hazel eyes and red hair, and as 965 Private Dalton he was posted to the 85th King's Light Infantry (Buck's Volunteers) at Waterford in Ireland. The 1851 census lists him as a soldier of the 85th Regiment stationed at Fulwood Barracks in Preston, and he was later stationed at Hull and Portsmouth. In 1853 the battalion embarked for service at Mauritius, where he was promoted to corporal on 1 July 1853, and drew his first entitlement to good conduct pay on 21 December 1854. He left the island three years later having been promoted sergeant on 7 September 1855. In 1856 he sailed with his regiment to the Cape, taking part in the Eighth Cape Frontier War. He re-engaged at Pembroke Docks on 21 December 1859, for a further 11 years' service.

He transferred to the Commissariat Staff Corps at Aldershot on 31 March 1862, being appointed colour sergeant on 1 June 1863. While stationed in Aldershot until 1867, he attended the Hythe School of Musketry in 1864, and on 7 February 1866, he was appointed clerk and master sergeant. His last tour of overseas duty was in Canada from 1868 to 1871, and he served during General Wolseley's Red River Expedition. The reorganisation of the Commissariat saw him transferred to the Army Service Corps on 1 April 1870, as second class staff sergeant, and on 1 July he was promoted to first class staff sergeant; the equivalent of a warrant officer. He discharged in London, on 28 November 1871, having received three good conduct badges, and he was awarded the Long Service Good Conduct Medal. Remarks on his discharge papers state: 'His conduct has been very good.'

By 1877 he was in South Africa serving as a senior officer. On 13 December 1877, he was appointed to British forces for the Ninth Cape Frontier War, for which he was mentioned in dispatches:

Mr Dalton, Acting Assistant Commissary, has been most energetic. The sole officer at Ibeka in that department, under great difficulties he increased the supplies, and provided three columns in their advances, and the stations in Galekaland, with the utmost regularity.

He and Louis Byrne rode through pouring rain on New Year's Day 1879, to join the British forces at Helpmekaar, and then they moved up to Rorke's Drift. James Dalton was highly praised for the part he played in the action at Rorke's Drift, and he is mentioned in several accounts by fellow defenders, praising his valour and initiative.

Private Hook stated:

Mr Dalton came up and said if we left the Drift every man was certain to be killed. He had formerly been a Sergeant-Major in a line regiment and was one of the bravest men that ever lived.

Mr Dunne recorded:

Dalton the lionhearted, as brave a soldier as ever lived, had joined us, and hearing the terrible news said, 'Now, we must make a defence!' It was his suggestion which decided us to form a breastwork of bags of grain, boxes of biscuits, and everything that would help to stop a bullet or keep out a man.

Doctor Reynolds reported:

My first move was to consult with Lieutenant Bromhead, and Commissary Dalton, Lieutenant Chard not having as yet joined us from the pontoon. We quickly decided that, with barricades well placed around our position, a stand could best be made where we were. At this period, Mr Dalton's energies were invaluable.

Lieutenant Chard reported:

There was a short but desperate struggle during which Mr Dalton shot a Zulu who was in the act of stabbing a corporal (Roland Miller) of the Army Hospital Corps, the muzzle of whose rifle he had seized, and with Lieutenant Bromhead and many of the men behaved with great gallantry; Mr Dalton dropping a man each time he fired his rifle. While firing from behind the biscuit boxes, Mr Dalton, who had been using his rifle with deadly effect, and by his quickness and coolness had been the means of saving many men's lives, was shot through the body. I was standing near him at the time, and he handed me his rifle so coolly that I had no idea until afterwards that he had been wounded so severely. He waited quite quietly for me to take the cartridges he had left out of his pockets. We put him inside our mealie sack redoubt, building it up around him.

Reverend Smith stated:

Mr Dalton, who is a tall man, was continually going along the barricades, fearlessly exposing himself and cheering the men, and using his own rifle most effectively. A Zulu ran up near the barricade. Mr Dalton called out 'Pot that fellow!' and himself aimed over the parapet at another, when his rifle dropped and he turned round, quite pale, and said that he had been shot. The doctor was by his side at once, and found that a bullet had passed quite through above the right shoulder. Unable any longer to use his rifle, he did not cease to direct the fire of the men who were near him.

Henry Harford recorded:

Mr James Dalton, who in the absence of Lieutenant Chard, devised all the rapid arrangements for the defence, as well as working like a Trojan himself with the men at the barricades and did much gallant work during the night. I noticed that directly Mr Smith or Mr Dalton showed themselves they received an ovation from the men, which was unmistakable.

Private Hitch stated: 'Mr Dalton was very active up till he was wounded.' Corporal Lyons noted: 'Mr Dalton deserved any amount of praise.'

He was sent to recuperate at Pietermaritzburg for six months. The medical records of Surgeon Blair-Brown are interesting to note:

James Dalton was hit in the right shoulder. The bullet entered about half-an-inch above the middle of the clavicle, and made its escape posteriorly at the lower border of the trapezius muscle. The course taken was curious, regularly running round the shoulder and down the back, escaping all the important structures. The wounds, like all those received at Rorke's Drift, were wide and open and sloughing when seen by me on 26 January. After the slough came away the usual tenax was applied. I had no antiseptic to use. I thought of quinine, which I knew was a wonderful preserver in animal tissue, and used a solution of that, experimenting in this case. It seemed to answer, as the wounds got well after being injected several times with it.

When the 2nd Battalion marched into Pietermaritzburg on 16 October 1879, it was recorded in the *Natal Witness*:

> The spectators in Church Street could not make out why one company of the noble 24th suddenly raised a deafening cheer when coming to the clubhouse. The fact was that B Company, the gallant defenders of Rorke's Drift, under Major Bromhead VC, had recognised amongst the spectators Assistant Commissary Dalton, one of the leaders on that night. May we ask why Mr Dalton has not yet received the Victoria Cross?

Evidence of the reason for this was given in document WO32 7386, dated 18 October 1879, which states:

> I think we are giving the VC very freely I think, but probably Mr Dalton has as good a claim as the others who have got the cross for Rorke's Drift defence. I don't think there is a case for Mr Dunne.

Consequently, Walter Dunne was overlooked.

The award to Commissary Dalton was announced in the *London Gazette* on 18 November 1879, which stated:

> For his conspicuous gallantry during the attack on Rorke's Drift post by the Zulus on the night of the 22nd January 1879, when he actively superintended the work of the defence, and was amongst the foremost of those who received the first attack at the corner of the hospital, where the deadliness of his fire did great execution, and the mad rush of the Zulus met with its first check, and where, by his cool courage, he saved the life of a man of the Army Hospital Corps, by shooting the Zulu who having seized the muzzle of the man's rifle, was in the act of assegaing him. This officer, to whose energy much of the defence of the place was due, was severely wounded during the contest, but still continued to give the same example of cool courage.

He received the medal from Major General Hugh Clifford VC, during a parade of the troops at Fort Napier in Pietermaritzburg, on

16 January 1880, 'Amid surroundings well calculated to make it impressive to participators and spectators alike.' He also received the South Africa Medal with 1877-78-79 clasp. For his gallantry Dalton had been awarded a permanent commission as sub-assistant commissary on 21 November 1879, back-dated to his temporary appointment in December 1877, and he became senior commissariat officer at Fort Napier. He was promoted assistant-commissary from 13 December 1879. He sailed to England in February 1880, and had an audience with Queen Victoria at Windsor Castle on 16 March 1880.

When Major Chard gave his verbal account of the battle to Queen Victoria, her private secretary noted:

Chard has been here this morning. I gather from all I hear that Dalton was quite as much (if not more) of the presiding genius here, as himself. He conceived the idea of joining the two buildings with mealie bags, etc, before Chard's arrival on the scene; though perhaps Chard would have done so, had he not found it in operation.

Little is known about the last years of his life. The 1881 census states that he was living in lodgings at 17 Cottage Grove in Lambeth, London, giving his age as 46. A man named Robert Dalton is listed as being a visitor at the address. He eventually returned to South Africa, making his living as a gold prospector. He owned shares in the Little Bess Mine at Barberton during the Transvaal gold rush days of 1884-86. He decided to spend the Christmas of 1886 with his old friend, former Sergeant John Sherwood Williams, at the Grosvenor Hotel in Port Elizabeth, Cape Province. After spending the day of 7 January 1887 confined to his bed, he died suddenly in his room during the night. He was in his 54th year, and had remained unmarried. He was buried in the Russell Road Roman Catholic Cemetery in Port Elizabeth, and a stone memorial was erected: 'by his old comrade Sergeant John Williams and Friends of Natal.' The centenary was celebrated with a wreath-laying ceremony at his grave. The Royal Corps of Transport purchased his medals in 1986, and they are now with the Royal Logistic Corps Museum at Aldershot. When the new military installation was established near Abingdon in Oxfordshire in 1992 they were named Dalton Barracks after him.

Eastern Province Herald for 10 January 1887
Illustrated London News for 6 December 1879
WO33/34/831–Transport

Mr Daniels was a civilian carpenter who took part in the defence.

He is believed to have been American, because his North American accent prompted the soldiers to nickname him 'Yankee Dan', but he may have been Canadian.

He was employed by the government to keep the ponts at the Buffalo River in good working order, because they were used to ferry the troops, transport and supplies across from Natal into Zululand. (also see Frederick Millne).

In his official report Lieutenant Chard stated:

> I desire here to mention for approval the offer of these pont guards, Daniels and Sergeant Milne, of the 3rd Buffs, who, with their comrades, volunteered to moor the ponts out in the middle of the stream, and there to defend them from the decks, with a few men to assist.

However, as Reverend Smith stated: 'Our defensive force was too small for any to be spared, and these men subsequently did good service within the fort.'

And in the report he submitted to Queen Victoria on 21 February 1880, Lieutenant Chard stated:

> I went round the position with them [Bromhead and Dalton] and then rode down to the ponts where I found everything ready for a start, ponts in midstream, hawsers and cables sunk, etc. It was at this time that the Pontman Daniells, and Sergeant Milne, 3rd Buffs, who had been employed for some time in getting the ponts in order, and working them under Lieutenant MacDowell, R.E., (Killed at Isandhlwana), offered to defend the ponts, moored in the middle of the river, from their decks with a few men. Sergeant Williams 24th and his little guard were quite ready to join them.

In his newspaper article of 23 July 1914, Private Caled Wood stated:

We were joined by Lieutenant Chard and one or two Engineers from the pontoon bridges, and another civilian who was with us acted as scout by riding to the top of the hill and telling us how near the Zulus were getting.

Although there were at least two men of the cloth in the camp at the time, Daniels was the only true civilian present.

In his 26 December 1913 report Private Wood recalled:

There was one little man amongst us whom the soldiers used to chaff about his size telling him he would make a nice soldier to defend his country. His height was only about four feet ten inches, and he was a carpenter employed by the government to attend to the pontoon bridge. One of the officers lent him a sword and relied upon his revolver only. The little man stood against the wall for some time with his sword ready for anything. At last he got his chance, a Zulu put his head above the wall and the diminutive carpenter brought him down, remarking 'there, shouldn't I make a soldier?' as he waved his sword triumphantly.

He is believed to have died in South Africa.

Lieutenant John Chard's official report dated 25 January 1879. Public Records Office, WO 32/7737.
Lieutenant John Chard's account of 21 February 1880
Ilkeston Pioneer for 26 December 1913–*Rorke's Drift: Story of Valour Retold by Ilkeston Veteran Who Was There*; by Private Caleb Wood
Nottingham Daily Express for 23 July 1914–*Ilkeston Hero of Rorke's Drift* by Private Caleb Wood

George Davies was a survivor of the defence.

He was born in 1853. He joined the army at Wrexham on 15 October 1874, aged 21 years, and as 470 Private Davies he was posted to the 2nd Battalion, 24th Regiment. He received orders for active service in South Africa, and sailed to the Cape with his battalion in February 1878. He took part in the Cape Frontier War, and during the Zulu War he was present at the defence of Rorke's

Drift. For his service in the campaign he was awarded the South Africa Medal with 1877-8-9 clasp. His name has not been traced on the muster rolls after 4 March 1881.

William Henry Davis was a survivor of the defence.

He was born at St Bartholomew's Parish in Camden Town, London, during the June quarter of 1853, and he was baptised at St Martins-in-the-field Church on 4 June 1853. His mother was named Emma but no name for father.

He had been employed as a porter before he enlisted at Bow Street Police Court in London, on 26 February 1877, aged 24 years and five months. He was somewhat diminutive, being described as just under five feet four inches tall, with a chest measurement of two feet ten inches. He had a dark complexion, hazel eyes and dark brown hair, and he had good muscular development. His religion was Church of England, and at the time of his attestation he had a broken upper front tooth. As 1363 Private Davis he was posted to the 2nd Battalion, 24th (2nd Warwickshire) Regiment, in 1 March 1877.

After short postings to Dover and Chatham, he received orders for active service in South Africa and sailed to the Cape with the battalion in February 1878. He took part in the Cape Frontier War, and during the Zulu War he was present at the defence of Rorke's Drift.

While still at Rorke's Drift he was granted a penny a day good conduct pay on 27 February 1879, which he forfeited in the following June. For his service he received the South Africa Medal with 1877-8-9 clasp.

He served at Gibraltar from 13 January to 11 August 1880, during which time he was hospitalised from 26 May to 12 June 1880, suffering with a stricture (inflammation), and he was confined in cells on 1 July 1880, charged with breaking out of the barracks and doing away with necessaries. He was tried by court martial and sentenced to 42 days imprisonment with hard labour, being released on 12 August 1880, to sail with the battalion to Secunderabad in India. It seems he suffered badly from hepatitis and haemorrhoids while he was there. On his return from the sub-continent on 27 May 1883, he transferred to the army reserve HQ, London District, in the following month, his character at that time being described as 'bad–latterly good.' He had received a fourth class certificate of education when he discharged from the army on 10 April 1889, his intended place of residence being 37 Johnson Street in Camden Town, London.

Soon after leaving the army William died at 180 Ebury Place in Pimlico, London, and after a service at St George's Church in Hanover Square, he was buried in an unmarked common grave situated near the chapel at Brompton Cemetery in West London, on 26 October 1889. He was aged 37. The grave reference E244.9 x 153.0 remains unmarked and overgrown.

Brompton Cemetery Burial Records
Friends of Brompton Cemetery

Thomas Daw was a survivor of the defence.

He was born on 8 July 1858, at his grandmother's house in Higher Street in Merriott, Somerset. He was the third child of four to Thomas Daw, a farm labourer, and his second wife, Priscilla, known as Ann (formerly Druce), who had married on 27 September 1852. Thomas senior had a daughter from his first marriage. They moved to 29 Piddletown in Haselbury Plucknett, Somerset, where Thomas Daw senior died on 8 November 1870, having suffered inflammation of the brain. By the time of the 1871 census Tom and his two brothers were working as agricultural labourers.

Thomas enlisted at Crewkerne in Somerset on 5 February 1877, where his description was given as five feet four and a half inches tall, with a florid complexion, brown hair and grey eyes. His muscular development was good and he had a 36 inch chest. His religion was Church of England. As 1178 Private Daw he was posted to the 2nd Battalion, 24th Regiment, at Brecon.

On receiving orders for active service in South Africa he sailed to the Cape with his battalion in February 1878. He served in the Cape Frontier War, being hospitalised in June 1878 suffering with dyspepsia, and he was hospitalised in Natal in August suffering with blisters caused by the long march across country. During the Zulu War he was present at the defence of Rorke's Drift, after which he was granted a penny a day good conduct pay from 6 February 1879, and he was transferred to H Company on 3 April 1879. For his service he received the South Africa Medal with 1877-8-9 clasp.

He served at Gibraltar in 1880, and on arriving in India in September 1880, he was hospitalised on several occasions with ailments such as dysentery, dyspepsia and venereal diseases. He was granted two pence a day good conduct pay from 6 February 1883, and on returning to England he was discharged at Gosport and posted to the first class reserve, Taunton District, on 31 May 1883. His character was described as clean, good and temperate.

Thomas obtained work as a wagon driver for the local wool factory. He married Emily Westcott (born in 1867) at Wellington Parish Church, on 26 May 1887, and in the following October Emily gave birth to Ernest Herbert, at Five Houses in Tone, Wellington, Somerset. Ada Priscilla was born in 1889, and Harold Percival was born in 1897. Sadly, Emily died two days after giving birth to a still-born child in 15 February 1906, and Ada died of pneumonia on 15 September 1909.

After seeing his sons return safely from service in the Great War, Thomas Daw died peacefully at his home on 23 May 1924, aged 65. The cause of death was given as 'carcinoma of the pancreas'. He was buried with his wife and daughter in unmarked grave number 2963 at Wellington Cemetery. His birth and marriage certificates state his name as Daw, but he was buried as Thomas Dawe. A new headstone was erected at the grave in 2010.

Birth certificate–Crewkerne FD126646
Father's death certificate–Coker, Yeovil FD126647
Marriage certificate–Wellington Y569854
Wife Emily death certificate–Wellington HD101890
Death certificate–Wellington HD101891

George Deacon was a survivor of the defence.

He was born as George Deacon Power on 23 August 1852, at 76 Hampden Street in the parish of St Mary's, Paddington, London (he stated that he was born in Kensington). He was the fourth son of six children to an Irish immigrant named William John Power, who worked as a guard for the Great Western Railway, and his wife, Mary Ann (formerly Deacon), who had married in Marylebone in June 1847. Following George's birth the family moved to Bromley Road in Paddington, and the 1871 census states that the family had moved to

22 Beringden Street in Kensington. He was educated at the Westbourne Park School, and then as a 'better' school in Notting Hill. He left school on 1865.

On 7 November 1870, George left his job as a clerk with the Great Western Railway to join the Royal Regiment of Artillery, where he trained with Louis Napoleon, the Prince Imperial, who was killed during the Zulu War. He served at Gibraltar from 1872 to 1875. He later served at the Purfleet magazine when 'the Fenians were about'. His father bought him out of the army for £30 and he gained employment with the London and North Western Railway.

However, he was not keen on civilian life, so he walked to Chatham on 10 November 1877, and using his mother's maiden name so his father could not trace him, he re-joined the army as George Deacon. The age on his service papers was given as 18 years, but he was aged 25. As 1467 Private Deacon, he was posted to the 2nd Battalion, 24th Regiment.

He received orders for active service in South Africa and sailed to the Cape with the battalion in February 1878. He took part in the Cape Frontier War, being confined for six days in March 1878. He was present at the defence of Rorke's Drift, and Private Hitch stated:

> Deakin [meaning Deacon], a comrade, said to me as I was leaning back against the biscuit boxes, 'Fred, when it comes to the last shall I shoot you?' I declined. 'No, they have very nearly done for me and they can finish me right out when it comes to the last.'

On 11 February 1879 he was confined for 14 days for refusing to obey an order, and it seemed that George was beginning to realise that army life was not for him, and he deserted at Pietermaritzburg on 9 September 1879. He stated that when the regiment went to Gibraltar early in 1880 he remained in South Africa, being stationed at Bloemfontein and Kimberley. He joined the Bechuanaland Police for a short while, and then saw service with Major Nesbitt's Light Horse in Basutoland. He said that he was a member of the party which was sent out to recover the body of the Prince Imperial.

He was said to have been in possession of three medals, which he kept in a black box that he would not allow anyone else to open but himself. They are likely to have been the South Africa Medal with

1877-8-9 clasp, which he claimed in 1920; the Cape of Good Hope General Service Medal with Basutoland clasp; and it was said that the third was the Khedives Bronze Star, which would have been for service in Egypt.

By 1884 he had set himself up in business as a provision's merchant in the Poplar district of London. On 26 November 1884, at the parish church in Poplar, he married Helena Teresa Sincock, who came from Tenterton in Kent, and was a well-travelled and educated daughter of Richard Sincock, a civil engineer. In 1887 Helena gave birth to twin daughters in Hackney, Middlesex, Helena Mercedes and Mary Elizabeth, and John George Homer was born in 1888. They then moved to 14 Wherstead Road in Ipswich, where William Donald Bain was born in 1890, Edward Richard was born in 1892, and Cecil Frederick was born in 1895.

George became a police officer on the Great Eastern Railway, becoming police inspector by 1891, and having moved to 184 Portway in West Ham, by the turn of the century, he became a chief inspector of railway police.

Helena died in August 1926, and George moved to the home of his daughter Helena, at Gantshill Crescent in Ilford, who had given up her career as a nurse to look after him. In June 1928 he was interviewed by a newspaper reporter at Thorold Road in Ilford, and George had although he had become blind from cataracts, he was described as being '... of a wonderful appearance, with chiselled features, with a high forehead and he has silvery grey hair.'

He was visited at Hill Crescent in Ilford by a *Star* newspaper reporter in 1931, by which time he had become bedridden. He died at the Romford Hospital on 16 February 1934, aged 81, and the cause of death was recorded as myocardial degeneration. He was buried with his wife in the City of London Cemetery on Aldersbrook Road in Little Ilford. Regimental representatives were present at his funeral, including Lieutenant Colonel Frank Bourne, and his death was reported in the April 1934 issue of the *South Wales Borderers Journal*. It was sold at auction on 16 September 1991.

Birth certificate–St Mary, Paddington y569854

Marriage certificate–Poplar AA997917

Death certificate–Romford W004553/D

Eastern Counties Times and Recorder for 29 June 1928

Michael Deane was a survivor of the defence.

He attested for 25 Brigade on 10 March 1877, and as 1357 Private Deane he was posted to the 2nd Battalion, 24th Regiment, at Brecon, on 26 January 1878, the unit having received orders for active service in South Africa. He took part in the Cape Frontier War, and during the Zulu War he was present at the defence of Rorke's Drift. He was entitled to the South Africa Medal with 1877-8-9 clasp, but he deserted while serving at Gibraltar on 22 July 1880.

Patrick Desmond was a survivor of the defence.

He was born in about 1857. There was a Patrick Desmond baptised in Cork on 29 January 1858, who was a son of Timothy and Brigid. His parents are believed to have come from Ireland to Pembrokeshire in Wales to escape the potato famine. There is no Patrick Desmond recorded for Pembrokeshire, but the 1881 census records a Patrick Desmond living in Richmond. If this is the Rorke's Drift man the census recorded that he was born at Innishannon in County Cork, Ireland.

He enlisted for the army, and at Fort Hubberstone in Pembrokeshire as 568 Private Desmond, and he was posted to the 2nd Battalion, 24th Regiment, on 15 April 1875, being transferred to G Company, 1st Battalion, on 15 July 1876. Just over a month later he was part of a unit of reinforcements which sailed to join the battalion for active service in South Africa. He gained the reputation as a notorious drunkard, and while there he was fined, forfeited pay or was imprisoned for drunkenness on numerous occasions from September 1877 to January 1879, and he was also imprisoned by civil power in South Africa from July to October 1878. When he was not in prison he served in the Cape Frontier War. He was assigned to store duties at Rorke's Drift, and during the defence he was slightly wounded by a slug which passed through the fleshy part of his thumb.

It was stated in newspapers at the time the unit returned home:
Among the men of the 1st Battalion of the 24th who disembarked were Sergeant Wilson, Lance-Corporal Roy, and Privates Desmond, Payton and Jenkins, who had been to the rear with prisoners...

However, while he was at Rorke's Drift, he was fined for drunkenness on 19 January 1879, and in a letter sent after 13 January, Colour Sergeant William Edwards of the 1st Battalion, who was killed at iSandlwana, stated: 'A man named Desmond of G Company got 50 lashes for insubordination.'

His wayward behaviour continued after the defence, being fined for drunkenness five times from 22 March to 22 August 1879. He was posted with the battalion to return to England, and arrived at Portsmouth on 2 October 1879. Still his bad behaviour continued, and he was fined for drunkenness and confined in cells several times in 1880, before being confined in a civil prison for a month. On his release on 15 November 1880, he was struck off and discharged from Pembroke Dock as a worthless character and notorious drunkard. He received the South Africa Medal with 1877-8-9 clasp.

The 1881 census states that a valet named Patrick Desmond, aged 23, and his brother John, aged 18, were living at 1 Marsh Gate Road in Richmond, Surrey, in the home of Frederick E. Perkins.

He returned to Ireland to marry Mary Ellen Dullia in about 1889, and there seems to have been a daughter named Catherine Ann, who was born at Dunmunway in County Cork, on 23 January 1896. In 1901 he was registered as a pauper inmate at the Union Workhouse of St George's in Hanover Square, London.

His campaign medal was requested to be forfeited by order dated 19 June 1906, but there is no record of it having been returned.

James William Dick was a survivor of the defence.

He is believed to have been born at Island Magee in County Antrim, Ireland, in about 1847. He had been a dock labourer before he enlisted at Belfast on 3 February 1865, to serve ten years, being described as five feet seven inches tall, with a fresh complexion, grey eyes and curly brown hair, and as 1697 Private Dick he was posted to the 2nd Battalion, 24th Regiment. He gave his next-of-kin as his mother, Mrs J. Dick of Island Magee. He served in India from 1865 to 1873, during which time he was granted good conduct pay of a penny a day in 1868, which had risen to two pence by the time he re-engaged at Secunderabad, on 18 November 1871. He was granted three pence a day good conduct pay on 6 February 1877.

He received orders for active service in South Africa and sailed to the Cape with his battalion in February 1878, taking part in the Cape Frontier War, and he was present at the defence of Rorke's Drift. He had forfeited a penny of his good conduct pay, which was restored to him soon after the defence. He was awarded the South Africa Medal with 1877-8-9 clasp, which was incorrectly inscribed as 'W Dick'.

He served at Gibraltar in 1880, and in India from 1880 to 1889, during which time he was awarded the Long Service and Good Conduct Medal with a gratuity of five pounds on 1 January 1884, and his good conduct pay had risen to five pence a day by 6 February 1888. He claimed his discharge as time-served at Secunderabad on 20 February 1889, his conduct being described as exemplary. His next-of-kin was his mother, Mrs J. Dick of Island Magee.

James died of chronic dysentery while serving at Secunderabad in India on 27 January 1897, aged 49, and he was buried at the Secunderabad Roman Catholic Cathedral. He was listed as a Chelsea Pensioner in official records, and burial records state that he was a 'Pensioned Private, 24th Rgt, South Wales Borderers'.

William Dicks was a survivor of the defence.

He was born at St Pancras in Islington, London, on 7 July 1847, being baptised with the surname Dickes, on 25 July 1847, at St Pancras Old Church. He was the only son of Joseph Dickes and Mary Ann (formerly Flood). He had a sister named Josephene Sebella, who was born on 14 December 1845, being baptised at the same church as William, and a sister named Anne.

He enlisted for 11 years' service at Westminster Police Court on 25 November 1864, being described as five feet six inches tall, with a fresh complexion, brown eyes and brown hair. As 1634 Private Dicks he was posted to the 1st Battalion, 24th Regiment, transferring to the 2nd Battalion on 1 February 1865. His next-of-kin was his married sister, Mrs Anne Franklin, of 42 Havelock Street in Islington, London.

He served in India from 1865 to 1873, and he was granted and forfeited good conduct pay on several occasions, being sentenced to six days in prison by his commanding officer in 1874. He was promoted to lance corporal on 17 September 1877, and his good conduct pay was at two pence a day and he had reached the rank of corporal on 14 November 1877, when he received orders for active service in South Africa, sailing to the Cape with his battalion in February 1878. While taking part in the Cape Frontier War, he was appointed lance sergeant on 13 May 1878, but having moved to Natal, he was tried and sentenced to be reduced to private on 16 September 1878, and spent the next two days in prison. During the Zulu War he was present at the defence of Rorke's Drift. For his service he was awarded the South Africa Medal with 1877-8-9 clasp.

He served at Gibraltar in 1880; and in India from 1880 until 22 January 1886, during which time he re-engaged at Secunderabad on 6 August 1882, to complete 21 years' service. He discharged at Gosport on 9 February 1886, and his conduct was described as very good.

He was admitted to the Royal Hospital in Chelsea, where he died on 19 October 1925; aged 78. He was buried in an unmarked grave with three other people on common land at the Islington and St Pancras Cemetery in East Finchley, London (grave 170-9v–286165), where George Smith had been buried earlier in the year.

His South Africa campaign medal was sold at auction in 2022.

William Doughty was a survivor of the defence.

He served as a corporal with the 2nd Battalion, Natal Native Contingent, and was a patient in the hospital.

Thomas Driscoll was a survivor of the defence.

He was born at Lower High Street in Dowlais, Monmouthshire, in August 1860, 'and went to the Catholic School there.'

He left his employment as a fireman at the Dowlais works to attest at Brecon on 29 January 1876, and as 971 (1525) Private Thomas Driscoll, he was posted to the 2nd Battalion, 24th Regiment, on 1 February 1876. He was described as being five feet five and a half inches tall, with a chest measurement of 34 inches. He had a sallow complexion, with grey eyes and brown hair. His religion was Roman Catholic.

He received orders for active service in South Africa on 2 December 1878. He took part in the Cape Frontier War, and during the Zulu War he was present at the defence of Rorke's Drift. He transferred to A Company on 29 January 1879, and for his service he received the South Africa Medal with 1877-8-9 clasp. He later served at Gibraltar and in India, being granted good conduct pay on 1 February 1880.

He left the army in 1888, and worked for the Ebbw Vale Company for 40 years. Shortly after the death of Queen Victoria he was working in the company's no. 1 mill when the roof fell in and broke his right ankle and he was incapacitated for six months.

He was living at the Cambrian Workmens' Home in Brierly Hill, Ebbw Vale when he was one of 25 Zulu War veterans who attended The Old Comrades Club of the 24th Foot reunion at the Victoria Barracks in Portsmouth on 30/31 March 1929, along with Henry Gallagher, John Jobbins, Henry Martin and John Williams VC.

Apparently, 'familiarly known as Tom Tambourine', he was interviewed by a local reporter in 1929, when he was described as unmarried and living alone, and being very feeble and practically blind. It was stated that he had done no work since 1925, and:

He had the misfortune to be knocked down by a motor car in the street at Ebbw Vale during last year [1928] and was taken to the Tredegar Infirmary, where he remained for two months. The accident severely shook the old man, and he has never completely recovered.

Thomas died at the Cambrian Workmens' Home in Ebbw Vale, on 20 June 1931, aged 77, and he is buried in the Ebbw Vale Municipal Cemetery.

South Wales Argus for June 1931
Western Mail for 24 January 1929

William Dunbar was a survivor of the defence.

In 1938 he told a reporter that he would be 88-years-old in May of that year. He stated that he had run away from home at the age of 13—because his father was 'very religious'. He added that he:

Served four years as an apprentice in the famous Black Ball Line, and then joined the American Navy. He returned to England, fell in love with a Liverpool girl, joined the Army and was sent to South Africa, and that was the last he ever saw of his sweetheart.

The Black Ball Line was a passenger line founded by a group of Quakers in New York, which ran between Liverpool and New York, and got its name from its flag, which was a black ball on a red background. It became defunct in 1878.

He enlisted at Newport on 20 June 1877, and as 1421 Private Dunbar he was posted to the 2nd Battalion, 24th Regiment, at Brecon, on 13 December 1877.

He received orders for active service in South Africa, and was appointed lance corporal on 1 February 1878, the day he embarked to sail to the Cape. He took part in the Cape Frontier War, being promoted corporal on 15 March 1878, but soon after arriving in Natal he was confined in cells, tried by court martial on 22 July 1878, and received 28 days imprisonment with hard labour and reduced to private.

He was present at the defence of Rorke's Drift, and evidently he was one of the sharpshooters posted behind the wagons in the south rampart, as Lieutenant Chard stated that during the first Zulu attack: 'a Chief on horseback was dropped by Private Dunbar, 24th.' Private Hook stated: 'One of my comrades, Private Dunbar, shot no fewer than nine Zulus, one of them being a Chief.' For his service he received the South Africa Medal with 1877-8-9 clasp.

He served at Gibraltar in 1880, and in India, from where he returned home on 9 October 1883. His intended place of residence was Newport in south Wales, but he eventually returned to South Africa.

He was interviewed by a reporter from the *Natal Mercury* at the Centenary Home for aged men in Durban in 1938, and he was known then as Charles Dunbar. He stated:

I've been in every war in this country since 1877... Gaika, Zulu, Basuto, Matabele... then the Boer War, where I was in the siege of Mafeking, and in the last war I started off by being drill instructor in Port Elizabeth, and ended up in the German west. After the war I got a job in the special water police in Durban, and then became a guard down at the docks.

He died at Hillcrest, Pinetown, Natal, on 29 January 1940, aged 82, one of the last surviving Rorke's Drift men, and he was buried at Stellawood Cemetery in Durban.

Natal Mercury for 1938

Walter Alphonsus Dunne was a survivor of the defence.

He was born on 10 February 1853, at 28 Victoria Street in Cork, Ireland. He was the third son of six in the family of twelve children born in Cork between 1845 and 1865 to James Dunne and his wife, Margaret (formerly Creedon). His father was the secretary of the Country Club at 80 South Mall in Cork, and later of St Stephens Green in Cork. The family were devout Roman Catholic, and Walter was baptised at Finbarr's South Catholic Church in Cork. He was educated at Queen's University in Dublin.

He joined the Control Department as sub-assistant commissary (second Lieutenant) on 9 April 1873, and served with the Commissariat Department in Dublin until October 1877. He was posted to South Africa, where he saw active service with the 1st Battalion, 24th Regiment, during the Ninth Cape Frontier War of 1878, and in the campaign against Sekhukhune in the north east of Transvaal, who was defying all attempts to prize him from his mountain stronghold. At the end of 1878, Assistant Commissary Dunne received orders to go to Helpmekaar in Natal where a force was being assembled for the invasion of Zululand, and he arrived exhausted after riding a hundred miles across country to take up his duties as senior commissary with the 3rd Central Column.

Commissary Dunne was mentioned in dispatches for his service during the defence of Rorke's Drift, and although Lord Chelmsford recommended that Dunne should be awarded the Victoria Cross it was not granted. Major Chard stated that Commissary Dunne had supervised the erection of the original defences and was later made responsible for building the inner defences, including the mealie bag redoubt meant as a last rallying point. When building the redoubt, Dunne, a tall man, encouraged the exhausted soldiers while standing on the growing pile of bags high above the defences, drawing fire on himself and ignoring any danger.

He took part in the re-invasion as a deputy commissary of supplies with the Flying Column, and he was in the square which destroyed the Zulu Army at the battle of Ulundi on 4 July 1879. He was in further action during the renewed Sekhukhuni Expedition, taking part in the successful assault on his stronghold in November 1879, for which he was mentioned in dispatches.

Two days after the battle he wrote a letter to a friend named Lieutenant Waneford describing the events at Rorke's Drift, and in February 1892, the Corps Journal later known as *The Waggoner*, published the third chapter containing his detailed account of the invasion of Zululand and the defence of Rorke's Drift, under the title *Reminiscences of Campaigning in South Africa, 1877-81*.

Mr Dunne remained in South Africa, where he was stationed in the Transvaal. When the Boer uprising began in 1880, he was again involved in a siege, this time by Boer commando units at the garrison town of Potchefstroom, a flashpoint of discontent. The 200 defenders, including women and children, had to survive behind a makeshift perimeter in an area about thirty paces square, their only protection against the elements being a few bell tents. Commissary Dunne sat on the parapet each Sunday reading the Roman Catholic service to the people of that faith. They held out under constant fire for three months until sickness and starvation forced them into dignified surrender in March 1881.

The ordeal affected his health and on returning to Natal he was nursed back to strength by friends, including Winifred, the daughter of John Bird, CMG, Treasurer of Natal, and they became engaged. After five years of active service in South Africa, Walter returned to England in April 1882, to be stationed at Aldershot. On his return to England in 1885 he and Winifred were married at Bath on 23 July of that year.

Just four months later he sailed for active service in north-east Africa, taking part in the decisive victory over Egyptian forces at Tel-el-Kebir on 13 September 1882. He returned to England, and in February 1885 he was posted back to north Africa to join the British forces station at the Red Sea port of Saukin in the Sudan, and he was present during the British advance against Dervish warriors at Hasheen on 19 March 1885.

He was transferred as a lieutenant colonel to the Army Service Corps on the establishment of that unit in 1888, serving on Mauritius, 1887-89, and he was DAAG of the Southern District, 1892-95; he was appointed Commander of the Bath for distinguished service in 1896, and was promoted colonel in 1897, becoming HAAG of the North-East District at York, a position he held until 1899. He was active in various public undertakings. While stationed at York he was president of the York Catholic Association, and he was a supporter of the Catholic Soldiers' Club in London. He sent a wreath to the funeral of Colonel Chard in 1897 on behalf of the Association.

From January 1900 he was assistant quartermaster general at Army Headquarters in Aldershot, representing the War Office on the Army Medical Advisory Board. He was considered for promotion to major-general in 1905, and in the same year he was appointed director of supplies and transport at Gibraltar, from where he retired from military service in February 1908.

It was reported that he travelled to Rome resigned to die, and that he would not pray for his own recovery, 'only that the will of God might be done.' He spent the last months of his life in the Hospital of the Little Company of Mary. This was a religious institute of women dedicated to caring for the sick, which began in Nottingham in 1877, and is similar to the Macmillan Nurses.

Having shown great bravery and resignation, Colonel Dunne died at The English Convent Home in Rome, on 2 July 1908, aged 55, sisters held lighted torches in their hands as the cortege left the hospital, and he was buried at the Verano Cemetery at Lazio in Rome (Burial niche (loculus) No. 5, 2nd Row of Gallery E). The letter he wrote from Rorke's Drift was sold at auction in 2014, and is now in the Museum of the Royal Welsh at Brecon.

Bennett, Lieutenant Colonel Ian H. W.: *Rorke's Drift: The Story of the Commissaries* (Two Parts), 1978
Catholic Press for 27 August 1908
Journal of the Army Service Corps for February 1892–*Reminiscences of Campaigning in South Africa by Commissary Walter Alphonsus Dunne, 1877-81*
Weekly Irish Times for 8 March 1879
Wellington Gazette for 15 July 1879

E

George Edwards was a survivor of the defence.

He was born as George Edward Orchard on 25 August 1855, at 5 Charles Street in the St James district of Bristol, and he was baptised in St James Church on 4 November 1855. He was the eldest son of three born to George Orchard, a master tailor, and his second wife, Anna (formerly Goodman), who he had married in Bristol in 1850. His first wife was Elizabeth Gadd of Bristol, who he had married on 4 July 1841. His siblings were Albert Thomas, born in 1857; and Frederick, born in 1859. George Orchard senior died on 30 April 1871, and George junior seemed to be jinxed when it came to employment. He was apprenticed to a shoemaker in John Street, Bristol, but his employer died, and he took a job at a boot factory near Stone Bridge in Bristol, which closed down. He headed for Wales, where he gained employment as a labourer in the building trade, but the business failed and closed down.

Perhaps not surprisingly, George went to the army recruiting office in Newport and enlisted on 23 November 1876, as George Edwards. His description was given as just over five feet four inches tall, with a fresh complexion, blue eyes and brown hair, and his religion was Church of England. As 922 Private Edwards he was posted to the 2nd Battalion, 24th Regiment. He served at Dover and Chatham, and from 15 June to 28 July 1877, he was attached to the Grenadier Guards in London, completing a course in training and drill.

He received orders for active service in South Africa and sailed to the Cape with his unit in February 1878. He took part in the Cape Frontier War, and on 17 July 1878, he made a remittance of two pounds to Anna Orchard. No other details of Anna being his mother were given to the paymaster owing to the fact that he had enlisted as George Edwards. George was up in front of his commanding officer in August 1878 charged with an offence which was unrecorded, but earned him eight days loss of pay and he was confined to cells from 23 to 30 August. He was fined seven shillings for drunkenness on 1 December 1878.

He was present at the defence of Rorke's Drift, and stated:

I remember well that when Lord Chelmsford rode in on the morning of the 23rd, I was sitting on a biscuit box drinking a cup of cocoa. For some reason he stopped to speak to me and asked me my opinion about the defence we had put up. There was only one answer I could make to him 'It was an act of providence.'

He wrote a letter to his father at St Luke's Road in Bedminster, and on 29 March 1879, the *Bristol Observer* carried a report under the title: *A Bedminster Man at Rorke's Drift*, in which he stated:

Our company was fighting hard from three o'clock in the afternoon until 6 o'clock the next morning, when we beat them off. These Zulus are a strong, savage, determined race of people, and we have not enough British troops out here for the war, so it will take a long time before it is over unless we get more troops as the enemy come in such large numbers.

It was also reported that: 'Pte Orchard and another comrade simultaneously fired at and wounded in the knee, the brother of the King of the Zulus, and he was taken prisoner in consequence.' He was also stated to have been present when the Prince Imperial was killed. For his service he received the South Africa Medal with 1877-78-79 clasp.

He served at Gibraltar, where he was fined a day's pay in March 1880, and again in April of that year. He was in confinement for seven days in May, and again confined for three days in June. He sailed to India, where he was awarded a penny a day good conduct pay from 9 June 1882. He arrived at Gosport on 27 January 1883, and was admitted to Netley Hospital until 6 February 1883. He was then posted to the 1st South Wales Borderers in Manchester to await discharge. He forfeited his good conduct pay while stationed at Manchester, and he was discharged to the first class army reserves on 1 April 1883. He received his final discharge at Brecon on 23 November 1888.

He gave his intended place of residence as Withy Mill in Paulton, Somerset, and it is thought that he found employment at Ashman's Boot Factory in Paulton.

He was described as a shoemaker when he married a domestic

servant named Rena Elizabeth Swift, at the Clutton Register Office, on 14 April 1884, and they lived at New Pit in Paulton. They had 11 children, all registered as being born in Clutton–Mabel Elizabeth was born in 1884, Sarah Hannah in 1885, William George in 1887, Albert Edward in 1888, who died at the age of three months. Mary Ellen was born in 1890, Edith Emily in 1892, Charles Frederick in 1894, Dennis Bertram John in 1897, Olive Rena in 1899, Herbert Ernest was born in 1903, and Florence Gertrude was born in 1907.

He was a member of the Royal Defence Corps, and he and Rena attended the Methodist Church. He attended the Northern Command Tattoo in 1934, and he gave an interview to the *Somerset Guardian* not long before he died, which appeared under the title: *Helped to Defend Rorke's Drift. Paulton Veterans Recollections.*

George died at New Pit in Paulton, Clutton, on 14 February 1940, aged 84, the cause of death being given as myocardia (heart failure), and he was buried at the Paulton Parish Cemetery with full military honours (section 25, row P, plot 25).

Birth certificate–St James, Bristol BXCC742637
Death certificate–Norton Radstock HD124784
Marriage certificate–Clutton AB215766
Bristol Observer for 27 March 1879
Somerset Guardian for 1 July 1932
The South African Wars: The Somerset Connection (Part Two), by J. C. Kenworthy

Abraham Evans was a survivor of the defence.

He was born on 7 February 1855, in Twyn-y-ffrwd, Abersychan near Pontypool, and he was baptised on 17 March 1855, at the Park Terrace Methodist Chapel in Pontypool. He was the fourth of six sons in the family of ten children to James Evans, a coal miner of Trevethin, and his wife Winifred (formerly Bratt–1829-1906).

James was joined at the pit by his three eldest sons, including Abraham. On 3 September 1879, Abraham's older brother, Paul, lost his life when he fell 30 yds down a pit shaft and was killed instantly. James Evans died of bronchitis and a fever at Garndiffaith in Trevethin on 27 September 1873, aged 48, and Winifred re-married in 1877.

Abraham enlisted into the Royal Regiment of Artillery at Newport, and as 1643 Gunner Evans he was posted to K Battery, 16th Brigade, at Woolwich. However, the unit became F Battery, 24th Brigade on 1 April 1874, and on 1 July 1877, it became known as N Battery, 5th Brigade. Gunner Evans was awarded a penny a day good conduct pay from 7 January 1878.

The unit received orders for active service in South Africa and embarked on the troopship Dublin Castle on 9 January 1878. They arrived at King Williamstown on 11 February 1878, to find that much of the heavy baggage had been ransacked. The unit saw active service in the Ninth Cape Frontier War, which ended in July 1878, and on 2 November the Battery was given orders to move to Greytown. They moved to Helpmekaar, followed by the order to move up to the Zululand border at Rorke's Drift. Gunner Evans was confined in hospital at Rorke's Drift suffering from dysentery. He left an account of his experiences in the *Free Press of Monmouthshire* for 18 April 1913.

Abraham and the other sick and wounded men were evacuated to Helpmekaar, where N Battery was camped, having been withdrawn from the field. When he returned to duty he re-joined his battery, and in June of that year Prince Louis Napoleon was killed by Zulus while he was out on patrol, and Abraham was on parade as the Prince's body left for transportation to England. Between July and October 1879, N Battery was in the Northern Transvaal, where Gunner Evans saw action against Chief Sekhukhune and the Pedi tribe, at which time he received news that his brother, Paul, had fallen down a pit shaft and was killed.

On 14 November 1880, N/5 was moved to Potchefstroom, where work began to reinforce the old fort. On 16 December 1880, the first shots of the first Boer (Transvaal) War were fired when Boer commando units laid siege to the town. During the siege Abraham was laid low with typhoid fever, and on 11 March 1881, he was hit in the back by a sniper bullet. The siege ended amicably on 23 March 1881. The Battery was inspected by Queen Victoria at Hay-on-Wye on 3 July 1882, and Abraham was brought to the attention of the Queen as being a defender of Rorke's Drift.

He requested service in Egypt, and as 10148 Gunner Evans, he was posted to I Battery, 2nd Brigade, 2nd Division, and embarked aboard the troopship *City of London* on 8 August 1882, arriving in Alexandria on 22 August. By 13 September 1882, he was fighting at

Tel-el-Kebir. While stationed at Abbussigeh Camp in Cairo, he sent an 18-verse poem to Mary Ann Williams which he had composed, entitled: *Recitation on Egypt.* The muster roll for 1883 shows Abraham in receipt of two pence a day good conduct pay. Abraham received his final discharge at Woolwich on 19 April 1883, at Woolwich. He had earned the South Africa Medal with 1877-8-9 clasp, The Egypt Medal with Tel-el-Kebir clasp, and the Khedives Bronze Star with Egypt 1882 clasp. A family story states that he used to have hallucinations that he was in the desert and the enemy was hiding in the sand.

Abraham returned to the home of his mother in Harpers Road, Victoria Village, Garndiffaith, and settled back into his former life as a coal miner in Trevethin. He married Mary Ann Williams at the Parish Church in Trevethin, on 5 November 1883, and they lived in Cwmavon Road, Garndiffaith. They moved to The Balance, Varteg, Abersychan, finally settling at Spring Gardens in Varteg. They had eight children; Benjamin James, born on 18 December 1884, Mary Valentine, born on 13 November 1886; Margaret 'Maggie' Hannah born on 2 February 1889; Elizabeth Ann, born on 14 January 1891; Rachel Tye, born on 23 August1892; Emma, born in 1894; John Leslie, born on 23 April 1897; and Alice Maud, born on 9 February 1899. Another baby was stillborn in 1902.

He wrote a letter to the *Monmouth Free Press,* which was published on 18 April 1913, and on 20 May 1914, the *Western Mail* published a story about him.

Abraham Evans died at his home in Spring Gardens, Varteg, Abersychan in Monmouthshire, on 4 May 1915, aged 60. The cause of death was given as 'hepatic disease' (liver disease). He was buried in an unmarked grave at the Wesleyan Chapel Yard, Varteg, Abersychan. Mary Ann died in 1946 and was buried with him. The grave was rediscovered, neglected and overgrown. The site was renovated and a memorial stone was erected at a rededication service in 2001. It was reported: 'Royal British Legion and other ex-service standards including those of the South Wales Borderers dipped smartly as a stone was unveiled at the head of the soldier's grave.' However, the new stone was destroyed by vandals and after the 'Gunner Evans Memorial Fund' was set up by various organisations, a replacement memorial was erected in 2002.

Abertillery Merlin for 5 September 1879
Birth certificate (Pontypool)
Birth certificates of children (all Pontypool)
Death certificate (Pontypool)
Father's death certificate (Pontypool)
Pontypool census 1891and 1901
Private article on the life of Abraham Evans compiled by his grandson, Thomas L. Roberts
War Office papers and muster rolls for N Battery (WO10/ 2530 and WO16/282, 283, 287 and 291)
Free Press of Monmouthshire for 18 April 1913
Western Mail for 20 May 1914

Edward Evans brought news of the Zulu advance on Rorke's Drift, but did not stay.

He served as 45/726 Private Evans with the 2nd Battalion, 3rd Regiment (The Buffs), the same unit as Sergeant Millne, and was attached to No. 1 Squadron, Mounted Infantry. He rode on to Helpmekaar after he had delivered the news.

According to Colonel Edward William Bray, 4th (King's Own) Regiment, 'He was ordered with two others to ride as hard as he could to Rorke's Drift to give them the alarm.' He is believed to have arrived at Rorke's Drift in the company of Private David Whelan of the 1st Battalion, 13th (Somerset) Light Infantry, who was also attached to the Mounted Infantry.

Under the title: *A Welsh Survivor from iSandlwana* the *Aberystwyth Observer* for 5 April 1879, reported:

Edward Evans, of Llawryglyn near Llanidloes [Montgomeryshire], was one of the few soldiers of the 24th Regiment who escaped from the iSandlwana disaster. Writing to his mother and brother [from Helpmekaar] on 3 February 1879, he says: 'Every day I have been running messages from the general to all the military posts on the Buffalo River, and, dear mother, don't grieve for me, for I am not to die in South Africa. With the help of God, there are no bullets made to kill me.'

Montgomeryshire Express and Radnor Times for 1 April 1879
Aberystwyth Observer for 5 April 1879
Y Genedl Gymreig for 10 April 1879
North Wales Express for 11 April 1879
Y Gwyliedydd for 17 April 1879
London Daily Chronicle for 25 June 1879
A Brave Fugitive: An Anonymous Account of iSandlwana: Studies in the Zulu War by Julian Whybra, 2012

Thomas Evans was a survivor of the defence.

He was born at Cilybebyll, Pontardawe, near Neath, in about 1855, the son of a stoker. By 1871 he was living with his family at Llwynypia, near Tonypandy, Glamorganshire. He was aged 15 and was working as a collier.

He enlisted at Monmouth in 1876, and as 954 Private Evans he was posted to H Company, 2nd Battalion, 24th Regiment. He received orders for active service in South Africa and sailed to the Cape with the battalion in February 1878. He took part in the Cape Frontier War, and during the Zulu War he was present at the defence of Rorke's Drift, probably as a patient in the hospital, although he does not mention it in his letter.

On 28 January 1879 he wrote a letter home in Welsh to his wife in Tonypandy, which appeared in the *Western Mail* for 29 March 1879, in which he stated:

> Dear wife—I send you these few lines to inform you that I was not among the unfortunate men belonging to our regiment who were killed on 22 January of this month. The camp was left in charge of some 850 privates and officers, and they were out (Allan) they were attacked and all killed excepting 20.
>
> The Zulus crossed into Natal and attacked another station (goraaf arall); but another company of our regiment poured out (geltwng Allan); such fire against them that they failed to force an entrance, and when they saw what number of men among them was being killed they set fire to the hospital and then retreated.
>
> I was in the midst of this fight and about a hundred of us killed about 600 of the enemy with a loss of 15 men among

ourselves.

On the following morning, what remained of our regiment came to us, and we are now waiting for others to come and take our place, because we have neither clothes nor anything else.

I do not suppose we shall go to the battlefield again, because our companies are so cut up that it will be hardly possible to form into a regiment (catrawd). I shall write again when that is possible, and give you full particulars...

He was tried for quitting his picquet without permission and confined for 14 days from 31 January 1879. For his service he received the South Africa Medal with 1877-8-9 clasp.

He served at Gibraltar in 1880, where he began to drink heavily and get into trouble with the authorities. He began to make a monthly remittance of seven shillings and six pence to 'Mrs Evans, Wife', from 30 April 1880. He was fined seven shillings and six pence for drunkenness on 12 May 1880, and he was fined ten shillings for drunkenness on 27 May 1880, being confined in cells, but he still managed to increase the remittance to his mother by three pence from 31 May 1880, although this was reduced to seven shillings at a later date. He was confined in cells on 3, 14 and 17 June 1880, and he was fined for drunkenness on 10 July 1880.

While he was with the First Class Army Reserve at Brecon in 1884, he served two terms of imprisonment–from 8 July to 11 August, for malicious damage; and from 13 August to 12 October, for assault. Both stretches included hard labour.

Abergavenny Chronicle for 11 July 1884
Western Mail for 29 March 1879

F

John Fagan was killed in action at Rorke's Drift.

He attested for the army on 13 December 1876, and as 969 Private Fagan he was posted to the 2nd Battalion, 24th Regiment, at Brecon. He received orders for active service in South Africa and sailed to the Cape in February 1878, taking part in the Cape Frontier War. He was confined by civil power in Natal, tried on 7 November 1878, and sentenced to five days imprisonment.

During the Zulu War he was present at the defence of Rorke's Drift, where he was killed in action. He was providing cover fire for the men who were evacuating the hospital when he was hit in the chest by a Zulu bullet, but he managed to keep hold of his rifle and remained at his post. Private Savage was interviewed by a newspaper which reported:

In the night time, when under fire, Savage heard a fellow soldier of the name of Fagan cry out for water, and managed to crawl along to help his disabled comrade-in-arms, who died before daylight next morning.

He was buried in the cemetery at Rorke's Drift and his name is inscribed on the monument. For his service he was entitled to the South Africa Medal with 1877-8-9 clasp, and his effects were listed as claim by his next-of-kin.

John Barker French was a survivor of the defence.

He was born on 6 August 1841, at 2 Dukes Lane in Kensington, London. He was the first child of four to William George French, a coachman, and his wife, Mary Ann (formerly Barker); who had married in Richmond-upon-Thames in September 1840. John was christened at St Mary Abbott's Church in Kensington on 3 October 1841. As the family increased they moved to a larger home at 2 Adam and Eve Yard in Kensington. John was working as a groom when he contracted erysipelas, a skin disease associated with dermatitis, which is passed from infected animals and can also affect the joints.

Consequently, John left his job at the stables and enlisted into the army at Westminster, London, on 16 December 1858. His description was five feet four inches tall, with blue eyes and brown hair. He had a thirty and three-quarter inch chest measurement, with a 'wiry' build. As 582 Private French he was posted to the 2nd Battalion, 24th Regiment. He was admitted to hospital on 12 May 1859, for treatment of his skin disease, which was to cause him problems throughout his army life.

He sailed from Cork to Mauritius on 10 March 1860, where he reached the rank of sergeant on 13 November 1861. However, he was tried by court martial on 18 August 1862, being sentenced to five days imprisonment and reduced to private. He received several promotions and demotions, never rising above the rank of corporal. He served in Burma from 6 October 1865, and he was sent to the hospital at Port Blair on the Andaman Islands, India, in June 1866, when his skin complaint flared up again. He returned to Burma, after which the regiment was posted to India, on 16 February 1869. He was invalided to Bombay on 17 February 1870, with his skin problem, and then he was sent to Netley Hospital on 8 April 1870. He was promoted to corporal on 16 July 1870.

While stationed at the Warley depot in Birmingham, he met Mary Priscilla Johnstone, of 2 Dukes Lane in Kensington, and they married at Kensington Parish Church on 13 April 1873.They had five children. Elizabeth was born in 1874, William James Alexander in 1876, Louisa Beatrice in 1877, Thomas George in 1880, and Ernest John in 1882.

While stationed at Aldershot John was in hospital suffering with another bout of erysipelas, which appeared to be lasting longer each time it erupted. He received orders for active service in South Africa, and his family accompanied him as he sailed to the Cape in February 1878. He took part in the Cape Frontier War, and during the Zulu War he was present at the defence of Rorke's Drift. He was promoted to sergeant on the day after the battle, and was transferred to G Company. However, on 24 June he was registered in the defaulters book and reduced to private.

He served at Gibraltar in 1880, returning to Brecon on 3 November 1880, where he was promoted to corporal on 9 February 1881. However, he was tried by court martial and reduced to private in the following August.

He discharged on 3 January 1882, having completed nearly 22 years' service, his conduct and character being described as good. His intended place of residence was 8 William Street in Kensington, the home of his mother, and, despite his condition, he gained employment as a stableman.

Sadly, Mary Priscilla died of blood poisoning on 22 September 1884, after giving birth to a still-born child at 8 William Street in Notting Hill, aged 34, and after a service at Kensington Church, she was buried in a common grave at Brompton Cemetery in West London (grave reference: N84.9 x 25.3).

He and his mother moved the family to live at Kintbury Cottage in Vine Terrace, Holland Street, Kensington, where his sister, Elizabeth found him to have dropped dead on the landing on 27 June 1895, aged 54, the cause of death being recorded as compression of the brain from sanguineous apoplexy (natural)–the rupture of a blood vessel. He was buried in a common grave at Hanwell Cemetery in London (section 92, grave 47).

Baptism notice for Kensington on 3 October 1841
Marriage certificate–Kensington G004747
Death certificate–Kensington Town R468801
Wife's death certificate–Kensington Town PAS6036909
West London Observer for 6 July 1895
Brompton Cemetery Burial Records
Friends of Brompton Cemetery

G

Patrick Galgey was a survivor of the defence.

He was born in Ireland in 1851. He was the son of Patrick Galgey, who was a chandler by trade. The *History of Cork* shows a Patrick Galgey of 2 Clifton Terrace in Cork, who may be Drummer Galgey's father.

Patrick junior attested in Cork as a boy soldier on 12 March 1865. He received a bounty of one pound, and he was described as: aged fourteen years, and being four feet seven and three quarter inches tall. As 1713 Private Galgey he was posted to D Company, 2nd Battalion, 24th Regiment. He was appointed drummer on 1 February 1866, which meant he received an extra penny a day. He remained in Cork for five years before being posted to India to join his company on 5 April 1869, at the age of eighteen. He was reduced to private at Secunderabad on 1 July 1870, but he was re-appointed drummer at Secunderabad, on 23 February 1872, and from 30 April 1872 he was in receipt of good conduct pay. He returned to the Warley depot on 1 October 1872. The muster rolls for 1 July 1873 show that he attended the Gravesend School of Musketry before postings at Warley, Aldershot, Dover and Chatham.

He received orders for active service in South Africa and sailed to the Cape with his battalion from Portsmouth in February 1878. He took part in the Cape Frontier War, and during the Zulu War he was present at the defence of Rorke's Drift. For his service he received the South Africa Medal with 1877-8-9 clasp.

He served at Gibraltar in 1880, where he was demoted to private, and he was discharged on 2 March 1880, having completed his army service of 15 years.

By 1881, Patrick was living at Top Row in New Town, Aberysrtuth, Monmouthshire, and he had gained employment as a labourer. Moving to London, he took lodgings at 24 Brand Street in Marylebone, and found work as a tailor's porter. He met Catherine Evans, who was 17 years older than him, and they lived together at 88 Newnham Street in Marylebone. They married at Marylebone register office, on 29 June 1891. By 1901 they had moved to 33 Great Quebec Street in Marylebone, and then they moved to 8 Circus Street in north-west London. At the age of 77, Catherine began to suffer the effects of senile dementia, and died in the Kensington registration district on 15 January 1913. She was buried in the Roman Catholic section of Kensal Green Cemetery. Six months later, on 5 August 1913, 61-year-old Patrick married Maria L. Eyles, who was aged 44, and lived at Greys Buildings in Marylebone. Patrick was described as being a shop porter.

Patrick was living at 110 Harrow Road in Paddington, when he died in Paddington Hospital on Harrow Road, on 11 August 1935, aged 84, the cause of death being given as a cerebral haemorrhage and arterial sclerosis. He was buried in an unmarked grave at Paddington Old Cemetery, London (section 3W, grave 9926), which remains overgrown and neglected. Maria was aged 88 when she died in the Ilford registration district in 1955.

First marriage certificate–Marylebone R475901
Second marriage certificate–Marylebone AB165872
Death certificate–Paddington West FC746873
History of Cork

Henry Edward Gallagher was a survivor of the defence.

He was born at Killenaule, Thurles in County Tipperary. Ireland, in March 1855, and he was baptised on 28 October 1855. He was the second child of Henry Gallagher, a merchant's clerk, and his wife, Mary (formerly Kennedy), His parents died while he was young, and it is believed that the church claimed the Gallagher's smallholding as payment for raising and educating the children. Henry became a clerk, and travelled to Liverpool in March 1874.

He enlisted into the army on 14 March 1874. He was just over five feet six inches tall, with a fresh complexion, amber eyes and dark-brown hair, and his religion was Roman Catholic. As 81 Private Gallagher he was posted to the 2nd Battalion, 24th Regiment, at Brecon. He was promoted to corporal on 11 March 1875. He was posted to Dover, where he gained a second class certificate of education in 1875, and he attended the Hythe School of Musketry in 1876. He was promoted to sergeant on 9 October 1877, aged only 22.

Henry married Caroline Maria Stanley, a domestic servant from Folkestone, at the Dover Registry Office, on 7 April 1877. Her father was a merchant seaman, and a member of her family had been in the service boat when Captain Matthew Webb swam the English Channel in 1875. At the time of the 1881 census they were living at the barracks in Brecon. They had six children. Caroline Lilian Gertrude was born in 1881, Henry Edward was born in 1883, William Alfred was born in 1885, Violet Elizabeth was born in 1888, Daisy Dorothea was born in 1890, and Lawrence Stanley was born in 1895. Henry, William and Lawrence enlisted in the army.

He received orders for active service in South Africa and sailed to the Cape in February 1878, taking part in the Cape Frontier War. He was present at the defence of Rorke's Drift, where, due to the continuous firing of his rifle, the heat made the breech of his weapon expand, which caused the powder to flash back, and from that day he had a permanent black mark burnt into his right cheek and the side of his nose. For his service he received the South Africa Medal with 1877-8-9 clasp.

He served at Gibraltar in 1880, where he extended his service to 12 years. When the regiment sailed for India he returned to Brecon, where he was promoted to colour sergeant on 26 January 1881, and when the unit became the South Wales Borderers on 1 July 1881, he was given the new regimental number 1590, and when he was posted to India in December 1882, and to Burma at the beginning of 1886. He was promoted sergeant-major on 9 January 1889, and served at Aden, where an ulcerated foot caused him to be hospitalised for the only time in his army career. He served at Malabar in India from 27 October 1893 to 9 January 1895, and on returning to England he was stationed at Hilsea, then Gosport. He served at Cairo in 1895, returning to England on 18 March 1897. While serving in Cairo his medals went missing and he had to get replacements.

Henry was discharged at Gosport, having completed over 23 years' service, and his conduct throughout his army career remained unblemished. His intended place of residence was Borstal House, 48 London Avenue, North End, Portsmouth. However, after only 24 hours as a civilian he was appointed barrack warden at Coleworth Barracks in Hilsea, a position he retained until 1911. He was described on discharge as being an exemplary soldier, with regular and temperate habits, and Army Orders for January 1911 announced that Sergeant Major Gallagher had been awarded the Meritorious Service Medal.

He was living in Corsham when he was one of 25 Zulu War veterans who attended The Old Comrades Club of the 24th Foot reunion at the Victoria Barracks in Portsmouth on 30/31 March 1929, along with Thomas Driscoll, John Jobbins, Henry Martin and John Williams VC. His retirement was spent at a house called 'Wistaria' 16 Augustine Road in Drayton Farlington, Hampshire, where Fred Hitch sometimes visited him.

He died of cardiac syncope and myocarditis–a massive heart attack–at his home on 17 December 1931, aged 75, and he was laid to rest at Christ Church Cemetery in Portsdown Hill, Hampshire, with semi-military honours. Caroline died on 7 July 1933, aged 74, and she was buried with him. A new memorial stone was installed at the grave, and a re-dedication service was organised in 2005.

Marriage certificate–Dover TF863854
Death certificate–Havant HC246
Wife's birth certificate–Elham, Folkestone PAS7007572
Wife's death certificate–North End and Buckland B361169
Henry Gallagher letter dated 30 March 1931
Private letters from Edward Lane

Edward Gee was a survivor of the defence.

He attested for the army in November 1872, and as 2429 Private Gee he was posted to the 1st Battalion, 24th Regiment, transferring to the 2nd Battalion on 1 January 1873. He received orders for active service in South Africa and sailed to the Cape in February 1878. He took part in the Cape Frontier War, and during the Zulu War he was present at the defence of Rorke's Drift. For his service he received the South Africa Medal with 1877-8-9 clasp. He was sent to Netley Hospital on 1 February 1880, and transferred to the army reserve.

James Graham was a survivor of the defence.

He was born as Daniel Sheehan near Cork in Ireland, on 28 April 1853. He left his job as a clerk to enlist into the army on 5 December 1870, and was posted to the 2nd Battalion, 6th (Warwickshire) Regiment. He was just under five feet eight inches tall. He gained a second class certificate of education, and by the end of January 1876 he had been promoted to sergeant, gaining a sergeant instructor of musketry certificate. However, he went absent without leave in the following June, for which he was tried and sentenced to be reduced to private. On 15 December 1876, he transferred to the army reserve at Liverpool District, having committed to six years at the time of his attestation.

He re-enlisted at Bin in Ireland, as 1123 Private James Graham, being posted to the 2nd Battalion, 90th Light Infantry. He said that he was born at St Mary's near Dublin, and stated that he had no previous military service. However, he was found out and convicted of fraudulent enlistment on 2 May 1877, lost his pension and good conduct pay, and was confined in military prison until 26 June 1877.

He received orders for active service in South Africa and arrived at the Cape on 11 January 1878. He took part in the Cape Frontier War, and while still on active service he was tried by court martial for desertion from the Liverpool District and had to forfeit the six years' service, pension and good conduct pay he had accumulated in the name of Private Sheehan.

Nevertheless, he continued his military service as James Graham, and by the time he took part in the defence of Rorke's Drift he had been promoted to corporal.

He later served in India, where he was promoted sergeant in May

1880, and all his forfeited service and pensions were restored to him on 16 March 1883. He reached the rank of colour sergeant with the 1st Lanark Rifle Volunteers, on 19 March 1887, and was discharged on 15 December 1891, after 21 years' service.

With the Anglo-Boer War looming, he was a foreman in the mobilisation stores, and he had been ill for ten days when he died of pneumonia at Winchester Street in Farnborough, Hampshire, on 24 February 1899, aged 46, and he was buried in the Aldershot Military Cemetery; where Edward Wilson had been buried eight years earlier.

Aldershot News for 4 March 1899

Robert Shedden St John Green was a patient in the hospital.

He was born in 1854, the son of Frederick Owen Green and his wife, Alice (formerly Shedden), who lived in Waterloo Road, Lambeth, London. He had two brothers; Harold, who was also known as John, and Frederick, who never married and survived into the London Blitz in 1940, and a sister named Alice, who never married and became a registered nurse. She came out of retirement to run the Cheltenham Hospital during the Great War. Frederick Owen Green moved to South Africa, and worked at the South African Glass Works in Cape Town.

The Natal Mounted Police (NMP) was formed as a para-military force by a retired British Army officer named Major John Dartnell, as the first line of defence in the colony, and the first man enrolled on 12 March 1874. Robert and Harold Green were based in Pietermaritzburg, where Robert joined the NMP on 31 August 1877, while Harold joined on 14 March 1878. The unit had been scouting the Natal-Zululand border since November 1878. Because of a problem with their horses the invasion force had already crossed into enemy territory when they joined the column, but they took part in the first skirmish with the Zulus at Sihayo's Kraal on 12 January 1879. Robert and Trooper Hunter were patients in the hospital on 22 January 1879, stricken with rheumatic fever.

A Roll of defenders compiled by Major Frank Bourne states that Robert was killed, but he escaped from the burning hospital, being wounded as he did so. Reverend Smith stated:

...and trooper RS Green (NMP) also a patient, all got out of the little end window within the enclosure. The window being high up, and the Zulus already within the room behind them, each man had a fall in escaping and then had to crawl (for none of them could walk) through the enemy's fire inside the entrenchment. Whilst doing this, Green was struck in the thigh with a spent bullet.

Robert discharged from the NMP on 30 April 1881, and Harold left the unit on 28 April 1884.

He died on 21 January 1925, aged 70, and is buried in Lazaretto Cemetery, Mossel Bay, Cape Province, South Africa.

H

James Hagan was a survivor of the defence.

He was born as James Egan at Neenagh, County Tipperary, Ireland, in 1857. Having previously served in the Royal Monmouth Militia, he enlisted with the name James Hagan at Monmouth on 23 March 1876, being just over five feet six inches tall, with a freckled complexion, grey eyes and light-brown hair. His religion was Roman Catholic. He gave his next-of-kin as his sister, Mary Ann Hagan. As 798 Private Hagan he was posted to the 2nd Battalion, 24th Regiment at Brecon. He obtained a fourth class certificate of education on 18 January 1877.

He received orders for active service in South Africa and sailed to the Cape with his battalion in February 1878. He took part in the Cape Frontier War, and during the Zulu War he was present at the defence of Rorke's Drift. For his service he received the South Africa Medal with 1877-8-9 clasp.

He was granted a penny a day good conduct pay in South Africa in July 1879, which he forfeited while serving in Gibraltar in June 1880, and it was restored while he was in India in June 1881. He returned to England on 24 November 1881, and transferred to the army reserve, 2nd Welch Regimental District, on 24 March 1882.

He married Catherine Julia Barry of Mountain Ash, at St Dubritius Chapel in Treforest, near Pontypydd, Glamorgan, on 8 July 1882, and they had five children.

He was re-called to army service in the 2nd Battalion, South Wales Borderers, on 3 August 1882, when he resumed his one penny a day good conduct pay, but he forfeited it a month later. He re-transferred to the army reserve, Cheshire Regiment District, on 8 February 1883, finally discharging at Brecon on 23 March 1888. His character was described as good.

James lived at 10 Meadow Street in Treforest. He died on 27 May 1916, aged 55, and he was buried in the Glyntaff Cemetery at Pontypridd.

A new headstone was erected at his grave in a dedication service held in 2009, during which time his great-grand-daughter recalled:

I grew up hearing my great-grandfather had fought and survived the famous Anglo-Zulu War. Members of my family had researched a James Egan and had said there were no records of him but when I asked my Aunt about him she showed me a scroll that had been wrapped up in a plastic bag for an eternity. I took it to the museum in Brecon and they explained it was given to survivors of the battle by the Mayor of Durban. I then got a copy of my great-grandfather's marriage certificate and contacted the church to see if they had any further information. They confirmed that his name was actually James Hagan and that he was buried in an unmarked plot in Glyntaff.

A commemorative blue plaque was unveiled at his former home in Meadow Street in 2024.

William Halley was a survivor of the defence.

He was born in Ireland in 1859. He attested for 25 Brigade on 3 March 1876, and as 1282 Private Halley he was posted to the 1st Battalion, 24th Regiment, transferring to the 2nd Battalion on 13 December 1877.

He received orders for active service in South Africa and sailed to the Cape with his unit in February 1878. He took part in the Cape Frontier War, and was promoted lance corporal on 17 July 1878. He served in the Zulu War, being present at the defence of Rorke's Drift.

He was promoted corporal on the day after the defence, was appointed master shoemaker on 29 January 1879, while he was still at Rorke's Drift, but he was reduced to private on 2 August 1879. For his service he received the South Africa Medal with 1877-8-9 clasp.

He was promoted to lance corporal on his arrival at Gibraltar on 21 February 1880, but he was reduced to private while in India on 10 January 1882.

He died of hepatitis while serving at Toungov (or Yougov), Thayetmyo in Burma, on 30 April 1887, aged 28; the informant being G. Bromhead VC, Major Commanding, Left Wing, 2nd/SWB. He was buried at Thayetmyo Military Cemetery. There seems to be no record of any claim for his effects, and his campaign medal was returned to the Mint on 23 November 1897.

John Harris was a survivor of the defence.

He was born at Crickhowell in Breconshire, in 1858. Having previously served in the Royal South Wales Borderers Militia, he enlisted for the regular army at Brecon on 15 January 1877, and as 1062 Private Harris he was posted to the 2nd Battalion, 24th Regiment. He was described as five feet six inches tall, with a sallow complexion, grey eyes and light-brown hair. His religion was Wesleyan. He was admitted to hospital at Brecon on 8 February 1877, suffering from anaemia, being admitted to hospital at Dover on 10 April 1877, suffering with the same complaint.

When the 2nd Battalion received orders for active service in South Africa it would seem that he had been granted permission 'For return home', and did not initially sail with his unit. However, he joined them on 1 July 1878, and apparently took part in the latter stages of the Cape Frontier War. He served in the Zulu War, and was present during the defence of Rorke's Drift. He claimed compensation for loss of kit at Rorke's Drift, and for his service he received the South Africa Medal with 1877-8-9 clasp.

He was admitted to the sick bay on board the ship transporting the regiment to Gibraltar on 26 January 1880, and he was admitted to hospital on their arrival. He was awarded a penny a day good conduct pay on 25 March 1880. He was brought before a medical board in Gibraltar and invalided on 12 July 1880. On his return to England on 24 July 1880, he was admitted to Netley Hospital suffering from chronic osteo-arthritis. He was discharged as unfit for further service on 14 September 1880, his character being described as good, his habits temperate, and he was in possession of one good conduct badge. An Injury Assessment Board held at the Royal Hospital, Chelsea, on 14 August 1880, confirmed that he was suffering from osteo-arthritis due to lying for months on damp ground, provoked and aggravated by climate and service. It was stated that he can eventually earn a living, and he was awarded a pension of seven pence a day for three years. His intended place of residence was Wandsworth, Surrey.

Garret Henry Hayden was killed in action during the fight for the hospital.

He was born in Ireland in 1852, the son of Charles Hayden, a cabinet maker. He enlisted in Dublin on 9 December 1865, and his description notes stated that he was five feet five inches tall. He gave his age as 18 but later information suggests that he enlisted as a boy soldier at the age of 13 and the latter figure has been mistaken for an eight by transcribers. As 1769 Private Hayden he was posted to D Company, 2nd Battalion, 24th Regiment, in India, on 11 July 1867. He was appointed drummer on 1 October 1868, but he reverted to private on 10 September 1873.

He married Margaret Ann Jones at Brecknock Register Office on 5 May 1877, when he gave his occupation as bugler, 2/24th Regiment. They set up home at 9 John Street in Brecon. Their only child, Mary Ellen, was born at the Barracks on 17 February 1878, and as Garret had received orders for active service in South Africa, and had sailed to the Cape on 2 February 1878, it must be assumed that he had missed the birth. Before leaving Britain, Garret had given his wife a small brooch as a keepsake, which is still owned by the family, and has been identified as the sept badge of the Irish 'Clan Dennis'.

He took part in the Cape Frontier War, and in the Zulu War he was killed in action during the defence of Rorke's Drift. He was a bedridden patient in a dangerously exposed room of the hospital being defended by Privates John and Joseph Williams. Private Hook stated:

John Williams had held the other room with Private William

Horrigan for more than an hour, until they had not a cartridge left. The Zulus then burst in and dragged out Joseph Williams and two of the patients, and assegaid them.

One of these was Drummer Hayden, and Sergeant Smith stated:

> We had thirteen killed and about eight wounded. Amongst the former was poor Drummer Hayden, who lived at the top of John Street. He was stabbed in hospital in sixteen places, and his belly cut open right up in two places, and part of his cheek was cut off.

He was buried in the cemetery at Rorke's Drift and his name is inscribed on the monument. His effects were claimed by his father. For his service he was entitled to the South Africa Medal with 1877-8-9 clasp.

Drummer Hayden had died never having seen his daughter. She died as Mary Ellen Jones in 1959 and was buried at Melksham in Wiltshire. His wife re-married in 1881 to a man named Job Jones.

Several of his descendants saw distinguished military service. His great-grandson, Kenneth Jones, served with the Welsh Guards. During the Falklands War in 1982 he was aboard HMS *Sir Galahad* waiting to disembark as part of British land forces when Argentine fighter planes attacked the ship and he was badly burned.

Birth certificate of his daughter–Brecknock CM96956
Marriage certificate–Brecknock 134
His wife's marriage certificate to her second husband

Patrick Hayes was a survivor of the defence.

He was born at Newmarket in County Clare, Ireland, on 9 September 1854. He enlisted at Ennis in County Clare, on 8 September 1868, and as 2067 Private Hayes he was posted to the 2nd Battalion, 24th Regiment. As a boy of 14, he was just over four feet eight inches tall, with a fresh complexion, grey eyes and light-brown hair. He was appointed drummer on 8 December 1869, and embarked for service in India on 29 December 1869. Having reverted to private, he returned home on 3 January 1873, and was appointed drummer on 1 April 1873.

He received orders for active service in South Africa and sailed to the Cape in February 1878, taking part in the Cape Frontier War, and during the Zulu War he was present at the defence of Rorke's Drift. For his service he received the South Africa Medal with 1877-8-9 clasp.

He re-engaged on 22 November 1879, and gained a second class certificate of education. He served at Gibraltar in 1880, and in India, where he reached the rank of corporal on 22 September 1885, and after reverting to private, he was appointed bandsman on 7 October 1887, while serving in Burma. Having returned to India on 10 November 1888, he was permitted to continue in the service beyond 21 years, on 29 October 1889. He returned home on 16 February 1892, being awarded a third good conduct badge on 9 September 1892. He discharged on 30 November 1892, being awarded a pension for life on the following day.

He became a civilian worker at the barracks in Brecon until he was over 60 years of age, and on his retirement he lived in Riverhall Street in Wandsworth Road, London.

Described as '...a grey-haired veteran living in a cosy house', he left an account in the *News of the World* for 22 January 1939.

Patrick died at Lambeth in London, on 4 October 1940, aged 86. He was buried with military honours provided by the East Surrey Regiment, in an unmarked grave at Lambeth Cemetery (plot V3-328), and Colonel Frank Bourne OBE, DCM attended his funeral. His widow was presented with his campaign medal, his Rorke's Drift bible and discharge papers, which are now at the regimental museum in Brecon.

News of the World for 22 January 1939
South Wales Borderers Regimental Journal for April 1940

Frederick Hitch was wounded in action, and was awarded the Victoria Cross for valour at Rorke's Drift.

He was born on 29 November 1856, at 7 Chase Side in Southgate, Edmonton, Middlesex (now Greater London), and was christened at the local Weld Chapel. He was the sixth son and ninth child of 11 to John Hitch and his wife Sarah (formerly Champness). His father was a journeyman boot and shoemaker, and the 1861 census shows the family at 7 Chase Side, and in 1871 at Chase Road.

It seems that Fred had committed some kind of petty crime for which he pleaded guilty at Westminster Police Court. In consequence of this he agreed to enlist into the British Army on 7 March 1877, and as 1362 Private Hitch he was posted to the 2nd Battalion, 24th Regiment, at Dover, on 11 May 1877. His physical description was given as: 'Five feet eight inches tall, with brown hair, hazel eyes and a fresh complexion.' He was only able to sign an X on his enlistment papers.

He served for a while at Chatham, then his unit received orders for active service in South Africa and sailed to the Cape with the battalion, taking part in the Cape Frontier War, and during the Zulu War he was present at the defence of Rorke's Drift.

After the battle he stated:

I had not had time to form an opinion as to whether the Zulus would take the fort or not. My only wish was—as I believe was that of every other man—to fight as hard as I could, and I did it until I was wounded. I crept to the rear, and with the assistance of Private Deakin, tied up my wound as well as I could by tearing off the sleeve of a greatcoat for the purpose. I then knocked about as well as I could, serving the others with ammunition until I became exhausted from loss of blood and fell down unconscious. I did not come to until the morning, just as peep of day, and then found myself in a stable. The Zulus, meanwhile, had retired, but were again advancing to attack us, and they saw the General and his column coming, and again retired.

After a tough journey of about 150 miles to Durban, which he described as being 'rather tough', he spent some time under medical care there, before being sent home on the *Tamar*. This voyage was full of its own horrors, as two children died and a Corporal Campbell jumped overboard and several men died of poisoning. Fred was unaware that he had been awarded the Victoria Cross, which had been announced on the day he had embarked on the *Tamar*. On arriving at Southampton it was reported:

Private Hitch, who still wears his right arm in a sling, was unaware of the honour conferred on him until his arrival back home. On being told, with much emotion he exclaimed: 'Have they given me the Cross?' On being assured that Her Majesty had been pleased to confer that distinguished recognition of his services upon him the poor fellow was completely overcome.

His award of Victoria Cross was announced in the *London Gazette* for 2 May 1879, which stated:

It was chiefly due to the courageous conduct of these men [Corporal William Allan and Private Frederick Hitch] that communication with the hospital was kept up at all. Holding together a most dangerous post, raked in reverse by the enemy's fore from the hill, they were both severely wounded, but their determined conduct enabled the patients to be withdrawn from the hospital, and when incapacitated by their wounds from fighting, they continued, as soon as their wounds had been dressed, to serve out ammunition to their comrades during the night.

He also received the South Africa Medal with 1877-8-9 clasp.

He was admitted to the Royal Victoria Hospital at Netley, where he had 39 pieces of broken bone taken from his shoulder, and a medical board decided that his arm was permanently disabled. He was discharged unfit for further service on 25 August 1879.

While he was a patient at the hospital, on 12 August 1879, Queen Victoria and Princess Beatrice sailed over from Osborne on the Royal Yacht Alberta to visit the hospital, and while she was there the Queen presented him with the Victoria Cross in person.

Fred returned to civilian life in London, and on 5 July 1881, he married Emily Matilda Meurisse, who was of German descent, at St Matthew's Church in Bayswater. They had made their home at Porchester Square in Westminster, and had six children. Their three sons all passed-out as drum majors at the Duke of York School. Frederick later joined the Metropolitan Police, and Charles served with the 60th Rifles and the South Wales Borderers.

The 1891 census shows Fred living with his family at 1 Epirus Mews on Epirus Road in the parish of St John's, Fulham, London, and he was self-employed as a cab proprietor, having bought a taxi cab and two horses and set up a small transport business in south London. While he was working at the Royal United Services Institute in Whitehall Cecil Rhodes visited and congratulated him on his bravery. By the time of the 1901 census the family had moved to 1 Epirus Mews, St John's Parish in Fulham.

His Victoria Cross was stolen from his coat, the family had to pay for a replacement, and Fred had to sign a declaration to return the medal if the original was found. He was presented with the replacement by Lord Roberts in 1908, and he wore his Victoria Cross at the coronation of King Edward VII in 1911.

He lived for a short time in 1910 in Pond House, Pond Place in Chelsea, and he was living in Duke Street in Chiswick when the age of the motor car began to make its mark he went to work as a taxi driver for the General Motor Cab Company in Chiswick. By 1912 he was living on his own in rented accommodation at 62 Cranbrook Road, Turnham Green in Chiswick. In those days when there was no power steering it must have been quite strenuous for Fred at times because of his injured arm.

During Christmas 1912 the drivers at his depot went on strike and he spent much of his time on picket duty in bitterly cold weather, which seems to have damaged his health, and on 6 January 1913, he complained of bad pains in his side. His landlady tried to comfort him but he collapsed and died, apparently in the arms of a neighbour, later in the day, aged 56. An inquest found that he had died of pleura-pneumonia and heart failure.

His funeral was an impressive affair, attended by John Fielding VC, Frank Bourne DCM, his friend Joseph Farmer (who was a Boer War holder of the Victoria Cross), and over a thousand London cab drivers. He was buried with military honours provided by the South Wales Borderers, at St Nicholas Churchyard in Chiswick Old Cemetery. His monument was paid for by public subscription, one of the donations coming from the family of Major Chard. The inscription reads:

To the Memory of Frederick Hitch VC, born 29 Nov 1856, died 6 Jan 1913. This memorial was erected by voluntary subscription to commemorate his heroic action at Rorke's Drift, 22 January 1879.

A London news special for 22 November 1929 reported under the headings: *Lost VC–Long Search Ends–Auction Find*:

> A romantic story of a son's search for his father's lost Victoria Cross was revealed today, when he purchased it in a London auction room for £65. It was won at Rorke's Drift in the Zulu War 56 years ago by Private Frederick Hitch, of the 24th Foot, now the South Wales Borderers. He bequeathed it to his eldest son, but it was lost. The never-ending search of his youngest son proved successful today. Curiously enough, he would have regained if at a considerably lower figure had it not been run up by another bidder. After the sale it was revealed that the other bidder had been a comrade-in-arms with the VC winner in the same regiment, who had been anxious to save one of the regiment's honours. He was not aware that Hitch's son was bidding.

A blue plaque was erected at the house where he died which states: 'Private Frederick Hitch VC, 1859-1913, Hero of Rorke's Drift, Lived and Died here.' His Victoria Cross is with the Regimental Museum in Brecon.

Chums for 11 March 1908
Daily Telegraph for 11 July 1910
Marylebone Mercury and West London Gazette for 11 January 1913
Penny Illustrated News for 21 June 1879
People for 4 October 1908
Private Frederick Hitch: Statement made on his being admitted to Netley Military Hospital in Southampton, published in *The Cambrian* newspaper on 13 June 1879.
Private Frederick Hitch: Eyewitness account held in the Regimental Archives of the South Wales Borderers at Brecon, and reproduced in *The Silver Wreath* by Norman Holme in 1979
Strand News and Gloucestershire Advertiser for 13 June 1879

Alfred Henry Hook was awarded the Victoria Cross for valour at Rorke's Drift.

He was born in Churcham, Huntley, near Gloucester, on 6 August

1850, the eldest son of three in the family of six children to Henry Hook (1828-1880) and his wife, Helen, Eleanor or Ellen (formerly Higgs–1831-1921). His father was an agricultural labourer, and their home was a house called 'Birdwood', known as 'Hook's Farm'. At the time of the 1861 census they were living in a cottage in Churcham (probably still the house where he was born), where Alfred, aged only ten, and his father, were recorded as working as wood-cutters. All Alfred's siblings had been born in Churcham, except the sixth child, Emily, who was born at Blaisdon in the Forest of Dean, Gloucestershire in 1863.

While living at Aston Ingham in Newent in Gloucestershire, Alfred met a local girl named Comfort Jones (1849-1900) and they married on 26 December 1870. He was described as a 'workman' on the certificate. The 1871 census records them as living in Pickle-nash in Newent, along with his wife's parents, John and Ann. They had three children born in Newent; Raymond John was born on 29 October 1871, Mary Henrietta on 19 September 1873, and Julia Ann on 16 May 1876.

He had enlisted into the Royal Monmouth Militia at Monmouth on 7 May 1869, and served with the unit until May 1874. He joined the regular army on 13 March 1877, and as 1373 Private 'Henry' Hook he was posted to the 2nd Battalion, 24th Regiment, at Monmouth, signing up for six years. He received orders for active service in South Africa and sailed to the Cape with his battalion in February 1878. He took part in the Cape Frontier War, and during the Zulu War he was present at the defence of Rorke's Drift. He left a detailed account of his experiences and his part in the action within the hospital.

Private Henry Hook was mentioned in dispatches, and his award of Victoria Cross was announced in the *London Gazette* on 2 May 1879:

These two men together [he and Private John Williams] one man working while the other fought and held the enemy at bay with his bayonet, broke through three more partitions, and were thus enabled to bring eight patients through a small window into the inner line of defence.

On 29 January he was one of the soldiers who transferred to G

Company to make up the numbers the unit had lost at iSandlwana; becoming orderly to Major Black. He remained stationed at Rorke's Drift, and on 3 August 1879 he became one of a very few number of men to be decorated with the Victoria Cross at the place where he had earned it, when General Wolseley pinned the medal to his chest. He also received the South Africa Medal with 1877-8-9 clasp.

Henry returned from Gibraltar to discharge from the army at Brecon on 25 June 1880, perhaps because his father was ill, as he died on 29 December 1880. His wife was apparently led to believe that 'Alfred' had been killed in action, which seems to have caused problems as he appears on the 1881 census as a domestic groom in Glendower Street in Monmouth, while Comfort and their children lived with her parents at Mount Pleasant in Newent, Gloucester. Comfort had become a gloveress (person who makes gloves).

Henry moved to London, where he lived in lodgings at Sydenham Hill, and gained employment as a general cleaner. He applied for a job at the British Museum, and after being recommended by Major Bromhead and Lord Chelmsford, he was taken on as an 'inside duster' from 26 December 1881. He was later appointed umbrella caretaker in the reading room at the museum, a position he held until his retirement. He became a member of the Loyal St James Lodge of Oddfellows in London; served as a corporal in the Bloomsbury Rifle Volunteers; and was sergeant, 19th Middlesex RVC, from April 1896 to January 1905. He was Sergeant Instructor of Musketry, 1st Volunteer Battalion, Royal Fusiliers, serving the unit for 20 years. A silver-plated memorial trophy bearing his name was presented to the British Museum Rifle Association, to be awarded for services to the Association. In the mid-1890s he moved to 4 Cumberland Street, Pimlico.

Although their marriage was not finalised until 25 August 1897, Comfort Hook married David Meyrick in Gloucester in June 1895, and after Henry met a local Islington girl named Ada Lettia Taylor (born in 1863) at a concert, they married on 10 April 1897, at St Andrew's Church in Islington. They had two daughters, Victoria Catherine was born in March 1899, and Letitia Jean was born in December 1902. In 1901 they lived at 25 Lesley Street, in the Lower Holloway district of Islington. Comfort died in 1900.

Henry had suffered from headaches, which were possibly caused by his wound, and by 1904 his condition had become serious. He was advised to return to his native county in the hope that the air would help combat his condition. He tendered his resignation, which took effect from 31 December 1904, and the museum trustees granted him a pension of 40 pounds a year. He was placed in the care of the Phoenix Lodge of Oddfellows at Gloucester, who recommended a doctor, and his family resided at 2 Osborn Villas in Rosebury Avenue, Gloucester.

Henry Hook died of pulmonary consumption on 12 March 1905, aged 54. His funeral was attended by thousands of people, and 23 regiments were represented. He was buried with military honours at St Andrew's Churchyard, Churcham. Fred Hitch attended the funeral with his son, who was one of the bearers. On 28 September 1906, his widow and daughters were present when a memorial cross was unveiled at his grave, and there is a memorial brass plate at Brecon Cathedral. His medals are in the South Wales Borderers Regimental Museum. His grave was renovated in 2008.

Death certificate–South Hamlet HC011951
Marriage certificate to Comfort Jones–Aston Ingham BO08604
Marriage certificate to Ada Taylor–Islington PAS46891/80
Macmillan's Magazine for May to October 1898
Private Alfred Henry Hook: *Stories of the Victoria Cross: Told by those who have won it*–published in the *Strand* magazine for January/June 1891.
Private Alfred Henry Hook: How They Held Rorke's Drift, published in the *Royal Magazine* for February 1905.

William Horrigan was killed in action during the fight for the hospital.

He was born at Cork, Ireland, in 1849. He enlisted into the 24th Regiment on 12 November 1863, and as 1861 Private Horrigan, he was posted to the 1st Battalion. He was just over 14-and-a-half-years-old. He re-engaged at Gibraltar 18 February 1873, and served in the Ninth Cape Frontier War, being stationed at East London in August and September 1877.

He may have originally been one of the men of G Company: 'who had been to the rear with prisoners...' but he was in the hospital at Rorke's Drift during the defence. He and three other patients, Privates Beckett, Adams and Hayden, were in the far end room of the building which had an outer door and no access to the interior. Privates John Williams and Joseph Williams were posted in the room with orders to defend them. When the Zulus attacked the hospital, they began to smash at the door trying to force their way in, and Private Horrigan was able to offer some assistance to keep them out while John Williams smash a hole through the partition with his bayonet as a means of escape. Private Horrigan escaped through the hole, but seems to have got disoriented, and he ran straight into the clutches of Zulu warriors entering by way of the verandah. He was seen to be thrown to the ground and stabbed to death.

He was buried in the cemetery at Rorke's Drift and his name is inscribed on the monument. His effects were claimed by his next-of-kin. For his service he received the South Africa Medal with 1877-8-9 clasp.

Arthur Howard was a survivor of the defence.

He was born on 2 May 1851, at Eynsford (pronounced Ainsford), near Farningham in Kent. He was the second son in a family of five children to William Howard, an agricultural labourer, and his wife, Maria (formerly Tucker). They had married at Dartford in 1842. All the Howard children were educated at the Eynsford village school.

Arthur began his working life as an agricultural labourer before becoming a groom, but by the beginning of 1871 he was unemployed. Consequently, on 28 April 1871, he enlisted in the Royal Regiment of Artillery at Woolwich Barracks in London. He was described as being five feet six and three quarter inches tall, with a fresh complexion, hazel eyes and brown hair. His chest measurement was thirty four inches, and he weighed 140 pounds. His muscular development was good and he had no distinctive marks.

He was posted to the 14th Brigade at Woolwich, where 2077 Gunner Howard transferred to the 15th Brigade, being posted to Newcastle-upon-Tyne on 20 August 1872. He was admitted to hospital for ten days in May 1873, suffering with primary syphilis. He was posted back to Woolwich on 5 May 1874, where he was back in hospital from 22 July until 14 August, being treated for ulcers on the left ankle. He was admitted to hospital with the same complaint on 9 January 1875, and discharged on 15 February 1875. On 17 April of that year he was posted to Newlodge in Ireland. He transferred back to the 14th Brigade on 29 April 1877, and on 1 August 1877, he transferred to the 5th Brigade, where he became the servant and batman to Major Arthur Harness.

The unit received orders for active service in South Africa and embarked on the troopship *Dublin Castle* on 9 January 1878. They arrived at King Williamstown on 11 February 1878, to find that much of the heavy baggage had been ransacked, and Gunner Howard was annoyed to find that his two sets of servant's clothes had been stolen, along with a clock belonging to Major Harness. The unit saw active service in the Ninth Cape Frontier War, and on 2 November the Battery was given orders to move to Greytown. They then moved to Helpmekaar, followed by the order to move up Rorke's Drift, where Arthur was admitted to the hospital on 18 January suffering with fever.

On 7 February 1879, he wrote a letter to his family from Helpmekaar describing the events, which was printed in the *Daily Telegraph*, on 25 March 1879, apparently to his dissatisfaction.

Arthur developed a good relationship with Major Harness. In a letter the major joked: 'Arthur Howard's correspondence is so large that I tell him he must provide separate mail arrangements, and that no government can stand the pressure he puts upon it.' By June 1879 Major Harness and Gunner Howard were camped on the banks of the Upoko River, and they were present at the battle of Ulundi on 4 July, for the final defeat of the Zulus. Harness describes Arthur as: 'always anxious to have a clothes-washing, in order, as he calls it, that we may start clean.' In a letter dated 7 September 1879, he hinted to his sister that he wanted Arthur to remain as his servant on his return home, by saying:

Arthur Howard is with me here. I have not mentioned to him my hope of getting leave, but if successful I intend telling him and getting him a passage home on a troopship if he likes to come. I have not made up my mind which is best; I shall send him to his friends of course on landing in England, I don't suppose you want him roaming about the village and garden.

On 14 October 1879 they boarded the *Edinburgh Castle* and arrived in Plymouth on 14 November 1879. Major Harness and Gunner Howard were posted to Hillsborough Barracks at Nether Hallam in

Sheffield, and then to The Cadets Academy on Woolwich Common in 1882.

Arthur had met a pantry maid called Frances Bird in Sheffield, and he found accommodation for here at 3 Woolwich Common. They married at the register office in Woolwich, on 24 May 1882. They had one child, who was known as Elsie, born in 1883, before Frances died of pneumonia aged 31 on 28 August 1889. Leaving Elsie with his sister in Sheffield, Arthur returned to Woolwich, from where he was discharged at his own request on 30 May 1890, with a pension of eleven pence a day. His character was described as 'exemplary'.

He obtained lodgings at 11 Adelphi Street in Nether Hallam, Sheffield, and found employment as a bookkeeper's clerk. By 1901 Arthur and Elsie had moved back to Woolwich, where he obtained employment as an ammunition case examiner at the Royal Arsenal factory, and took lodgings at 1 Parry Place in Plumstead. As his sight and general health gradually deteriorated with age, he retired from his job at the Royal Arsenal and took employment as a night watchman. He eventually retired for good and survived on his pension and savings.

On 14 February 1930, the *Daily Mirror* published a report that it had been announced in Australian newspapers that he had died in Sydney, after complaining of an old assegai wound received in the historic Drift fight. To which Arthur had expressed great surprise when he was informed of the report. The report went on to say: 'Although he is blind, he is an active man, and takes a keen interest in present day affairs.' Arthur added:

I was at Ulundi too, where we beat the Zulu Armies in forty minutes. I never received a wound of any sort from an assegai, or from anything for that matter. How Sydney Art Gallery can have a picture of me leaving the burning hospital carrying another man over my shoulder is more than I can understand. It certainly cannot be a picture of me. It was as much as I could do to leave the building myself, without carrying anyone else. I think the Australian report must be incorrect in the name.

It was indeed a case of mistaken identity.

Arthur Howard died on 15 July 1935, aged 84, at St Alfege Hospital, Vanbrugh Hill, Greenwich, London, the cause of his death being reported as senility. His home address at that time was his lodgings at 7 Harton Street in Deptford, London. He was buried in an unmarked grave in Brockley Cemetery in Lewisham, London (plot Y, grave 614), which had been purchased by his landlord, Walter Tanner. A new headstone was unveiled at the grave in 2012.

Daily Mirror for 14 February 1930
Daily Telegraph for 25 March 1879–Letter from Arthur Howard
Lloyds Weekly Newspaper for 30 March 1879
Birth certificate (Farningham)
Service records WO97/3095
Marriage certificate (Woolwich)
Death certificate (Greenwich East)
Wife's death certificate (Woolwich Arsenal)
War Office papers and muster rolls for N Battery (WO10/ 2530 and WO16/282, 283, 287 and 291)

Sydney Robert Hunter was killed in action at Rorke's Drift.

He was born in September 1856, at Barnet in Hertfordshire, the son of Sergeant Robert Hunter, who at the time of Sydney's death lived at Union Street in Barnet, and was described as a, 'deservedly respected fellow townsman.'

Sydney was a great friend of Lord Panmure, whom he visited at Seymour House, and stated: 'I loved Hunter as a brother.' It was recorded:

He went to the Transkeian front on 31 May 1878, got his discharge from the FAM Police. He then went up to Natal, to the war there, and joined the Natal Rifles. Damp and exposure laid him up in hospital with rheumatic fever, and his last letter to us was written from the hospital in Pietermaritzburg. He must, after this, have got better and crossed the Tugela.

He had been residing at Helpmekaar when he joined the Natal Mounted Police, and he was killed in action at Rorke's Drift. Lieutenant Chard reported:

Trooper Hunter, escaping from the Hospital, stood still for a moment hesitating which way to go, dazed by the glare of the burning hospital, and the firing that was going on all around. He was assegaid before our eyes, the Zulu who killed him immediately afterwards falling.

He was aged 22. Three pounds were found on his body, and a document recording his death states that his possessions were 'two saddle rings'. These were given to his commanding officer, Major John Dartnell. He was buried in the cemetery at Rorke's Drift and his name appears on the monument.

A letter announcing his death was sent to his father, and in June 1880, his father wrote a letter to the authorities in Natal, seeking the balance of his late son's estate, in which he added:

...my wife, who is now on her death bed, has never recovered from the shock of the sad news of his death. PS I am truly a great sufferer from that cruel and uncalled for Zulu War.

Barnet Express for 17 May 1879

J

David Jenkins was a survivor of the defence.

He was born in about 1847, at Defynnog in Brecknockshire, Wales. He was the son of Thomas David Jenkins, a tailor and draper. The 1861 census states that he was aged 14, and was a boarder at 1 Lower Road in Defynnog, being employed as an apprentice currier to a farmer.

He had served with the Carmarthenshire Artillery Militia, and gave up his job as a skinner to enlist for the regular army at Brecon, on 19 June 1874, and as 295 Private D Jenkins he was posted to G Company, 1st Battalion, 24th Regiment. He was five feet five and a half inches tall, with blue eyes and dark brown hair. His religion was Wesleyan.

He served at Gibraltar from 16 October to 27 November 1874. He was posted to Cape Town, South Africa on 28 November 1874. He lost privileges and was imprisoned for breaking out of barracks and going absent without leave several times during 1875, and he was hospitalised several times before being posted to King William's Town on 3 January 1876, where he was hospitalised suffering with a venereal disease. He deserted on 21 November 1876, and was hospitalised from 9 December 1876, with a contusion in the foot after being run over by a wagon when in a state of desertion. He re-joined and was placed in confinement on 8 December 1876, being tried and imprisoned for desertion from 8 December 1877 to 15 April 1878, and his former service towards good conduct pay and pension was forfeited. He was posted to Cape Town on 18 April 1877, where he was hospitalised for a week, and he was posted back to King William's Town on 8 August 1877. He served in the Cape Frontier War, being in confinement from 6-9 August 1878, and he was imprisoned from 19 August to 1 November 1878, for leaving his post while on picquet duty in Natal.

He was present at the defence of Rorke's Drift, where, about two hours into the battle the Zulus launched a particularly fierce assault. Lieutenant Chard was using his revolver to help to keep the enemy at bay when Private Jenkins suddenly ducked the officer's head down as a Zulu slug just missed him. It was stated in newspapers at the time the unit returned home:

Among the men of the 1st Battalion of the 24th who disembarked were Sergeant Wilson, Lance-Corporal Roy, and Privates Desmond, Payton and Jenkins, who had been to the rear with prisoners...

He wrote a letter to his father at the Tanner's Arms, Davynock, on 26 January 1879, which was published in the *Merthyr Express* on 22 March 1879, which stated:

Just a few lines to let you know that I am one of the ten that escaped out of the five companies. The remainder were cut to pieces,–in fact cut in bits–with those savages. Oh I never saw such a sight. Please to pray to God to continue to save my life. Please go to Isaac Lewis. His son Thomas is alive but is still in hospital with the fever. He had a very narrow escape. He crept on his hands and knees and came from the hospital to the fort through all the firing.

He arrived back in Portsmouth on 2 October 1879, and was posted to Gosport, being hospitalised on 18 October. He was tried and imprisoned for drunkenness, before being posted to Colchester on 26 November 1880. He transferred to the 1st class army reserve, Brecon District, on 11 June 1882, his character being described as fair. He was re-called to the colours at Brecon on 1 August 1882, and he was posted to Salford on 29 August 1882. He was appointed lance corporal 1 November 1882 to 7 February 1883, received good conduct pay of a penny a day from 24 January 1883, and obtained a second class certificate of army education. He transferred to Brecon on 8 February 1883, to complete his service, and transferred to the Cardiff District, 11 August 1883 to 24 May 1884. He discharged from the first class army reserve Brecon on 10 June 1888.

He married Annie Downey in Battersea, London, on 14 June 1880, giving his address as 7 Howey Street. They had seven boys. Thomas M. was born in 1882, William in 1883, David D. in 1885, Harry W. in 1888, Stanley T. in 1891, Frederick J. in 1894 and John J. in 1896. From 1884 to 1903 the family lived at 52 Bryn Melyn Street, St. Marks, Swansea, before moving to 13, where David worked for the Swansea Corporation and Harbour Trust as a clerk and storekeeper.

He died at 52 Bryn Melyn Street in Swansea, on 20 August 1912, aged 66, and he was buried in Cwmgelli Municipal Cemetery in Swansea (section D grave 945). His wife died in 1939 and is buried with him. There is a memorial stone at the grave.

The Ladies' Rorke's Drift Testimonial Fund presented a holy bible to all the known defenders of Rorke's Drift, and David's was donated to the Brecon Museum by his family. The museum also has the bibles presented to William Bessell and Charles Mason (Frederick Herbert Brown).

Brecon County Times for 26 April 1879 and 22 August 1912
Merthyr Express for 22 March 1879
South Wales Daily Post and Herald of Wales for July 1904

James Edmund Jenkins was killed in action during the fight for the hospital.

He was born on 29 October 1848, at 18 Broad Street in

Littledean, near Cinderford, Gloucestershire. He was the third child in a family of six to Griffith Jenkins and his wife, Fanny (formerly Limbrick). James, who apparently preferred to be called Edmund, was educated at the local Dame School in Littledean, from about 1855, later attending Littledean Parochial Primary School until he passed his Labour Exam at the age of 10. He started work as a dram boy just before his 11th birthday in the local Iron Ore Mine, and by 1861 he was labouring in a coal mine.

He enlisted at Monmouth on 18 July 1876, and as 841 Private Jenkins he was posted to the 1st Battalion, 24th Regiment. He was sent with a draft of the battalion for active service in South Africa, which arrived on 2 August 1877, serving in the Cape Frontier War. He may have originally been one of the men of G Company: 'who had been to the rear with prisoners...' but he was in the hospital at Rorke's Drift on 22 January 1879, presumably suffering with fever, as Surgeon Reynolds stated:

The only men actually killed in the hospital were three... The names were Sergeant Maxfield, Private Jenkins, both unable to assist in their escape, being debilitated by fever, and Private Adams...

Reverend Smith stated that as the patients were trying to escape from the Zulus through holes in the partitions: 'One poor fellow (Jenkins), venturing through one of these was also seized and dragged away...'

He was buried in the cemetery at Rorke's Drift and his name is inscribed on the monument. His effects were claimed by his next-of-kin. For his service he received the South Africa Medal with 1877-8-9 clasp. There is a memorial at Brecon Cathedral, and his name was added to the family headstone in Littledean. The inscription read: 'Also of Edmund, Their son, Who Was Killed in Battle at Isandula, Zululand, South Africa, Jan 22nd 1879, Aged 30 Years.' The area was cleared to make way for a play area for the Sunday school children, and the headstone is now against the wall.

John Samuel Jobbins was a survivor of the defence.

He was born on 18 July 1856, at Queen Street in Bedwelty, Newport, Monmouthshire, the second child in the family of six to

William Jobbins and his wife, Harriett (formerly Greenaway), who had married in the parish of St George's, Bristol, on 17 August 1851. They moved to Malthouse Lane in Trevethin in 1864, and by the age of 15 John was working as a puddler at the local iron works. His siblings were George, Harry, William, Mary and Sarah.

He enlisted in the Monmouthshire Militia on 8 January 1876, being described as having a 37 inch chest. He enlisted for the regular army in Pontypool on 11 January 1877, being described as five feet seven inches tall, with a chest measurement of 37 inches, fair complexion, with hazel eyes and brown hair, and as 1061 Private Jobbins he was posted to the 2nd Battalion, 24th Regiment. He received orders for active service in South Africa, and sailed to the Cape with the battalion in February 1878, taking part in the Cape Frontier War. In mid-1878 his father was unemployed, so he began making remittances of two pounds to his mother. He wrote many times to his parents letting them know how he was, and for his service he received the South Africa Medal with 1877-78-79 clasp.

He served at Gibraltar in 1880, and in India, returning to England from Secunderabad in January 1883, where he was discharged to the first class reserves. During his six years with the colours he had received two good conduct badges.

He gave his intended place of residence as Osborne Road in Pontypool, Monmouthshire; the home of his parents. By 1884 he had found work as a labourer in Llantarnum, Cwmbran. It was here that he married Elizabeth Wilmott, on 13 October 1884, at the parish church, and by 1886 they had made their home at 24 Chapel Lane in Pontypool, where John found work at the local steelworks, and then as an underground worker at the local pit.

They had eight children, all born at Chapel Lane, Crumlin Street, Pontypool. Elizabeth was born on 20 September 1886, James on 6 January 1889, William on 10 April 1891, Harriet Maud on 31 May 1893, Sylvia Leah on 5 July 1895, Mary Ann on 9 November 1897, John Samuel on 3 May 1900 and Evan on 12 August 1902. By 1900 John was working as a colliery roadman and moved to lodgings at 32 Railway Parade in Pontypool, while Elizabeth and the children moved to Rose Cottage, 6 Pear Tree Road, Abersychan, before the house at 31 Railway Parade became vacant and John took over the tenancy for his wife and children.

He lost his original campaign medal and he had to have a

replacement made. He was living in Pontypool when he was one of 25 Zulu War veterans who attended The Old Comrades Club of the 24th Foot reunion at the Victoria Barracks in Portsmouth on 30/31 March 1929, along with Thomas Driscoll, Henry Gallagher, Henry Martin and John Williams VC. He was present at the ceremony for the Laying up of the colours at Brecon Cathedral in 1934, and in the same year he attended the Northern Command Tattoo in Gateshead.

After lying seriously ill for some time, John died of old age in his home at 33 Machine Meadows in Pontnewynydd, on 22 September 1934, aged 78. He was buried with full military honours in the same grave as his wife at St Cadoc's Parish Church in Trevethin, Pontypool (plot Y grave 37).

The grave site had become overgrown, and in 2013 it was cleared and his grave was renovated by members of the local Veterans' Association. In 2017 a road on the Penygarn Heights Estate in Pontypool was named 'John Jobbins Way'.

Parents' marriage certificate–St George, Bristol AB206841
Marriage certificate–Llantarnam TWA815831
Elizabeth birth certificate–Pontypool WCN029211
James birth certificate–Pontypool WCN029210
William birth certificate–Pontypool WCN029209
Harriet Maud birth certificate–Pontypool WCN029208
Sylvia Leah birth certificate–Pontypool WCN029207
Mary Ann birth certificate–Pontypool WCN029204
John Samuel birth certificate–Pontypool WCN029205
Evan birth certificate–Pontypool WCN029206
Death certificate–Pontypool HC085385
Free Press of Monmouthshire for14 September 1934
Hereford Times and Monmouthshire Beacon for 29 March 1879
Western Mail for 25 September 1934

Evan Jones was a survivor of the defence.

He was born as Evan Cosgrove on 10 April 1853, at Nantyglo in Aberystruth, Abergavenny, Monmouthshire, the first child of five to John Cosgrove, who was a blast-furnace filler at the steel works, and his wife, Tabitha (formerly Evans). Evan was sometimes known as Patrick. John and Tabitha were natives of Nantyglo, and they married at Aberystruth Parish Church on 8 November 1852.

John eventually moved his family to 19 Armoury Row in Manmoel, Ebbw Vale, where he obtained employment as a hot bank haulier. By 1871, Evan and his three younger brothers had found work as rollers in the steelworks, and the family moved to 31 Armoury Row.

Evan joined the Monmouthshire Engineers Militia at Abergavenny, on 17 February 1875, before enlisted into the regular army at Brecon on 19 July 1877, using the name Evan Jones, and giving a false age. He was described as five feet four inches tall, with a fresh complexion, grey eyes and light brown hair. His chest measurement was 39 inches and he weighed 140 pounds. 1428 Private E. Jones he was posted to the 2nd Battalion, 24th Regiment, at Brecon.

He received orders for active service in South Africa and sailed to the Cape in February 1878, taking part in the Cape Frontier War, and during the Zulu War he was present at the defence of Rorke's Drift, where he is said to have used his fists when all else failed. For his service he received the South Africa Medal with 1877-8-9 clasp. He wrote a letter home to his brother from the camp at Dundee in South Africa on 7 July, in which he defends his Commander-in-Chief, Lord Chelmsford, against the criticism he received for his tactics during the campaign.

He was appointed drummer while serving at Gibraltar on 30 July 1880, and attained a fourth Class certificate of education while in India on 8 March 1882. He chose to revert to private on 31 October 1884. He was posted to Burma in 1886, where he was again appointed drummer on 17 December 1887, and returned to India in 1888. He re-engaged at Ranikhet in 1889, as bandsman with the Gloucestershire Regiment. He transferred back to the South Wales Borderers, with effect from 30 December 1892, and while he was in India he was a member of the Governor's Band at Bombay. He was posted to Aden in 1893, and in October of that year he was posted back to India. He arrived at Gosport on 26 November 1893, by which time he had been overseas for 15 years.

He was appointed lance corporal and reverted to drummer on several occasions during 1894-95. He was admitted to hospital with a fractured hand on 11 March 1896, and while in hospital he was appointed to the 4th Militia Battalion of the South Wales Borderers, for duty on the permanent staff. He was promoted lance corporal on 1 September 1897, and he was awarded five pence a day good conduct pay on 21 July 1898.

He was living at 16 Mount Street in Welshpool, in 1898, and retaining the surname Jones, he married Alice Evans (formerly Pugh), at Forden Registry office, on 15 October 1898. He was described as a musician, and Alice was a widow with four children, Alice, born in 1885, Richard, born in 1887, William, born 21 June 1890, and Agnes, born in 1895.

Evan discharged on 17 October 1899. However, the Boer War began, and he attested at Welshpool on 17 March 1900, for short service of one year in the Royal Northern Reserve Battalion. He was stationed at Pembroke Dock and was discharged again on 16 March 1901, when the regiment was disbanded. From around 1902 to 1915, Evan served with the Montgomeryshire Yeomanry, and when the Great War began he re-attested for the 2nd/7th Welsh Fusiliers, at Aberystwyth, on 15 April 1915. He passed as fit for territorial force home service at the age of 62. The *Montgomery County Times* ran a story about his career under the title *A Welshpool Veteran: Over 40 Years Service and Still in the Army*.

He was promoted corporal on 24 August 1916, acting lance sergeant on 7 August 1917, and when hostilities ended he was discharged on 15 February 1919. However, he re-enlisted soon after his discharge as a private in the Northumberland Fusiliers. It is believed that he was posted to Germany and served as part of the army of occupation in 1919 and 1920. He received his final discharge on 10 February 1920, while in his 67th year.

Evan died on 29 July 1931, aged 78, at his home at 18 Union Street in Welshpool, the cause of death being given as 'carcinoma of rectum' (bowel cancer). He was buried with military honours in St Mary's Churchyard in Welshpool. A cross marked his final resting place until 2022 when a new memorial stone was placed at his grave. His rare combination of medals is now the property of the National Museum of Wales.

Birth certificate–Aberystruth, Abergavenny WCN060376
Marriage certificate–Forden, Montgomery and Salop WNXZ200008
Marriage certificate parents–Aberystruth
Death certificate–Welshpool, Montgomery WDXZ087298

Montgomery County Times and Shropshire and Mid-Wales Advertiser for 27 February 1915
Merthyr Express for 8 August 1931

John Jones (970) was a survivor of the defence.

He was born at Caedraw near Merthyr Tydfil, Glamorganshire, and he attested for 25 Brigade at Merthyr on 13 December 1876. As 970 Private Jones he was posted to the 2nd Battalion, 24th Regiment, on 22 January 1877, a date which had great significance to him two years later.

He received orders for active service in South Africa, and sailed with the unit to the Cape in February 1878. He took part in the Cape Frontier War, and during the Zulu War he is believed to have been present at the defence of Rorke's Drift. For his service he received the South Africa Medal with 1877-8-9 clasp. He served at Gibraltar in 1880, and in India, from where he returned on 29 January 1883.

He wrote a letter to his mother which makes no mention of the defence of Rorke's Drift, and suggests that he was with Chelmsford's reconnaissance column during the action at iSandlwana. Another letter written by a fellow Caedraw soldier, named James Bell, seems to confirm this, but proof that he was not a defender has not been corroborated.

A South Wales newspaper entitled *The Pioneer* published an article which is believed to have been about him on 23 May 1914: *Old Merthyr Soldier's Reward–Hero of Rorke's Drift in Lodging House.*

> John Jones an old soldiers, living in a common lodging house at Riverside, Merthyr, is one of the few remaining heroes of the defence of Rorke's Drift in 1879. Jones, who is a man of 60 years of age, has found that, like many of his fellows who serve their country faithfully in other walks of life, his reward has been poverty.
>
> Jones spent most of his life in the army, having joined the Warwickshires in 1876 at Merthyr, served in the Zulu War, served in India, took part in the South African War, for which he received two bars. For his service in the Zulu War he obtained a medal and clasp. He has however, been assisted by friends who have helped the old man to avoid the taint of

pauperism.

Carmarthen Journal for 28 March 1879
Western Mail for 18 May 1914
The Pioneer for 23 May 1914

John Jones (1179) was a survivor of the defence.

He was born at Merthyr Tydfil, in 1853. He had served in the Cardiff Militia when he enlisted for the regular army at Tredegar in Monmouthshire, on 2 February 1877, and as 1179 Private Jones he was posted to the 2nd Battalion, 24th Regiment, at Brecon. He was described as five feet five-and-a-half inches tall, with a dark complexion, blue eyes and light-brown hair. His religion was Church of England. He was charged with drunkenness and placed in confinement on 22 July 1877, being tried and fined two days later.

He received orders for active service in South Africa and sailed to the Cape with his battalion in February 1878. He took part in the Cape Frontier War, and during the Zulu War he was present at the defence of Rorke's Drift. For his service he received the South Africa Medal with 1877-8-9 clasp.

He served at Gibraltar in 1880, and in India. He obtained a 4th class certificate of education, and on returning to England he discharged to the army reserve on 28 June 1883, giving his next-of-kin as D Morgan, cousin, High Street, Merthyr Tydfil, Glamorgan. His character was described as very bad and his habits were intemperate. He received his final discharge at Brecon on 6 February 1889.

Robert Jones was awarded the Victoria Cross for valour at Rorke's Drift.

He was born at 5 Ty Newydd in Clytha, Monmouthshire, on 19 August 1857, the fourth of five sons in a family of seven children to Robert Jones, 'a farmer of thirty-three acres', and his wife, Hannah (formerly Fryer). He was christened at Penrhos in Monmouth. He became a rural worker like his father, the 1871 census stating that at the age of 14 he was employed at and living in the Drybridge Farm, in the St Mary's Parish district of Monmouth.

His father is said to have greatly disapproved when he joined the army at Monmouth on 10 January 1876, and as 716 Private R. Jones he was posted to the 2nd Battalion, 24th Regiment. He was described as being five feet seven inches tall, and having a fresh complexion, grey eyes and brown hair.

He received orders for active service in South Africa, and sailed to the Cape with his unit in February 1878. He served in the Cape Frontier War, and during the Zulu War he was present at the defence of Rorke's Drift. For his conduct at the defence of Rorke's Drift, Private Robert Jones was mentioned in dispatches, and his award of Victoria Cross was announced in the *London Gazette* on 2 May 1879:

> In another ward, facing the hill, Private William James and Private Robert Jones defended the post to the last, until six out of the seven patients it contained had been removed. The seventh, Sergeant Maxfield, 2nd Battalion, 24th Regiment, was delirious from fever. Although they had previously dressed him, they were unable to induce him to move. When Private Robert Jones returned to endeavour to carry him away, he found him being stabbed by the Zulus as he lay on his bed.

He received the medal from Lord Wolseley while still on active service at Utrecht in the Transvaal, on 11 September 1879. He also received the South Africa Medal with 1877-8-9 clasp. His service in the campaign left him with one bullet and four assegai wounds, and he left an account of the part he played in the action at Rorke's Drift.

He served at Gibraltar in 1880, and in India, from where he returned to Britain on 25 November 1881. He transferred to the Army Reserve, was recalled for service on 2 August 1882, and transferred back to the Army Reserve on 7 February 1883. He finally discharged from the army on 26 January 1888.

He married Elizabeth Hopkins at Llantilio, Crosseny, Monmouthshire, on 7 January 1885, and they had five children. Alice Margaret was born in Monmouthshire in 1886, Edith Emily in Peterchurch on 7 October 1888, Robert at Peterchurch in 1892, Lily Rose at Peterchurch on 10 December 1895, and Ellen, known as Nellie, was born at Peterchurch in 1898. In 1891 Robert was living at The Lodge in Dorstone, Hereford, while his wife and girls were 'visiting friends' at Ewyas Harold in Hereford. They went to live in the village of Peterchurch, Herefordshire, and Robert gained employment for Major De La Hay, a retired officer, at the nearby Crossways House. The family home was at Rose Cottage, on Rose Farm, and they also acquired some land in the village of St Margaret's. Robert had been wounded close to his eyes and sometimes suffered severe pains in his head.

In August 1898 he collapsed, and although he recovered his wife noticed a change in his character. On the morning of 6 September he changed his clothes and put on his best shoes. He was seen to be acting strangely before he went to work, and when he arrived he asked to borrow the Major's gun and two cartridges and went into the garden, presumably to shoot birds. The gun was heard to go off, and he was found dead with the back of his head blown away. An inquest found that he had committed suicide whilst of unsound mind. He was aged 41. Two days later he was given a modest military funeral, and members of his old regiment attended as he was buried in St Peter's Churchyard.

The official report concerning his death was published in the Hereford Journal for 16 September 1898:

Dr McMichael said on Tuesday morning he was called to Crossways and got there about nine o'clock. He went in the garden, found the body, turned it over and examined it. There was a large hole in the back of the roof of the mouth, and the top of the head was blown out. There was no mark of powder on the face, and from the position of the wound the muzzle of the gun must have been put in his mouth and then discharged. The deceased was a big man with long arms, and would have no difficulty in holding the gun in such a position and firing it with his right hand. That was what, in his opinion, took place. He attended the deceased about three weeks ago. It was drink that was the matter with him then. The deceased had a sore throat. He had recently had scarlet fever in the house. He had doctored him at intervals for four years; he had never complained to him about his wounds. Death must have been instantaneous.

Robert Jones was known to be a good father, and he was a talented amateur poet. A poem of his is preserved at the Regimental Museum.

His is the only Victoria Cross of the seven gained by the 24th Regiment at Rorke's Drift which remains in private hands, as part of the collection owned by Lord Ashcroft.

Carmarthen Journal for 28 March 1879
Hereford Journal for 16 September 1898
Radnor Express for 15 September 1898

William Jones was awarded the Victoria Cross for valour at Rorke's Drift.

He was born in Bristol in 1839, and his family descendants believe him to be the one born on 16 August 1839, at 5 Lucas Street, Castle Precinct. He was the second son of four in the family of five children to a stonemason named William Jones (born in 1806 at Cwmcarvan in Monmouthshire), and his wife, Mary Ann (late Martin, formerly Lancastle–born in 1816 at Llanon in Carmarthenshire). The Wesleyan Methodist Chapel at Coleford in the Forest of Dean, Gloucestershire, records the baptism of William and James Jones, on 22 March 1840, and the 1851 census records a family living in East Dean, near Ross-on-Wye, which may be them. William served an apprenticeship as a shoemaker before entering the army, and there are records of a shoemaker named Jones who lived in Cowell Street in Evesham, Worcestershire, who may have been William.

He enlisted at Birmingham on 21 December 1858, and as 593 Private W. Jones he was posted to the 2nd Battalion, 24th Regiment. He was described as being five feet five inches tall, with a sallow complexion, dark brown eyes and brown hair. While serving at Mauritius he was promoted corporal on 1 September 1859, but he was reduced to private on 5 September 1860. He re-engaged at Rangoon on 10 January 1868, to complete 21 years' service, and he also served in India.

He married Elizabeth Goddard at the Wesleyan Methodist Chapel in Farnham in Hampshire, on 25 May 1875. He was posted to Dover, where a child named William was born on 15 November 1876, who was sent to live with his grandparents in Farnham.

He received orders for active service in South Africa and sailed with his battalion to the Cape in February 1878, taking part in the Cape Frontier War. His wife went with him, but she died of tuberculosis on 11 October 1878. During the Zulu War he was present at the defence of Rorke's Drift. For his service during the Zulu War Private William Jones was mentioned in dispatches, and his award of Victoria Cross was announced in the *London Gazette* on 2 May 1879:

> In another ward, facing the hill, Private William James and Private Robert Jones defended the post to the last, until six out of the seven patients it contained had been removed. The seventh, Sergeant Maxfield, 2nd Battalion, 24th Regiment, was delirious from fever. Although they had previously dressed him, they were unable to induce him to move. When Private Robert Jones returned to endeavour to carry him away, he found him being stabbed by the Zulus as he lay on his bed.

He was examined by a medical board at Pietermaritzburg on 3 September 1879, which found that he was suffering from chronic rheumatism. He was sent to Netley Hospital, and on 2 February 1880, he was discharged as 'unfit for further service due to chronic rheumatism of the joints.' He was in possession of three good conduct badges. He also received the South Africa Medal with 1877-8-9 clasp. He was decorated by Queen Victoria at Windsor Castle, on 13 January 1880.

His intended place of residence was 174 Lupin Street in the Aston district of Birmingham, and by the time of the April 1881 census he was named as a warehouseman visiting Charles and Elizabeth Goddard at Court 3, 6 Love Lane in Duddeston, Aston, Birmingham. A child named Albert Ulundi (Frodsham) was born there on 12 May 1881, and Elizabeth (Frodsham) was born on 19 June 1883, at 7 Holt Street in Duddeston, Aston, Birmingham. Albert's unusual name suggests that he may have been fathered by William, and he and Elizabeth are the only two children who had their names changed to Jones. By the time of the 1891 census the family home was 8 Luxton Street, Duddleston, Aston, Birmingham. Charles had moved out of the house and William was recorded as a boarder.

He moved to Rutland Street in Chorlton-on-Medlock, Manchester, and by 1901 he lived at 7 Ash Street in Miles Platting. In the early 1880s he made several appearances at Harry H. Hamilton's *Panstereorama* in places like the Theatre Royal in Preston, to recite his account of the defence, and he appeared in *Buffalo Bill's Wild West* when it came to Lancashire in the late 1880s.

An item exists which is dated 1 August 1895, and consists of the metal regimental number and sphinx taken from the uniform of William Jones. It seems to have belonged to William Henry Dugan, who produced what is believed to be the first painting of the defence of Rorke's Drift. Dugan also painted some of the backdrops for Hamilton's shows, and it is likely that he met Jones during that time. However, William could not get regular employment because of his health, and he was also forced to pawn his VC to provide for his family. It is now with the regimental museum.

William was aged 61 when he married Elizabeth, at St Augustine's Church in Newton Heath, Manchester, on 16 July 1901. In 1912 they were living at 72 Sanderson Street in Collyhurst, Manchester, when William was found wandering the streets in an 'impoverished' condition and his wife had to collect him from Bridge Street Workhouse in Salford. He died at his daughter's home, 6 Brompton Street in Ardwick, Manchester, on 15 April 1913, aged 73, and he was buried with military honours at Philips Park Cemetery in Manchester; where Joshua Lodge and John Lyons had already been laid to rest.

A ceremony was held at the cemetery in 2007 to commemorate the unveiling of new headstones for William. The plaque commemorating William's burial and deed went missing for some time, and in 2011 it was returned to its rightful place, along with two new plaques and gravestones dedicated to Joshua Lodge and John Lyons sited opposite the war memorial.

The Era for 6 February 1886
Strand Magazine for January-June 1891
Manchester Evening Chronicle for 9 February 1911
Bristol Times for 18 February 1911

Peter Judge was a survivor of the defence.

A letter published in the *Rosscommon and Leitrim Gazette* for 5 April 1879, stated that he was a native of Boyle in County Rosscommon, Ireland. He is believed to have attested for the army in late 1872, and as 2437 Private Judge he was posted to the 2nd Battalion, 24th Regiment, in January 1873. He was awarded a good shooting prize.

He had brothers named Peter and Charley who served with the 88th Connaught Rangers in South Africa.

He received orders for active service in South Africa, and sailed to the Cape with his unit in February 1878. He took part in the Cape Frontier War, and during the Zulu War he was present at the defence of Rorke's Drift. He made a monthly remittance of one pound to a Mrs Judge beginning in March 1879. For his service he was awarded the South Africa Medal with 1877-8-9 clasp. He served at Gibraltar in 1880, and on his return to England from India on 29 January 1883, he transferred to the army reserve.

According to the Chelsea Hospital Records, Private Judge was discharged from the 2nd Battalion, 24th Regiment on 12 May 1882, to join the Volunteer Cape Infantry Regiment on South Africa.

The Cape Infantry Regiment was raised in 1882 to garrison the Transkei, and the Colonial Government paid its expenses. It was officered by colonials and manned by Imperial reservists. It recruited in the London area and families were allowed to travel with the recruits. It was disbanded after a few years.

In June 1887, even though he had presented official documentation of his discharges from the 2nd/24th Regiment, and the Cape Infantry Regiment, he failed in an attempt to join the Cape Police at Kimberley. However, it seems that he remained in the Kimberley area, as there is evidence that he had joined the Kimberley Regiment. There is also evidence that he was alive in 1905.

His campaign medal came up for auction in 2025.

Rosscommon and Leitrim Gazette for 5 April 1879
Chelsea Hospital Records
Cape Infantry Regiment discharge book
Government House Records of the Cape Archives Repository

K

Patrick 'Frank' Kears was a survivor of the defence.

Frank Kears was born in Ireland in about 1858. He was the eldest child of Francis 'Frank' Kears, believed to have been a blacksmith, and his wife, Margaret, who left Ireland to try to make a better life. In

1872 they lived at 99 Charter Street in the centre of Manchester, where Lord Shaftesbury was to establish the Charter Street Ragged School and Working Girls Home in 1892.

Francis senior had been earning a living as a hawker when he died that year. Patrick's mother was pregnant at the time of his father's death, and she is believed to have had a daughter in Blackburn. By the mid-1870s they lived at 41 Fontenoy Street in Liverpool, and Patrick found work as a labourer. Unfortunately, Margaret had taken to drink.

Frank served with the 2nd Royal Lancashire Militia, and he enlisted for 25 Brigade at Liverpool on 6 December 1876. He gave his name as Patrick and his place of birth as Liverpool, and he was described as being just under five feet five inches tall, with a fresh complexion, blue eyes and brown hair. His religion was Roman Catholic and he had a star on his left hand. As 972 Private Kears he was posted to the 2nd Battalion, 24th Regiment.

He received orders for active service in South Africa, and sailed to the Cape with his unit in February 1878. He took part in the Cape Frontier War, and during the Zulu War he was present at the defence of Rorke's Drift. For his service he received the South Africa Medal with 1877-8-9 clasp.

He was admitted to hospital with enteric fever in Pietermaritzburg on 17 June 1879, and he was re-admitted on 20 July suffering with debility. He was examined by a medical board on 23 July, and was recommended for a change of climate. He was sent to Netley Hospital on 3 October, and at Brecon in April 1880 he was admitted to hospital suffering from bronchitis.

He married Annie Lewis on 16 November 1880, at St Mary's Chapel, St John the Evangelist, Brecon. They had five children. Honor was born in 1882, Amy Ethel in 1884, Ellen Florence in 1885, and Francis junior in 1888. Sadly, he died after four days. Margaret was born in 1889.

Patrick was discharged to the first class army reserve on 1 February 1883, his conduct being described as very good, and his habits were good. Following his discharge the family moved to 3 Davies Street in Brynmawr, Crickhowell, near Abergavenny, where Patrick obtained employment as a railway porter. At certain times the family moved to 99 King's Street, and then to 6 Hitchman's Court, both addresses being in Brynmawr.

He was charged and tried for having been absent without leave from the army reserve, the result of the hearing was an acquittal, and he was discharged from the first class army reserve at Brecon, on 8 December 1888.

The 1901 census shows Annie Kears still residing in Brynmawr, but there was no sign of Patrick. The marriage certificate of one of his daughters states that her father was a sailor, suggesting that Patrick had gone to sea. A Patrick Kears died at the Rosscommon County Home in Ireland, on 16 March 1932, aged 75, and it is believed that this is the former 972 Private Patrick Kears.

Marriage certificate–St John's, Brecon TWA743482

James William Keefe was slightly injured during the defence.

He was born on 28 May 1857, at 19 Little East Street, St Giles and St George, London. He was the only child of James Keefe, a general labourer, and his wife, Ellen (formerly Vickers). His mother died of tuberculosis in the Vinegar Yard Workhouse, St Giles, on 6 February 1867, and James was placed in the care of his aunt and uncle in Aldersgate, St Botolph, London.

James enlisted as a boy soldier at the Marlborough Police Courts, on 3 March 1871. His army records show his age as 'apparently' 14 years and ten months, but James had given himself an extra year. He was four feet seven and a half inches tall, with a fresh complexion, grey eyes and brown hair. It is also noted that he had a scar on his forehead. His next-of-kin was his aunt: A. Baines, Holdgate Street, London. As 2381 Boy Keefe, the 1871 census records that he was stationed at Chatham, having been posted to the 2nd Battalion, 24th Regiment. By May 1871 he had attained the age of 15 and was given the rank of 'lad', and having attained the age of 17 on 4 May 1873, he was promoted to private, and he was appointed drummer on 21 October 1873. He was awarded and forfeited good conduct pay and badges on several occasions.

He received orders for active service in South Africa and sailed to the Cape with his battalion in February 1878. He took part in the Cape Frontier War and in the Zulu War. He was the company bugler during the defence of Rorke's Drift, where he was slightly injured when a bullet grazed his scalp. For his service he received the South

Africa Medal with 1877-8-9 clasp, which is now at the regimental museum.

While serving at Gibraltar in 1880, he was fined for drunkenness. He re-engaged in India on 18 December 1880, to complete 21 years' service. He reached the rank of corporal on 22 January 1884, and having gained a second class certificate of education, he was awarded two pence a day good conduct pay on 1 May 1884, and received a third good conduct badge on 1 January 1886. However, he was reduced to private and forfeiting good conduct pay in April 1886. He served in Burma from 9 July 1886 to 7 December 1887, when he returned home. He was promoted lance corporal at Brecon on 2 January 1888, and his good conduct pay was restored on 24 July that year.

He married Margaret Bury Ellis at the Brecon Register Office, on 17 April 1889, and his cousin Robert of the South Wales Borderers was a witness at the wedding. They had four children. Ellen Margaret was born in 1889, James Hardy was born at Brecon Barracks on 4 April 1891, William George in 1892, and Ellis John Bury was born at Armoury Row in Ebbw Vale on 31 March 1894, after his father's death.

He became a sergeant with the 3rd Volunteer Battalion, South Wales Borderers, on 15 April 1890, being appointed to the permanent staff on 22 September 1891. He was promoted colour sergeant on 4 March 1892, and soon afterwards he was permitted to continue his service beyond 21 years.

However, he was diagnosed as suffering from an aortic aneurism (a swelling of the main artery), which caused his sudden death at his home, 20 Armoury Terrace, Ebbw Vale, Blaenau, Gwent, on 18 September 1893, aged 36, and he was buried in Ebbw Vale Cemetery.

His sons served with the South Wales Borderers. James Hardy served with the 1st Battalion from 1905 until 1930, when he retired as a QMS, and he re-enlisted for service in the Second World War. Ellis and William served with the 2nd Battalion in Gallipoli, where they were both killed in action in 1915, and their names appear on the Helles Memorial.

Birth certificate–St Giles and St George BXCB310537
Mother's death certificate–St Giles South, Middlesex DYA822819
Marriage certificate–Brecknock Register Office

James Hardy birth certificate–Brecknock WBXZ185853
Ellis John Bury birth certificate–WBXZ 185855
Death certificate–Tredegar, Bedwelty, Monmouth HC087
South Wales Daily News for 19 September 1893
South Wales Star for 19 September 1893

John Key was a survivor of the defence.

He attested for the army at Secunderabad in India on 28 August 1871, and as 2389 Private Key he was posted to the 2nd Battalion, 24th Regiment. He was appointed drummer in 1873, but reverted to private on 25 September 1877.

He received orders for active service in South Africa and sailed to the Cape in February 1878, where he was appointed lance corporal on 3 May 1878, and soon after taking part in the Cape Frontier War he was promoted corporal on 3 July 1878. During the Zulu War he was present at the defence of Rorke's Drift.

He was appointed lance sergeant in A Company on 19 February 1879, and transferred to H Company on 31 March 1879. For his service he was awarded the South Africa Medal with 1877-8-9 clasp. Some modern researchers cast doubt on his status as a defender of Rorke's Drift but this has not been corroborated. He was promoted sergeant on 20 March 1880, and was placed on the unattached list at Secunderabad on 1 March 1884.

His South Africa Medal was sold at auction in 2011 and again in 2021.

Michael Kiley was a survivor of the defence.

He attested for 25 Brigade at Brecon, on 24 April 1877, and as 1386 Private Kiley he was posted to the 2nd Battalion, 24th Regiment.

He received orders for active service in South Africa, and sailed to the Cape in February 1878, where he took part in the Cape Frontier War. He was confined by civil power on 7 October 1878, being sentenced to five days imprisonment with hard labour. He made remittances to Helen Kiley and Mary Sullivan. During the Zulu War he was present at the defence of Rorke's Drift.

He was one of several soldiers to be transferred to G Company on

29 January 1879, and on the following 11 March he was confined in cells on a charge of insubordination, was tried by court martial and was sentenced to receive 50 lashes and fined one pound. He was confined by civil power on 26 September 1879. He was sent to the general depot on 1 January 1880. For his service he received the South Africa Medal with 1877-8-9 clasp, which is now the property of the regiment.

In a newspaper article of 1915 a John Kiley stated that he was a defender of Rorke's Drift.

L

David Lewis was a survivor of the defence.

He was born as James Owens on 29 May 1852, at Gorsgoch in Llanboidy, Whitland, Carmarthenshire. He was one of two sons in the family of seven children to David Owens, a farm labourer, and his wife, Anne (formerly Thomas). He was educated by monks at nearby at Whitland Church School, where he is said to have taken pride in his handwriting and could write in copper-plate. In his early teens he travelled to Swansea, where he gained employment at the tinworks at Swansea Docks, before becoming a weaver. He married Emma McIndoe at Swansea, on 28 March 1875. Emma was a widow with two children, who was 11 years his senior, and they had two children; Amy, and David Lewis, born on 12 November 1876.

Soon after his son's birth he went to Brecon to enlist on 9 December 1876. He used a false name, and as 963 Private David Lewis he was posted to the 2nd Battalion, 24th Regiment, having his allowances made payable to his sister, Emma. He was described as being five feet nine inches tall, with a fresh complexion, grey eyes, and brown hair.

He received orders for active service in South Africa, and sailed to the Cape in February 1878. He took part in the Cape Frontier War, and during the Zulu War he was present at the defence of Rorke's Drift. For his service he received the South Africa Medal with 1877-8-9 clasp.

He began to show signs that he had a heart problem and he was invalided to England, where he was discharged on 1 August 1879; his character being described as indifferent. An injury assessment board held at the Royal Hospital, Chelsea, on 12 August 1879, confirmed that he was suffering from valvular disease of the heart, caused by being under canvas for six months and constantly exposed to climatic vicissitudes. It was considered that he ought to earn after a time, and he was awarded a pension of six pence a day for six months, which was cancelled by the Adjutant General's list dated 11 August 1879.

He returned to his family in Swansea as James Owens and resumed his work as a weaver. Early in 1928 he went into work on his day off to collect his wages, and while he was there he saw a girl using a machine without a safety guard. As he was pointing out the danger a serious accident occurred and he lost an eye. On 7 May 1928, he applied to the Royal Hospital for financial help in obtaining a glass eye, which cost 28 shillings (£1.40p).

He was present at many funerals of Rorke's Drift men, and attended a number of reunions at Brecon.

He died on 1 July 1938, at his son's home, 12 Kemble Street in Brynmill, Swansea, aged 87, and he was buried with military honours at Bethel Cemetery in Sketty, Swansea. A wreath was sent by a number of surviving Rorke's Drift men, Frank Bourne, Patrick Hayes, Thomas Lockhart, George Edward Orchard, William Cooper, and George Mabin's son, William.

Thomas Lewis was a survivor of the defence.

He was born on 6 October 1854, at 9 Winston's Row, Llanfaes St David's in Brecon. He was the only son of three children to Isaac Lewis, and his wife, Annie (formerly Lloyd). Their occupations were described as: 'servants in husbandry'. The 1861 census shows them as living at 3 Forge Cottages in Brecon, then they moved to Lower Pontwilliam, and in 1871 they lived at Priory Mill House in Brecon.

Brecon being a garrison town, it was not surprising when Thomas enlisted into the army on 24 November 1874. However, he chose the Royal Regiment of Artillery as opposed to his local unit the 24th Regiment, and 458 Gunner Lewis was posted to N Battery, 5th Brigade.

The unit received orders for active service in South Africa and embarked on the troopship *Dublin Castle* on 9 January 1878, taking part in the Ninth Cape Frontier War, and late in 1878 they received orders to move up to Rorke's Drift to prepare for the invasion of Zululand, and Thomas arrived there having been promoted to bombardier. His older sister, Margaret, married Sergeant George Chambers, an instructor of musketry with the 1st/24th Regiment. He was also stationed at Rorke's Drift and moved on to iSandlwana with his regiment, where he was killed in action on 22 January 1879.

Thomas was in the hospital at Rorke's Drift having been injured in a wagon accident. A letter by Private David Jenkins stated:

> Dear Father, please go personally or write a letter to Isaac Lewis, Pendre, Brecon and tell him that... His son Thomas is alive but is still in hospital with the fever. He had a very narrow escape. He crept on his hands and knees and came from the hospital to the fort through all the firing.

After the battle Bombardier Lewis developed fever and was taken to hospital in Pietermaritzburg. He remained in South Africa, and on 14 November 1880, N/5 was moved to Potchefstroom, where there was fear of a Boer uprising and work was begun to reinforce the old fort on 22 November. On 16 December 1880, the first shots of the first Boer War were fired at Potchefstroom when Boer commando units began to lay siege to the town. The siege ended amicably on 23 March 1881. On 24 April 1881, he was tried and sentenced to be reduced to gunner, with the loss of good conduct pay. However, on 19 December 1881, his good conduct pay was restored and backdated for 225 days. On 3 July 1882 he was presented before Queen Victoria at Windsor Castle.

Because his service papers have not survived his date of discharge is not known. In civilian life the first job was a prison officer, but he resigned from the prison service, apparently being unhappy with the treatment of prisoners. In early 1898 he gained employment with a London transport company driving horse-drawn trams in Highgate, London, refusing to use a whip on any of his horses, and when the age of the motor engine began to make its mark his new job description was that of a motorman.

He met a nurse named Annie Price and they married. Annie suffered more than one miscarriage before giving birth in 1898 to their first child, Thomas, at 6 Eton Grove in Islington. This was followed in 1899 by the birth of Gladys, at 7 Hampden Court in

Islington. Rita was born in 1901, at 34 Despard Road in Islington. Irene was born in 1903, but she died in the following year. Florentina was born in 1905, and in the summer of 1910 Annie announced that she was expecting another child.

However, on 12 August 1910, Thomas suffered severe stomach pains and vomiting, and was admitted to the Richmond Ward of The London Hospital, Whitechapel, ten days later, and on 23 August he was operated on by Surgeon Hugh Rigby to remove his appendix. On 30 August, after he had suffered great pain, it was decided to remove four stitches from his wound to insert a tube to syringe it internally with carbolic. On the following evening his wound was re-opened by the surgeon who found a new pelvic abscess. The hospital notes of 12 September state that Thomas was reported to be 'going on nicely'. However, on the following day Mr Rigby found it necessary to operate on him again. The nursing reports on 26 September state: 'a fair amount of discharge was still being drained from the wound, but the patient felt well in himself.' The last entry in the nursing notes was on 19 October, which stated: 'discharge diminishing by day.'

Thomas had been in hospital for 71 days, and on 1 November he showed signs of recovery. He was sat in a chair in the ward reading a book waiting to be discharged when he collapsed and died. According to his death certificate Thomas had died of a pulmonary embolism (blood clot) aged 56. However, the post mortem report state findings of: 'Small amounts of fibrin along a sinus which leads to a puss-soaked gauze swab.' It would seem that the surgeon had left a swab inside the wound following one of the operations, which had caused infection. He was buried on 5 November 1910, in Highgate Cemetery (grave: 37970). A stone plaque memorial dedicated to him was placed at the cemetery.

Birth certificate–Brecknock CM969266
Death certificate–Mile End Old Town DYA591678
War Office papers and muster rolls for N Battery (WO10/ 2530 and WO16/282, 283, 287 and 291)
Weekly Mail for 22 March 1879

Henry Lines was a survivor of the defence.

He was born on 12 April 1844, at Chipping Warden in Northamptonshire, and he was christened there on 30 June 1844. He was the second of ten children to Edward Lines, a sawyer, and his wife, Ann (formerly Lovell). Henry began his working life as an agricultural labourer.

He enlisted in Birmingham on 11 October 1864, and as 1528 Private Lines he was posted to the 2nd Battalion, 24th Regiment. He was described as: five feet, five inches tall, with a fresh complexion, hazel eyes, and dark-brown hair. He had a somewhat chequered army career. He was posted to Mauritius on 23 August 1865, and then he moved to and from various stations in India and Burma between 1865 and 1869. He lost and re-gained good conduct pay several times, and he had reached the rank of sergeant on 13 August 1869, when, on 14 January 1870, he was tried and sentenced to six months imprisonment, and reduced to private. Private Lines re-engaged in Secunderabad on 10 July 1871, for such term as would complete 21 years' service. He was posted to the Warley Depot in Birmingham, where he arrived on 4 January 1873, and then to Aldershot on 19 December 1873, and he also attended the Hythe School of Musketry, where he received a good shooting prize. He was posted to Dover, and on 1 June 1876, he was appointed lance corporal, being reverted back to private three months later. He was hospitalised numerous times during his army career for almost every ailment a British soldier on overseas duty was prone to, such as syphilis, fever, dysentery, jaundice, bronchitis, contusions, abscesses, bubo, an inflamed gland of the groin and orchitis (inflammation of the testicles).

He received orders for active service in South Africa, and sailed to the Cape in February 1878, being appointed lance corporal on board ship on 16 February 1878, but he reverted back to private on 16 April 1878. He took part in the Cape Frontier War, and during the Zulu War he was present at the defence of Rorke's Drift. For his service he received the South Africa Medal with 1877-8-9 clasp.

He gained a third class certificate of education in September 1881, and he was promoted corporal on 31 January 1882. However, he was tried by Court Martial on 7 March 1883, for breaking out of barracks, being sentenced to three days imprisonment, and reduced to private. He was posted to Gosport, and was discharged on 18 December 1883: 'due to a reduction in his second term, and a reduction in rank from the rank of corporal', and his conduct was described as good. He received a pension of eleven pence a day, and gave his intended place of residence as Chipping Warden.

Henry found work as an agricultural labourer, and lodgings in Lower Boddington, not far from Chipping Warden. However, in 1885 he was living with Ann Berry at 102 Maysoule Road in Battersea, London, and they married at the local parish church on 27 October 1885. They moved back to Lower Boddington where they took up residence in Bradshaw Cottages. By 1901 they had moved to Bake House in Lower Boddington, where Henry still worked as a general farm labourer, and he continued to state his age as three years less than it actually was.

Henry Lines died of carcinoma of the rectum (bowel cancer) and exhaustion, on 22 April 1904, at his home, 18 Lower Boddington, aged 60, and he was buried in plot 243, at St John's Churchyard in Upper Boddington. His South Africa medal was sold at auction in 2022.

ICI Individual record of baptism
Death certificate–Cropredy, Banbury DYB440547
Marriage certificate–Battersea MXD234617
Muster and Payroll entries WO12/WO16 and WO97 3297

David Lloyd was a survivor of the defence.

He was born on 11 May 1853, at Llanfair Clydogau, Lampeter in Cardiganshire, Wales.

He had worked as a collier, and previously served with the Royal South Wales Borderers Militia when he enlisted for the regular army at Brecon on 5 June 1877, and as 1409 Private Lloyd he was posted to the 2nd Battalion, 24th Regiment. He was five feet four and a half inches tall, with a fresh complexion, grey eyes and brown hair. His religion was Church of England.

He received orders for active service in South Africa, and sailed to the Cape in February 1878. He took part in the Cape Frontier War, and during the Zulu War he was present at the defence of Rorke's Drift. For his service he received the South Africa Medal with 1877-8-9 clasp.

He served at Gibraltar, and in India, where he was granted a penny a day good conduct pay on 10 July 1882. He returned to Britain on 1 December 1883, transferred to the army reserve, Cardiff district, and then he transferred to the Brecon district on 25 May 1884. He discharged on 5 June 1889, his habits being described as intemperate and his conduct as bad.

He married Mary Price at Merthyr Tydfil on 21 January 1885, and the couple settled at 4 Dare Street in Aberdare. He died on 15 February 1916, and he was buried in an unmarked grave at Aberdare New Cemetery (plot Y14/3). A new headstone was placed at his grave, and a rededication service was held in 2018.

The new headstone reads: 'Pte David Lloyd, 2nd/24th Regiment of Foot, Defender of Rorke's Drift, South Africa. Born in Lampeter, May 11, 1853; died 4 Dare Street, Aberdare, February 15, 1916.' Also his wife, Mary Lloyd, died April 1, 1920, aged 59.

Thomas Lockhart was a survivor of the defence.

He was born 15 March 1857, at St Michael's Parish in Ancoats, Manchester. He worked as a fitter before enlisting at Derby, on 6 February 1877, and as 1176 Private Lockhart he was posted to the 2nd Battalion, 24th Regiment, at Brecon. He was described as being five feet nine and a half inches tall, with a fresh complexion, dark-grey eyes and brown hair. His religion was Church of England.

He was awarded a good shooting prize following a musketry course in 1878. He received orders for active service in South Africa, and sailed to the Cape in February 1878, where he took part in the Cape Frontier War. During the Zulu War he was present at the defence of Rorke's Drift. For his service he received the South Africa Medal with 1877-8-9 clasp.

He was granted one penny a day good conduct pay from 7 February 1879. He served at Gibraltar in 1880, and then he returned to Brecon. He transferred to the 1st Battalion, which seems to have prompted a difficult time for him. He forfeited his good conduct pay on 5 September 1881.

In the same month he broke out of barracks at Colchester, where he was attacked by 'soldiers who remain unknown of the Colchester garrison, who waylaid and maliciously ill-treated him without provocation or notice'. This presumably means he was punched about the face and head, because he was admitted to hospital at

Colchester on 30 September 1881, with a contusion (black eye), and suffering from the effects of an epileptic fit. An invaliding board held at Colchester on 6 February 1882, declared that he was suffering from a permanent condition of epilepsy–induced by an injury to the head. This had caused a fracture of the orbit (eye-socket), and the displacement of certain other bones. He was left with a scar on his left temple. The injury may have affected his eyesight because it was considered that his disability would seriously interfere with his powers of supporting himself. He was declared unfit for further service and discharged on 6 April 1882. His conduct was described as fair, and his habits were regular. A second Injury Assessment Board held at the Royal Hospital, Chelsea, on 13 June 1882, confirmed the previous findings. A Court of Inquiry concerning the incident found that the injury had taken place when he was absent, when not on duty, and he was awarded a pension of six pence a day for eight months.

His intended place of residence was 41 Butler Street in Ancoats, Manchester, but he later emigrated to South Africa.

He lived in the gold-mining town of Krugersdorp in the Transvaal. On 4 February 1900 he enlisted as 3927 Corporal Lockhart with F Company of Thorneycroft's Mounted Infantry, for service in the Boer War. He was present at the Relief of Ladysmith; the battles of Tugela Heights and Laing's Nek; and operations in the Transvaal and Orange Free State. He discharged on 9 November 1900, and went to live in Johannesburg.

In July 1938, he was one of the Rorke's Drift survivors who sent a wreath to the funeral of fellow defender, James Owens (David Lewis). He was one of the very last survivors of the defence of Rorke's Drift when he died in 'The Old People's Home' at Krugersdorp on 25 June 1943, aged 85. His funeral took place at St Peter's Church and he was buried in Krugersdorp Cemetery.

Joshua Lodge was a survivor of the defence.

He was born on 1 September 1856, at 11 Fletcher's Square, City Road in Hulme, Manchester, the only son and oldest child of four to Henry Lodge, an iron moulder, and his wife Elizabeth (formerly Tetlow). All the Lodge children were christened at Manchester Cathedral. Shortly after Joshua's birth, they moved to Stanby Street in

Hulme, and then to Eagle Street, off Oldham Road, Manchester.

Joshua left his job as an engine fitter to enlist into the army at Ashton-under-Lyne, on 3 March 1877, and as 1304 Private Lodge he was posted to the 2nd Battalion, 24th Regiment, at Chatham. Two weeks later he received orders for active service in South Africa, and sailed to the Cape in February 1878. He took part in the Cape Frontier War, and during the Zulu War he was present at the defence of Rorke's Drift. For his service he received the South Africa Medal with 1877-8-9 clasp.

He received one penny good conduct pay from 1 March 1879, and from 17 March he made a remittance of one pound a month to his mother. He served at Gibraltar in 1880, and in India, where he reached the rank of corporal on 1 January 1882, but he was reduced to private soon afterwards. He returned to England on 1 May 1883, and after being confined in cells, he was discharged to the army reserve at Gosport, on 28 June 1883. He received his final discharge from the military service at Manchester on 28 June 1889, at which point he gave his intended place of residence as the Albion Inn, 2 Bank Street at Red Bank, Manchester.

He married a Yorkshire girl named Sarah, and the 1901 census records him as living at 16 Green Lane in the parish of St Thomas in Ardwick, and he was working as a compositor letter press printer. In 1906 he was stated to be living at 17 Broughton Street in Ancoats, Manchester, and he was working in an iron foundry.

However, it seems that he had declined into alcoholism, and he was admitted to the Ancoats Hospital, where he died on 26 July 1906, aged 49. The cause of death was given as 'rupture of an artery in the cortex, accelerated by excessive drinking.' He was buried at Phillip's Park Cemetery in Manchester (Church of England section I, grave 2302); where John Lyons had already been laid to rest and William Jones VC would later be buried. In 2011 memorial plaques dedicated to Joshua Lodge and John Lyons were erected opposite the war memorial, and new memorial stones were placed at their graves.

Death certificate—Ancoats HC667795
Manchester Evening News for 27 July 1906

Thomas Levi Luddington was a survivor of the defence.

He was born on 14 December 1855, at Lavendon, close to the northern border of Buckinghamshire, and he was christened in that town on 3 August 1856. He was the fourth son in a family of ten children to an agricultural labourer named James Baker Luddington and his wife, Ann (formerly Brittain). His mother died in childbirth in 1858. The family moved to London, and the 1861 census shows them living at 34 Dean Street, Islington, where James was employed as a 'dust controller's labourer'.

Thomas left his job as a locksmith to enlist for the British cavalry at Westminster, on 30 April 1874, and as 1509 Trooper Luddington, he was posted to the 8th Hussars. He was described as five feet six and a half inches tall, with a fresh complexion, hazel eyes, and brown hair. His religion was Church of England, and it was stated that he had 'rather flat feet'. He transferred to 48 Brigade on 30 June 1874, and as 91 Private Luddington he was posted to the 2nd Battalion, 2nd (Queen's Royal West Surrey) Regiment. He transferred to the Army Hospital Corps (AHC) at Aldershot, on 1 September 1876, with the regimental number 3037. He was posted at Devonport until October 1878, when he received orders for active service in South Africa, where it arrived on 7 November 1878, and during the Zulu War he served under Surgeon Reynolds at the defence of Rorke's Drift. For his service he received the South Africa Medal with 1879 clasp.

He was promoted to second corporal in June 1879, and obtained a fourth class certificate of education, being classed as a professional AHC, and he arrived back at Aldershot on 18 March 1880. He was posted to Malta from 15 September 1880 until August 1881, when he purchased his discharge and arrived in England on 2 October 1881. However, he re-enlisted at the Westminster Police Court on 6 October 1881. The Army Hospital Corps had been re-designated as the Medical Staff Corps, and he was posted to Aldershot as 4580 Private Luddington, later reverting to his old regimental number of 3037.

He arrived at Devonport on 17 April 1883, where he married a Devonport girl named Jessie Harper, a widow with a daughter, on 28 April 1884. She was the daughter of a courier (licensed waterman) named Peter Sleep and his wife Kate, who were natives of St Germans in Cornwall. Jessie had married Sergeant Arthur Harper of the 32nd (Cornwall) Light Infantry, who was stationed at Aldershot, in Stoke Damerel in December 1877, and Jessie Maude had been born at St Germans in March 1879.

He received orders for active service in Egypt on 27 August 1884, from where he took part in the Nile Expedition to try to relieve General Gordon at Khartoum. For his service he received the Egypt Medal with Nile 1884-85 and Gemaizah 1888 clasps, and the Khedives Bronze Star. He passed the exams for his second class education certificate on 10 April 1886, and on 1 May 1886 he was promoted to corporal, returning to Aldershot from Egypt in March 1889.

Thomas and Jessie married for a second time, at the Stoke Damerel Register Office on 12 August 1889. Official documentation confirms that the first marriage was legal.

The 1891 census shows Thomas as being stationed at Aldershot, with his wife, step-daughter Ethel Linda Harper (Luddington), and Thomas, who is stated to be a nephew, but it is known that he was born to Jessie while Thomas was in Egypt. William George Ernest was born at Fromley on 8 February 1894, and soon afterwards Thomas and Jessie were married for a second time in Stoke Damarel, Devonport. He discharged on 3 May 1896, having received the Long Service and Good Conduct Medal.

Thomas became the landlord of The Naval Reserve public house at 6 Pembroke Street, Stoke Damerel, where George Francis was born in 1897. By 1900 he was the landlord of the Friendship Inn at 19 Cannon street, Devonport, before moving to 15 Fort Street, where Jessie died in 1911. Thomas died of a heart attack, brought about by chronic bronchitis, in a lodging house at 5 Prospect Row, Devonport, on 22 March 1934, aged 78, and he was buried with his wife in Weston Mill Cemetery (section: general B, grave: 4498). A new headstone was erected at the grave during a re-dedication service in 2009.

William George Ernest Luddington became captain of the Royal Navy rugby union team, and he was capped 13 times for England, during which they suffered only one defeat, winning the Grand Slam on two occasions. He was killed in action in 1941 while serving in the Malta Convoys on HMS *Illustrious*. His name is inscribed on the Plymouth Naval Memorial, and items of rugby memorabilia associated with him are on display at the Museum of Rugby in

Twickenham.

Birth certificate–Olney, Newport Pagnell–BXCB243491
1884 marriage certificate–Stoke Damerel AB020072
1889 marriage certificate–Stoke Damerel MXA689133
William George Ernest birth certificate–Frimley BXCB 289710
Death certificate–Devonport South, Plymouth DXZ752145

Henry Lugg was a survivor of the defence.

He was born on 9 March 1859, at Northlew near Clovelly, Devon. He had travelled to South Africa with fellow Devonians, Edward and Henry Camp, of Barnstable, whose sister, Mary, Harry was courting, and they all joined the Natal Mounted Police on 22 May 1878. The Natal Mounted Police was formed as a para-military force in 1874 by a retired British Army officer named Major John Dartnell, as the first line of defence in the colony, and they had been scouting the Natal-Zululand border since November 1878. Because of a problem with their horses the invasion force had already crossed into enemy territory when they joined the column. They had a skirmish at Sihayo's Kraal, and after the engagement Harry was ordered to ride to Pietermaritzburg with dispatches. He was eager not to miss the further advance into Zululand, so he made a pony express-style ride, using ten horses in relays, and he was back at Rorke's Drift 17 January. However, his efforts were in vain. As he crossed the river his mount lost its footing and crushed his knee as it fell, causing him to have to go into hospital.

During the defence of the garrison on 22 January he manned a loophole in a kitchen extension of the hospital, from where he could get a good shot at any warriors who reached the outer wall of the building. When the Zulus had moved off he was limping about among the bodies outside the compound when he saw a rifle and went to pick it up. As he did so, a warrior who was lying close by pretending to be dead, suddenly grabbed the weapon and jumped up, jamming the muzzle against Harry's body. Harry heard the trigger click, but the rifle misfired, and before the Zulu could recover he dropped on him and stabbed him with his hunting knife. He managed to rescue his spurs from the ruins of the hospital, although they were burnt black, and while hospitalised in Pietermaritzburg, the

17th Lancers presented him with a commemorative belt, which he is said to have worn every day.

He and Edwin Camp bought a store and hotel at Umbango in the Port Shepstone area of Durban. They celebrated a double wedding in Durban in 1881, when Harry married Mary Camp, and Edwin married Harry's sister, Marion. Harry became active in the formation of a local volunteer regiment named the Umzimkulu Mounted Rifles in 1884, which was amalgamated with the Alexandra Mounted Rifles, which in turn amalgamated to form the Natal Mounted Rifles (NMR) in Durban in 1888. The NMR consisted of two units, but in 1894 one was separated and re-designated the Border Mounted Rifles, with Captain Henry Lugg as second-in-command.

In 1895 he became a District Adjutant on Colonel W. J. Royston's staff, who was then commanding the Natal Volunteers. He held an intriguing variety of Government posts, including conservator of forests, field cornet and collector of dog tax. Harry died at the home which he had called 'Lynton', in Port Shepstone, on 27 October 1927, aged 68. He left a widow and five sons, one of whom Harry Camp Lugg became a respected Zulu linguist and writer. In his book *A Natal Family Looks Back*, he stated: 'The firing was so fast and furious that rifle barrels got red hot', and in proof of this, the forepiece of the carbine Henry Lugg used during the defence, which was still in possession of the family a century later, was found to have been so badly scorched that a piece had to be cut off the end to prevent it splintering. The family also had his spurs and hunting knife.

Bristol Mercury and Daily Post for 5 April 1879
Western Times for 1 September 1899

Thomas Michael Lynch was a survivor of the defence.

He was born at Limerick in Ireland, in September 1858. He left his job as a letter sorter with the post office to enlist in London on 20 November 1876, and as 942 Private Lynch he was posted to the 2nd Battalion, 24th Regiment. He was just over five feet four inches tall, with a fresh complexion, blue eyes and brown hair. His religion was Roman Catholic.

He received orders for active service in South Africa, and sailed to

the Cape in February 1878. He took part in the Cape Frontier War, and on 21 November 1878 he was granted a penny a day good conduct pay. During the Zulu War he is believed to have been present at the defence of Rorke's Drift, and for his service he received the South Africa Medal with 1877-8-9 clasp.

He served at Gibraltar in 1880, and in India, where he was appointed drummer on 1 June 1882, and his good conduct pay was increased to two pence on 21 November 1882. He returned to Britain on 20 January 1883, and transferred to the army reserve as a drummer on 30 March 1883.

He joined the Cameron Highlanders on 11 October 1884, before transferring to the permanent staff with the 4th Battalion, Argyle and Sutherland Highlanders, on 14 January 1885, with whom he gained a third class certificate of education. He was confined by civil power for 17 days in March 1888, and forfeited a penny a day of his good conduct pay. He was discharged from the Stirling depot on 25 April 1888, in consequence of his having been convicted of theft, his character being described as indifferent. His next-of-kin was his mother, of Covent Garden, London.

John Lyons was one of the oldest defenders.

He was born at Kallaloe, near O'Brien's Bridge in County Clare, Ireland, in March 1837. He worked as a labourer before joining the British Army to escape the horrors caused by the terrible potato famine. He enlisted into the 87th Regiment—later The Royal Irish Fusiliers (Princess Victoria's), at Ennis in County Clare, on 31 March 1859. He was described as being just under five feet eight inches tall, with a fresh complexion, grey eyes and red hair. On 1 July 1861, he transferred to A Company, 2nd Battalion, 24th Regiment, as 1441 Private Lyons. He was granted one penny a day good conduct pay from 31 March 1862. He then served on the sugar island of Mauritius until 5 October 1865, and in India from 6 October 1865 to 5 January 1973. His good conduct pay rose to four pence a day on 31 March 1875.

He received orders for active service in South Africa, and sailed to the Cape with his battalion in February 1878. He took part in the Cape Frontier War, and during the Zulu War he was one of the oldest soldiers present at the defence of Rorke's Drift. He was admitted to hospital at Rorke's Drift for ten days from 25 February 1879, being treated for Bright's Disease, which was caused by severe exposure to wet and cold weather, and he was recommended to return to England. For his service he received the South Africa Medal with 1877-8-9 clasp, and a copy of the Address by the Lord Mayor of Durban was forwarded on to him in Brecon.

He was admitted to Netley Military Hospital in Southampton, on 10 June 1879, and was examined by a Medical Board on 16 July. He was found to be 'suffering from general debility at the Cape, 1879.' 'A very clear and honest case of a worn-out soldier, scarcely able to earn anything for his family.' He was discharged as unfit for further service on 4 August 1879. His character was described as 'very good' and his habits 'temperate'. His intended place of residence was Manchester.

He had worked as a bricklayer's labourer, and died on New Year's Day, 1 January 1900, aged 60, at 41 High Burton Street in St George's Parish, Hulme, Manchester, cause of death being acute pneumonia and cardiac failure. His son, James H. Lyons, was present at his death. He was buried at Philips Park Cemetery in Manchester (Roman Catholic - section F grave 103); where Joshua Lodge and William Jones VC would later be laid to rest. In 2011 memorial plaques dedicated to John Lyons and Joshua Lodge were erected opposite the war memorial, and new memorial stones were placed at their graves.

Death certificate HC703987
WO Form 83

John Jeremiah Augustus Lyons was dangerously wounded in action at Rorke's Drift.

He was born on 23 August 1844, at Sowhill in Trevethin, Monmouthshire. He was the oldest surviving child of John Lyons (or Lions), and his wife, Mary (formerly Gahean, sometimes spelt as Gain or Gane).

Following the death of his father in 1857, John and his mother moved to lodgings at Morgan's Houses in Gibson's Square, Trevethin, where John went to work as a labourer, before joining the Hanbury Corps of the Monmouthshire Rifle Volunteers. He joined the 57th (West Middlesex) Regiment in June 1864, and in the following year he was on active service in New Zealand, where a Maori uprising had to be put down, for which he received the New Zealand Medal, 1845-66, with 1863-65 clasp.

After six years he was posted to India, where he transferred to the 63rd (West Suffolk) Regiment, and remained on the sub-continent for four years. He transferred to the 24th Regiment at Cardiff on 24 January 1874, and as 1112 Private Lyons he was posted to the 1st Battalion, being appointed lance corporal on 13 February 1877. He transferred to the 2nd Battalion on 22 February 1877, and was promoted to corporal on 26 November 1877.

He received orders for active service in South Africa, and sailed to the Cape in February 1878, where he took part in the Cape Frontier War, and a local newspaper reported: 'He was present at the battles of Haynes Hill, Rubula Heights and the Perie Bush.' He made remittances to his mother and wrote to her on a regular basis. During the Zulu War he was dangerously wounded during the defence of Rorke's Drift. For his service he received the South Africa Medal with 1877-8-9 clasp.

In a letter published in the *Cambrian* newspaper on 13 June 1879, he stated:

...after we had been fighting between two and three hours, I received a shot through the right side of the neck, the ball lodged in the back striking the spine, and was not extracted until five weeks afterwards. My right arm was partially disabled. I said: 'Give it to them, Allen, I am done, I am dying...'All I could do as I lay on the ground was to encourage the men, and I did so as long as I could open my mouth.

Lieutenant Chard reported:

I saw Corporal Lyons hit by a bullet which lodged in his spine and fall between an opening we had left in the wall of biscuit boxes. I thought he was killed, but looking up he said: 'Oh Sir, you are not going to leave me here like a dog?' We pulled him in and laid him behind the boxes where he was immediately looked to by Reynolds.

Surgical Experiences in the Zulu and Transvaal Wars by D. Blair Brown, states:

When engaged in the defence of Rorke's Drift he received a bullet in his neck near the posterior margin of the sterno-mastoid on the left side, about the upper portion of the middle third of its length. Only wound, that of entrance was present.

He complained of great pain in the neck on the slightest movement. When in bed, the pillow caused an increase in this. He had lost almost all use of his arms and hands, especially the right one, which he described as quite dead. Painful twitchings were experienced in the arms. Whenever he wished to move his head from the bed, someone had to support it between their hands before he could do so.

At Rorke's Drift several surgeons tried to find the bullet, but were unsuccessful. In the above condition he came under my care at Helpmekaar, 26 January, four days after the injury. Next day I put him under chloroform and made a prolonged attempt to find the bullet. The course I found it had taken was in a direct line with the spinal cord. I made a free opening in the middle line as far down the course as possible, and again attempted to reach the bullet. I found by digital examination now that the processes of two adjacent vertebrae were smashed. I could also feel the spinal cord itself. Pressure thereon instantly caused the patient to turn pale and the pulse to be almost imperceptible, and necessitated the immediate withdrawal of the chloroform and the adoption of artificial respiration. I took away several pieces of the vertebral processes which were lying loose, but had to give up attempting to reach the bullet. The case continued much as described for some time.

He was sent to the base hospital at Ladysmith, and on taking over the medical charge of that hospital a month later, I found my old patient much in the same condition. He was suffering greatly from the pain in his arms and wished to have them both off, to relieve him from it. On examination, on making firm pressure, I found a distinct hard substance beneath the ligamentum nuchae which was not present on former occasions. On consultation with the surgeon-general of the forces; who happened to be on a tour of inspection at the time, I cut down upon it and enucleated an ordinary round bullet with a rather long rough process extending from its smooth surface. This wound healed rapidly, but the original one continued to discharge slightly for a long time. In a few days the pain entirely disappeared from his arms, and their use nearly returned. He was shortly after sent home to England.

A footnote to the doctor's report stated: 'The gallant fellow bore the excruciating pain of the operation without making the slightest murmur, though he was not under the influence of chloroform or any other anaesthetic.'

Corporal Lyons arrived back in England at Spithead on 8 June, and was taken to Netley Military Hospital. He was given a civic reception when he finally returned to Pontypool. He was discharged from the army as medically unfit for further service, on 22 September 1879, and an Injury Assessment Board held at the Royal Hospital in Chelsea, on 30 September 1879, found him to be:

Suffering from the effects of a gunshot wound to the neck in the action at Rorke's Drift. The condition will long continue critical and he can do light work only.

He was awarded a pension of six pence a day for six months. He had the slug which had caused his injuries mounted on a chain, which he wore for special occasions.

A newspaper report on 12 December 1879 stated that he had joined the Corps of Commissionaires in London. However, by the end of 1880 he had returned to Wales. He obtained employment as a labourer at an iron works, and lived at 9 Mary Ann Street in Cardiff. Living nearby was a spinster named Elizabeth Ann Evans, and they married at the register office in Cardiff, on 3 January 1881, and lived at Albion Hill in Pontypool. They moved house regularly, before settling at 70 Wharf Road in Newport, and John had a variety of jobs, including a coal miner and a postman in the Eastern Valley postal service.

They had six children, William John was born in 1881, Philip Henry in 1882, Thomas Augustus in 1885 (died in 1892), James

Jeremiah in 1888, Ellen Jane in 1892, Margaretta in 1894. Philip was killed in action while serving with the Royal Marines in the Dardanelles, and James was wounded while serving in Gallipoli with the South Wales Borderers. Two of his sons went to live in Australia.

John Lyons died of pneumonia and heart failure at his home on 1 May 1923, aged 79, and he was buried with military honours in an unmarked grave at St Woolos Cemetery in Newport, where John Murphy and Alfred Saxty would later be laid to rest. Unfortunately, his medals have been mislaid, but in 1936 Elizabeth donated the bullet and watch chain to the Regimental Museum at Brecon.

At the time of his death the *Western Mail* for 3 May 1923, reported under the title *Belated Claim to VC: Newport Hero of Rorke's Drift Dies Unknowing*–that Newport sympathisers were making a claim to the War Office that he should be awarded a belated Victoria Cross, as his name was apparently on the Horse Guards roll of Victoria Cross heroes. As is usually the result of such claims, it was unsuccessful.

A plaque was placed at the grave of John Murphy, and new headstones were erected at the graves of John J Lyons and Alfred Saxty in 1996.

Surgical Experiences in the Zulu and Transvaal Wars by D. Blair Brown
Pontypool Free Press for 8 March, 5 April, 19 April, 14 June and 20 September 1879
Western Mail for 3 May 1923

M

George William Mabin was a survivor of the defence.

He was born in Culver Street, St Augustine's, Bristol, on 5 October 1848, the oldest of seven children to George Mabin, of Dartmouth, and his first wife, Frances (formerly Howe). His father's middle name is given as James on his marriage certificate and Jellard on George's birth certificate. His parents had married at St Michael's Church in Bristol, on 5 January 1847. His siblings were Samuel Henry, born in 1852; Frances Ann, born in 1856; Florence Esther, born in 1858; Federick Christopher Alphonsos, born in 1860; Mary Ann Lellard Julia, born in 1861; and Oscar Horatio Griffith, born in

1864.

His father was a mariner, who had become the landlord of The Plough on Culver Street. It seems that George had a good relationship with his father, as on his seventh birthday his father composed a special acrostic poem for him. While George senior was at sea in 1855, Frances became the licensee of the Royal Oak on Charles Street in Bristol, and on his return the family moved to 14 Elbroad Street in Bristol, where George Jellard earned a living as a sail-maker, before taking over the Elephant and Castle on Merchant Street in Bristol. However, Frances died in 1865, and George senior married Hannah Robbins in the following year. At the time of the 1881 census George senior was a widowed greengrocer of 71 Thunderbolt Street in the St Stephen's Parish of Bristol, and his daughter, Florence Esther, lived with him.

They were living at the Bay Horse at Lewin's Mead in Bristol, when George enlisted into the 2nd Battalion, Rifle Brigade (Prince Consort's Own), on 29 May 1868. He was five feet six and a half inches tall, with a fresh complexion, grey eyes and brown hair. He had 'two small blue dots on his left forearm.' 1566 Private Mabin gained a second class certificate of education on 29 November 1869, and was promoted corporal on 3 July 1870. He was appointed as military staff clerk on 19 May 1872, and promoted sergeant, being promoted colour sergeant on 20 May 1875.

He had been posted to the Western Heights in Dover on 30 August 1870, where he met Mary Elizabeth Ranger (born at Brighthelmston in Brighton on 2 August 1855), and they were married at St Mary's Church in Dover, on 3 January 1872. Three children were born in the next few years; Gerald George in Hulme Barracks, Manchester on 7 July 1873, Florence Gertrude in Dover on 29 April 1875, and Samuel Edward in Dover on 5 May 1877.

Colour Sergeant Mabin was appointed to the District Officer at the Cape of Good Hope, on 6 June 1878, and sailed to South Africa on the SS *Nubian*. His wife apparently went with him. He was serving at Rorke's Drift as clerk to Major Henry Spalding, who was in charge at Rorke's Drift on 22 January 1879, until he famously went to Helpmekaar to hurry forward a detachment of the 24th Regiment, leaving Colour Sergeant Mabin at the depot to catch up with paperwork or just enjoy some free time. On leaving, Major Spalding stated: 'Nothing will happen'—and he intended to be back the same day.

In an account given in 1914, George stated:

I was sitting at my office tent door at the station. We did not
expect any trouble. Just after three in the afternoon, a man,
hatless and bootless, rode up on an exhausted horse; he halted
at the tent and I immediately asked him what had occurred.
'Good God, the camp is taken and they are coming here!' We
had scarcely finished our preparations when the approaching
Zulus were observed coming round the spur of the Oscarberg
Mountain. There were eighty-six of us bearing arms, and we
prepared to sell our lives as dearly as possible. The first man I
ever killed in my life was a big Zulu. As he advanced he took
cover behind anything that presented itself. He dropped behind
a rock prior to making another rush, when I covered the rock
with my rifle, and as he rose to come out again I pulled the
trigger, and he leaped at least five feet in the air and dropped
dead. About seven in the evening the Zulus attempted to fire
the hospital, lighting tufts of grass and attaching these to their
assegais and throwing them into the thatched roof of the
building which was soon alight. The flames, as a matter of fact,
aided us, because by their light we were able to distinguish the
Zulu as they formed into bodies for succeeding rushes. I was
on the look-out and discovered a movement on the Zululand
side of the river. Owing to the light, I could not determine
what was happening; whether they be friends or enemies
approaching. But in the next ten minutes I found they were
mounted men, and to our intense joy it proved to be the
General at the head of the remainder of the column, and their
approach was the signal for the full flight of the Zulus.

George stated that his only wound was a very slight one on the shin,
made by a spent cartridge. He was promoted to sergeant major on 19
February 1880, being appointed superintendent clerk to the General's
Staff, at Fort Napier, Pietermaritzburg, where the aptly named fourth
child, Albert Napier was born on 20 April 1880.

Sergeant Major Mabin saw active service during the uprising in the
Transvaal in 1881. He was present at the engagement with Boer
commando units at Laing's Nek on 28 January, at Ingogo on 8

February, and he was standing close to General Colley when he was shot dead during the disastrous engagement at Majuba Hill on 27 February. It was during this campaign that George earned himself the nickname 'The Fighting Clerk'.

He was posted back to England, and on 8 December 1882, a son named William was born at 6 North View in Stapleton Road, Bristol. By 1884 he was garrisoned at The Castle in Cape Town, where five more children were born; Frances Mary Catherine, on 11 August 1884; Reginald Victor, on 19 August 1886; Blanche Amy on 28 April 1888; Harold Edgar, on 20 March 1890; Maud Millicent, on 2 November 1893; and their 11th and last child, Gladys Elsie, was born on 2 January 1897.

As part of the celebrations for Queen Victoria's diamond jubilee he was one of only two men to receive the Cape of Good Hope Meritorious Service Medal with an annuity, dated 25 June 1897. Sergeant Major Mabin was discharged at Aldershot on 31 May 1898, after an unblemished military career.

He returned to South Africa as a civilian in 1900, where he took employment as a clerk for the Governor of the Cape. His wife died in 1906, at their home at 20 Williams Street in the district of Woodstock, Cape Town. He wrote a letter to his son, William, announcing her death:

> You will understand that it is with sorrowful feelings I pen these few words to you. Poor mother has gone to rest; there was not much hope for her some weeks before her death, but I advised Bert to keep the worst from you in order not to sadden your holiday more than possible. Even now I know it would have been mother's wish that you should not in any way curtail your trip; though of course I can understand that this blow must have a very sorrowful effect on the remainder of your holiday in England. Remember me to all, and wishing you the best you can desire; believe me—Your Affectionate father.

A few years later George married Sarah Annie Stroud, but he was widowed again in 1920.

On 3 April 1935 he gave an interview to newspapers, and on being asked if he still celebrated the action he replied:

Lord, bless you, no. There have been too many anniversaries of that battle. I was in other battles just as bad. And there will be a lot more anniversaries before I go.

The report also stated:

Mr Mabin, aged 87, lives in Woodstock, and claims to be the last survivor of that epic stand in the Zulu War of 1879. He now lives with his daughter, and spends his time gardening.

The family lived at 48 Strand Street in Woodstock, Cape Town, at the time of his first wife's death in 1906, before moving to 20 William Street in Woodstock. He developed malignant tumours on his thigh and lung, and on 23 October 1938, he underwent an operation at the Groote Schuur Hospital in Cape Town (famous for the world's first heart transplant). However, he did not fully recover and died on that day, aged 90. The official cause of death was 'Sarcoma of thigh, Secondary sarcomatosis of lung; Operation for removal of Sarcoma of thigh.'

He was buried alongside his wives in the family plot 12487 at Maitland Road Cemetery in Cape Town. His obituary described him as: 'an exemplary husband and father, a soldier, and a veteran of Rorke's Drift.' The Maitland Road Cemetery Record of Internment states the following were buried in the same plot: 16 July 1906–Mary E. Mabin; 2 February 1916–Claude D. Mabin; 6 January 1920–Sarah Annie Mabin; 16 October 1928–Thelma Mabin; 24 October 1938–George William Mabin.

Birth certificate–St Augustin, Bristol 3469B
Marriage certificate–St Mary, Dover TD410538
Death certificate–Cape of Good Hope
Cape Times for 22 January 1914 and 3 October 1928
Maitland Road Cemetery Record of Internments

John Manley was a survivor of the defence.

He was born at Barrackton in Cork, Ireland in about January 1850. He joined the British Army at Cork on 16 April 1864, and attested on the following day. He was aged 15 years 3 months and was five feet one inch tall. He was appointed drummer at Brecon on 1 December 1866, reverted to private on 14 July 1868, and as 1731 Private Manley he was posted to A Company, 2nd Battalion, 24th Regiment, in about December 1868. He was appointed drummer on 1 January 1869, and reverted to private on 7 August 1876. It seems that he saw service in India some time before he went to South Africa.

This was a difficult time for him, because soon after being reduced to private he was confined by civil power from 13 to 16 August 1876, and on 13 September 1876 he was sent to jail for a month for assaulting a woman who was a barmaid at the Gaiety in Dover, who he thought had stolen from him. He was also confined by civil power from 1 to 12 October 1876.

He received orders for active service in South Africa and sailed with his battalion to the Cape in February 1878. He took part in the Cape Frontier War, and during the Zulu War he was present at the defence of Rorke's Drift, having been a patient in the hospital. For his service he received the South Africa Medal with 1877-8-9 clasp, which gives his rank as drummer, and was not issued until 17 June 1881. He made a payment of two pounds to Miss Manley (sister) on 26 May 1879.

He went with his unit to Gibraltar, but he was sent to Netley Military Hospital from Casement Barracks early in 1880, suffering with sunstroke, from where he transferred to the Army Reserve on 2 March 1880. He returned to the depot at Brecon from 2 to 13 August 1882, and transferred back to the army reserve for service with the 28th (Gloucestershire) Regiment, being promoted to lance corporal on 27 January 1883. His last muster period was at Portsmouth from 1 April to 30 June 1883.

At the time of his death it was reported:

He had served 18 years with the colours, twelve with the 24th Foot, now the South Wales Borderers, and six with the 28th Foot [later the North Gloucestershire Regiment]. He left the service with the rank of sergeant, and became in civilian life a painter and decorator.

He was charged with criminally assaulting a woman at Stoke Bishop near Bristol on 9 January 1885–'while the worst for drink'. He was stated to be aged 34. The report stated that while he was in India he had been reduced from the rank of corporal for drunkenness, but that was the only thing against him. He had an attack of sunstroke and was invalided home. He was a married man with two children. Apparently in tears, he stated that he had no recollection of the offence and 'tendered his deepest regret for having molested her.' Colour-Sergeant Strait of Gloucester gave him a good character. He pleaded guilty to an attempted assault, for which a jury found him guilty, and he was sentenced to be imprisoned for 18 months with hard labour.

He was married to Ellen Carroll and they had six children, and in about 1915 he settled with them at 5 Frederick Terrace on Livingstone Street in Nottingham, where he became a house painter. They worshipped at St Edward's Roman Catholic Church on Bluebell Hill.

John died in October 1924, and he was laid to rest with military honours provided by the Nottinghamshire and Derbyshire Regiment in an unmarked grave at Carlton Cemetery in Nottingham. A new memorial stone was unveiled at his grave in 2014, which states: 'In honoured memory of John Manley–soldier who fought at Rorke's Drift–Jan. 1879. Born 1849, Died 1924.'

Beeston Gazette and Echo for 25 October 1924
Dover Chronicle for 16 September 1876
Gloucester Journal for 7 February 1885
Nottingham and Midland Catholic News for 1 November 1924

James Marshall was a survivor of the defence.

He was born on 9 November 1857, in the Hitchin Union Workhouse in Hertfordshire, and he was christened at St Mary's Church in Hitchin, on 15 January 1858. He was the middle son of three born to Dinah Marshall, who was unmarried; Samuel having been christened at St Mary's on 4 February 1853, and Augustus, who was born at Hitchin in March 1861, and died in December 1862.

Dinah married John Bates at Arlesey in Bedford, on 16 October 1861, and James took his step-father's surname, although no formal adoption took place. Two more children named Eliza and John were born at Biggleswade before John Bates was killed in a farming accident at Arlesey on 28 November 1865, aged 55. In 1871 the family were living at 17 Hitchin Hill.

He left his job as a chimney sweep to enlist in the army on 4 December 1876, at Bow Street Magistrates Court in London, and as 964 Private James Marshall he was posted to the 2nd Battalion, 24th Regiment at Brecon. His description was given as five feet six inches tall, with a fresh complexion, hazel eyes and brown hair, and his religion was Church of England. He was hospitalised at Dover in May 1877 suffering with gonorrhoea, and in the following September he was charged with fraudulent enlistment, having been found out that he was two years younger than he had stated, and he was imprisoned for nearly three months, and his former service towards good conduct pay and pension was forfeited.

He received orders for active service in South Africa, and sailed to the Cape in February 1878, and took part in the Cape Frontier War. On 19 October he was sentenced to 21 days imprisonment for 'loss of necessaries'. During the Zulu War he was dangerously wounded during the defence of Rorke's Drift. For his service he received the South Africa Medal with 1877-8-9 clasp.

Caleb Wood stated:

When the Zulu's became thick round the hospital, one soldier named Marshall, whom we all regarded as a bit peculiar, and different from the rest of us, stood his ground for a second or two while we were taking our position ten yards away. We shouted 'Come here you silly...!' When he saw where we were he turned about and came, but at the risk of his life, for he was followed by the enemy. Hastily turning around with his fixed bayonet, he brought down three Zulus with the point from the guard.

He served at Gibraltar in 1880, and in India, and spent several stints in hospital suffering with febricula, a mild form of malaria (chills). He arrived back in England on 29 May 1883, and was discharged to the army reserve on 29 June 1883, his character being described as: 'fair, latterly good.' Having given an intended place of residence in East Chatham, James eventually settled in Nottinghamshire.

He settled in Redmile Road in Elton, near Nottingham, where he worked as a labourer. He married Martha Upton (formerly Millington), on 21 June 1887, at Hyson Green Parish Church near Nottingham. Martha already had two daughters named Mabel and Mary Ann, and together they had six more children: Rosella was born in 1888, Jesse Millington in 1890, James Leonard in 1891, Grace May in 1893, William Herbert in 1900 and Noel Millington, on Christmas Day 1905. During the Great War, Jesse served with the Royal Engineers, and James became a sergeant with the South Nottinghamshire Hussars. During the Second World War Noel served as a fireman with the Royal Air Force.

By 1890 they had moved to Parson's Buildings in Mansfield, shown on the census as Forest Cottages, and James worked as a cowman. The family then moved over the county border to Bottesford in Leicestershire, where James worked as a farm labourer. They moved back over the county border to Village Street in Thoroton, Nottinghamshire, where James and Martha rented a shop, along with an allotment where he grew fruit and vegetables to sell in the shop, and they kept pigs. Shortly after the turn of the century, they moved to 11 Maud Street in Nottingham, and in 1907 they moved to 71a Gawthorne Street in Nottingham, before moving to 17 Clipstone Lane in Ruddington, finding employment as a gardener.

Martha died at Station Road in Ruddington, on 10 January 1916, and in 1918 James left the village and returned to Nottingham, where he obtained employment as an office caretaker. He died of pneumonia on 5 November 1930, four days before his 73rd birthday, at his home, 12 Bertha Terrace, Brierley Street, Nottingham, and he was buried with his wife in Shaw Street Cemetery, Ruddington (section 11, grave 2). Fellow defender Robert Tongue was already laid to rest in the cemetery, and Caleb Wood would be laid to rest there a few years later. A service of re-dedication was held at his grave in 2010.

Birth certificate–Hitchin, Hertford and Bedford BXBZ112492
John Bates death certificate–Biggleswade HC990657
Martha Marshall death certificate–Wilford, Nottingham DYB179680
Death certificate–Nottingham South-West FC906908

Henry Herbert Martin was a survivor of the defence.

He was born on 3 April 1857, at West Lydford in Somerset, his birth was registered at Evercreech near Shepton Mallet, and he was baptised at West Lydford Parish Church. He was the second son of five, and the fourth child of ten, born between 1851 and 1876, to an agricultural labourer named Thomas Martin, and his wife, Anne Maria (formerly Appleby), who had married at West Lydford Parish Church on 3 March 1851, and made their home at Park Farm in West Lydford. Having received some education at the Binegar Church of England School, Henry was able to read and write, and worked as an agricultural labourer, and in a quarry, before leaving home to lodge at Monnow Street in Monmouth.

He joined the Royal Monmouthshire Militia on 23 November 1875, his description being given as just under five feet, six inches tall, and his religion was protestant. He gave his age as 21 years, although he was actually only 18 and a half. He enlisted for the regular army at Newport, Monmouthshire, on 10 February 1876, and as 756 Private Martin he was posted to the 2nd Battalion, 24th Regiment, at Brecon, on 10 March 1876.

He received orders for active service in South Africa, and sailed to the Cape in February 1878. He took part in the Cape Frontier War, and during the Zulu War he was present at the defence of Rorke's Drift. For his service he received the South Africa Medal with 1877-8-9 clasp.

He served at Gibraltar in 1880, and in India, where he began receiving one penny good conduct pay from 4 September 1880. He served in Bombay and Poona, before being shipped back to England as time expired, on 28 October 1881. While awaiting his discharge at Brecon he was fined five days' pay and forfeited his good conduct badge and pay. He was discharged to the first class reserve on 11 February 1882. He returned to his parents at New Inn, West Lydford. He was recalled for duty at Brecon on 2 August 1882, for a short period before receiving his final discharge from the army on 10 February 1883.

He gave his intended place of residence as Lenor's Grove in Shepton Mallet, Somerset, but he moved to Pilton in Somerset, where he obtained lodgings at Carnards Grove. He married Mary Jane Warment at the parish church in Pilton on 24 April 1885, and they lived with Polly's parents at Beard Hill in Pilton. By 1901 Polly had lost her hearing, and they had moved to Belvedere Cottage in Gurney Slade, Somerset, where Henry worked in a slate quarry, eventually becoming a foreman.

He was one of 25 Zulu War veterans who attended The Old Comrades Club of the 24th Foot reunion at the Victoria Barracks in Portsmouth on 30/31 March 1929, along with Thomas Driscoll, Henry Gallagher, John Jobbins and John Williams VC.

He was active in establishing the Ashwick and Binegar branch of the Royal British Legion Club, which opened on 10 December 1930. When the Duke and Duchess of York visited Wells on 27 May 1933, to inspect the annual parade of the British Legion, Henry was introduced to them.

Henry Martin died of cardiac failure, chronic bronchitis and asthma, on 25 January 1937, at his home in Gurney Slade, aged 79, and he was buried in an unmarked grave at Binegar Churchyard. In 1965 a stone cross was erected at his grave site, and a memorial portrait was unveiled in Binegar Memorial Hall.

Birth certificate–Evercreech, Somerset–CN358018
Death certificate–Shepton Mallet, Wells HD109959
Marriage certificate–Pilton, Shepton Mallet MXC236601
The South African Wars: The Somerset Connection (Part Three) by J. C. Kenworthy

Charles Mason was a survivor of the defence.

He was born as Frederick Herbert Brown on 5 December 1854, at 20 Barbican, St Giles Parish in Cripplegate, London. He was the youngest of four children to Charles Brown, a City of London police officer based at Bishopsgate, and his wife, Mary Ann (formerly Mason). By 1861 they had moved to 3 Greenwood Rents in Bishopsgate. His mother died in 1864, and his father, who had become a detective constable, married Ann Johnson, and another child was born to the family. The 1871 census shows that the family lived at 53 Bartholomew Close in Bishopsgate, and at that time Frederick worked as a lamp maker.

He left his job as a solder maker to enlist at Bow Street Magistrates Court on 26 February 1877, and as 1284 Private Charles Mason he was posted to the 2nd Battalion, 24th Regiment, at Brecon.

He was described as just over five feet six inches tall, with a fresh complexion, hazel eyes and brown hair. He had lost several upper teeth (probably in a workshop), and his religion was Church of England. He gave his next-of-kin as his sister, E. Schooley, 57 Skinner Street. He was hospitalised with a sprain injury, treated for tonsillitis, and he was fined for drunkenness, all early in his army career in 1877, but he gained his fourth class certificate of education at Chatham.

He received orders for active service in South Africa, and sailed to the Cape in February 1878. He took part in the Cape Frontier War, and during the Zulu War he was present at the defence of Rorke's Drift. On 8 February 1879, he wrote a letter home from Rorke's Drift in which he stated that he had been on guard duty before the Zulus attacked them. For his service he received the South Africa Medal with 1877-8-9 clasp. He was actually issued with two South Africa medals by mistake, the edges being engraved with both upright and sloping lettering.

He served at Gibraltar in 1880, where he began to receive one penny a day good conduct pay, and in India, where he was hospitalised on several occasions, and his good conduct pay was increased to two pence a day. He embarked for England on 1 May 1883, and was discharged to the first class reserve on 28 June 1883, his character being described as fair, latterly good, and his intended place of residence was given as Finsbury in London.

However, on 30 October 1884, he returned to the colours as a private in the South Wales Borderers, his good conduct pay being resumed at two pence a day. He was posted to Ireland, and then to India, where his unit arrived on 28 September 1885, returning to Ireland on 12 October 1886. He returned to the depot at Brecon on 13 April 1887, being placed in D company. He was hospitalised several more times, and lost all his good conduct pay. He discharged on 26 February 1889, his character being described as: 'latterly good for ten months since April 1888,' giving his intended place of residence as the Lion Coffee Tavern at 105 The Street in Brecon.

Reverting to his real name of Frederick Herbert Brown, he was visiting his sister, Caroline, when he gave her the Rorke's Drift bible, and the illuminated address he had received from the Mayor of Durban.

An emigration and passport application in the name of Frederick

Brown, aged 37 years, male, unmarried, gives a departure date of 15 April 1890, from Liverpool, destined for Halifax, Canada, and the 1891 census for Canada shows a Frederick H. Brown living and working in Montreal, Quebec, before crossing the border into the USA.

It is thought that he returned to England and settled in Old Southgate, London, where he died after an accidental fall in 1936, aged 81. However, his family believe that he lived in Liverpool, where he was admitted to the Walton Workhouse in 1905, and he died in 1918. They believe he was buried in a communal grave at Walton Park Cemetery having possibly been a victim of the flu epidemic of that year.

The bible presented to him by The Ladies' Rorke's Drift Testimonial Fund was presented to the Brecon Museum by his family. His grandson, Captain Reginald Schooley, was killed in action while serving with the Royal Welch Fusiliers during the D-Day landings in Normandy, France, in June 1944.

Birth certificate–Cripplegate BXCD411181

Robert Maxfield was killed in action in the hospital.

He was born in 1855, at Llangarron in Herefordshire. He enlisted at Newport on 30 July 1875, and as 623 Private Maxfield he was posted to G Company, 2nd Battalion, 24th Regiment at Brecon, in the following month. He and his mother are believed to have had a shop in Monmouth.

He received orders for active service in South Africa, and he was promoted to sergeant on 1 February 1878, the day he embarked to sail with his unit to the Cape. He took part in the Cape Frontier War, being awarded a good shooting prize in 1878. During the Zulu War he was a patient in the hospital at Rorke's Drift suffering with fever, where he was killed by the Zulus. Henry Hook reported:

Privates William Jones and Robert Jones... kept at it with bullet and bayonet until six of the seven patients had been removed. They would have got the seventh, Sergeant Maxfield, out safely but he was delirious with fever and, although they managed to dress him, he refused to move. Robert Jones made a last rush to try and get him away like the rest, but when he went back into the room he saw that Maxfield was being stabbed by the Zulus as he lay on his bed.

He was buried in the cemetery at Rorke's Drift and his name is inscribed on the monument. For his service he received the South Africa Medal with 1877-8-9 clasp. His effects were claimed by his mother, brothers and sisters.

His brother, Charles, died at 6 Chesson Road in Fulham, aged 49, and after a service at Fulham Church, he was buried in a common grave at Brompton Cemetery in West London (reference: J228.9 x 165.3).

Brompton Cemetery Burial Records
Friends of Brompton Cemetery

Jesse Handcock Mayor was a survivor of the defence.

He was born in Ireland in November 1859, possibly in Dublin; the son of Joseph Thomas Mayor (1830-1897) of the Royal Navy and the 86th (Royal County Down) Regiment; and his wife, Mary Jane (formerly Lynch).

Jesse joined No. 7 Troop of the Frontier Armed and Mounted Police (later the Cape Mounted Rifles), and was posted to the Transkei in about October 1877, when he took part in the Ninth Cape Frontier War of 1877-78. He was discharged on 25 July 1878, on the reduction of the forces. He then enlisted as corporal, 1st Battalion, 3rd Regiment, Natal Native Contingent, in November 1878, for service in the Zulu War.

He had been caught below the knee by a Zulu assegai at Sihayo's Kraal, and an excerpt from *Surgical Experiences in the Zulu and Transvaal Wars, 1879 and 1881,* states:

The next case is a very interesting one. Private J. H. M., of the 1st Battalion, 3rd regiment, Native Contingent, was present on the 12 January 1879 at the attack on Sirayo Kraal, the first encounter between our troops and the Zulus. Several prisoners were taken and were being disarmed, when one of them, being irritated by our friendly Kaffirs, tried to force his escape, and, assegai in hand, stabbed right and left at every one. This patient was one thus injured. A bandage was applied, and he was conveyed to Rorke's Drift for treatment. While there several outbursts of severe haemorrhage occurred from the wound, and, though the bleeding points were searched for by all the surgeons at that camp, it could not be permanently stopped, breaking out again after a day or more, or whenever the local means of arrest were withdrawn.

This patient was one of those in the hospital at Rorke's Drift on the memorable 22nd of January, and managed, under fire, to hop out from one building to the other. He therefore had four marvellous escapes within a few days—first, that of the stab at Sirayo's Kraal; secondly, the escape under fire from the hospital at Rorke's Drift; thirdly, the frequent profuse haemorrhages; and fourthly, the operation.

On the 15th of February he left Helpmakaar for the base hospital. He afterwards returned to duty and joined 'Buller's Horse', with which famous body he went through all the reconnaissances and battles, including Ulundi, without any inconvenience.

His name appears on the Roll of men serving with Lonsdale's Horse in the NNC which appeared in the *Cape Mercury* for 27 January 1879. On 6 August 1879, while at King Williamstown, he was employed as a clerk and storekeeper with the Commissariat Department, and he served in Pondoland. He was discharged as services no longer required on 13 October 1879. His South Africa Medal was issued on 2 May 1884, of which there was also a duplicate issue, and he applied for the 1877-8-9 clasp in the following month, when he was residing at 104 Caledon Street in Cape Town.

On 13 April 1881, he enlisted as a trooper in A Troop of Baker's Horse for service during the Basuto Gun War of 1880-81, being promoted to corporal on 21 May 1881. He received his cattle prize money in 1883. Corporal Schiess served in C Troop of the same unit.

On 17 November 1887 he enlisted as a private in the Cape Garrison Engineers, having gained the rank of sergeant major when he resigned on 1 July 1892. Two weeks later he enlisted as a pioneer in the Duke of Edinburgh's Own Volunteer Rifles; discharging on 1 January 1899. He gained employment as a clerk at 37 Regent Street in

Salt River, Cape Town.

He married Johanna (Annie) Catherine Coskey (1866-1928), and they had three daughters—Edith Maude 'May' (later Greef–1895-1970), who was born in Cape Town; Charlotte 'Lottie' and Nelly. Their son was Joseph Thomas Mayor, who served in the Great War with the 2nd South African Infantry, and was killed on 10 October 1916 at Delville Wood on the Somme.

On the outbreak of the Second Anglo-Boer War he enlisted as 2228 Trooper Mayor in Roberts's Horse. He saw active service during the operations for the relief of Kimberley, and the actions at Driefontein and at Paardeberg. He deserted the regiment at Bloemfontein on 17 January 1901, and at Cape Town he enlisted as a private in the Western Province Mounted Rifles, with the service number 474, taking part in operations in Cape Colony. On 9 April 1901, he went back to the Duke of Edinburgh's Own Rifle Volunteers (Colonial Light Horse) as 439 Trooper Mayor in E Company of the 2nd Battalion, for operation in Cape Colony.

His final employment was as a clerk with the South African Railways and Harbours, and he died at 5 Roberts Road in Woodstock, Cape Town, on 10 September 1915, and he was buried in Maitland Road Cemetery in Cape Town.

WO33/33

Michael McMahon was awarded the Distinguished Conduct Medal for gallantry during the defence, but it was cancelled later.

He was born at Rathkeale in Limerick, Ireland, in about 1856. At the age of 18 he attested at Lanark in Scotland, on 27 April 1874, and as 362 Private McMahon he was posted to the 64th (South Staffordshire) Regiment at Limerick in Ireland. He was posted to Glasgow, and then to Portsmouth, where he was promoted lance corporal on 19 April 1876. He had begun his army career well, but he started to get into trouble because of excessive drinking and spent a lot of time in the guard room and in a military prison at Aldershot, and was reduced to private.

He transferred to the Army Hospital Corps at Aldershot on 15 February 1877, as 3359 2nd Corporal McMahon. He was probably with the same Army Hospital Corps unit as Privates Luddington and

Miller which was posted at Devonport until October 1878, when it received orders for active service in South Africa.

The unit arrived on 7 November 1878, and he served under Surgeon Reynolds during the defence of Rorke's Drift. As the hospital patients were being evacuated across the compound to the inner defences, several Zulus scaled the ramparts and attacked them. McMahon was one of the men who ran out to help them, assisting Private Robert Cole in particular. Doctor Reynolds stated: 'I am glad to say that the men of AHC behaved splendidly.'

He was promoted to lance corporal on 1 March 1879, and for his gallantry he was mentioned in dispatches, and on 15 January 1880 he was recommended to receive the Distinguished Conduct Medal. However, this was cancelled two weeks later 'for going absent without leave and stealing certain items.' For his service he received the South Africa Medal with 1879 clasp.

John Meehan was a survivor of the defence.

He was born in Limerick, Ireland, and he attested for the army in about March 1871. He appears on the Muster Roll for 1 January 1873, and as 2483 Private Meehan he was posted from the depot at Warley, being appointed drummer on 7 August 1876. In June 1877 he was sentenced to 42 days imprisonment with hard labour, of which 11 days were remitted.

He received orders for active service in South Africa and sailed with his battalion to the Cape in February 1878. He was awarded a good shooting prize in 1878. He took part in the Cape Frontier War, and during the Zulu War he was present at the defence of Rorke's Drift. For his service he received the South Africa Medal with 1877-8-9 clasp.

He served at Gibraltar in 1880, and returned from India for discharge on 29 January 1883. He died in Limerick.

Rowland Herbert Miller was a survivor of the defence.

He was born on 25 May 1855, at Te Aro, Cuba Street, Wellington, New Zealand. He was the fourth son of six to Edward Miller, a native of London, and his wife, Frances Ann (formerly Brown), who had emigrated from England with three of the children on the

Carnatic and arrived in New Zealand on 10 December 1853 to set up as sheep farmers, before Edward gained a senior position at the Wellington branch of the Bank of New South Wales, and he also became the mathematical examiner to Wellington College. All six Miller boys attended Mr Fennimore's School in Willis Street, and went on to Grammar School, where Rowland gained a first in history and a second in Latin.

Rowland travelled to England, where he enlisted into the British Army at Horfield in Bristol, on 2 July 1874, and as 248 Private Miller he was posted to the 37th Brigade, being described as five feet nine inches tall, with a fresh complexion, blue eyes and dark brown hair, and he had a slight burn mark on the back of his hand. He left the infantry, and on 1 October 1876, he signed on for 12 years with the Army Hospital Corps as 3169 Private Miller. He was promoted corporal on 3 January 1878. He married Elizabeth Ellen Few, on 2 April 1878, at St Mary's Church on Northgate, Canterbury, Kent, and they had one son, Rowland Herbert Henry, born in Chelsea in 1885.

He was posted at Devonport until October 1878, when his unit received orders for active service in South Africa, where it arrived on 7 November 1878, and he served under Surgeon Reynolds during the defence of Rorke's Drift. Lieutenant Chard reported: 'There was a short but desperate struggle during which Mr Dalton shot a Zulu who was in the act of stabbing a corporal (Roland Miller) of the Army Hospital Corps, the muzzle of whose rifle he had seized...' He was promoted sergeant on 2 July 1879, and for his service he received the South Africa Medal with 1878-9 clasp.

The *Otago Witness* for 29 November 1879, carried the devastating story of the *Wellington Tragedy* that his brother Clarence had murdered his father and mother and then had taken his own life. All the deeds carried out with an ordinary carving knife. The report stated, 'A brother named Sydney... committed suicide recently by shooting himself, and another brother is in the lunatic asylum in Sydney.'

He returned to England on 15 May 1880. British forces were struggling with a serious uprising by the Transvaal Boers, and on 24 January 1881, the day they had suffered heavy losses at Spion Kop, Rowland was posted to South Africa with British reinforcements. He returned to England 12 months later. On 10 August 1882, he was posted to Egypt for his last tour of overseas duty, and returned to Aldershot on 9 June 1883. Unfortunately, by this time he was beginning to have difficulties with his sight. In spite of this he was promoted to second staff sergeant on 8 April 1886. However, he appeared before a medical board in London on 14 May 1886, which concluded that he was suffering with hypermetropia and astigmatism of the eyes and was no longer fit for overseas duties. On 8 June 1886, he re-engaged with the Medical Staff Corps, but on 19 January 1887, he was in hospital under observation for mental weakness.

He married Mary Brehaut, on 18 December 1889, at St Mary's Presbyterian Church in South Stoneham in Southampton, and they had three children; William Edward was born in 1891, Madeline Frances Mary in 1893, and Gertrude Ellen in 1895, but she only survived for 18 months. The family home was Alderney House, Grand Bouet, Guernsey, and after discharging from the army in 1895, it is thought that Rowland found employment in a nursery and market garden owned by Mary's uncle. The 1901 census has Rowland and his family living at 135 Upton Park, West Ham, London, where he was working as a watcher for the Customs and Excise, but they later moved back to Alderney. His time of death can be estimated as between 1925 and 1932.

Marriage certificate to Elizabeth Few (Canterbury–WOO1574)
Marriage certificate to Mary Brehaut (South Stoneham–G009037)
Otago Witness for 29 November 1879

Frederick Augustus Millne was a survivor of the defence.

He was born on 18 February 1854, at 2 Suffolk Place, Holly Street in Hackney, London. He was the only child of David George Millne and his wife, Mary Ann (formerly Slate). Mary died in 1857, and within a year David married her sister, Frederick's aunt, Louisa Marie, and they had three children. Fred was reasonably well educated and when he left school he became a clerk.

He enlisted into the 2nd Battalion, 3rd Regiment (The Buffs), at Lambeth, on 4 June 1872. 2260 Private Millne was five feet five and a half inches tall, with a chest measurement of thirty-four and a half inches. He had a fair complexion, grey eyes and brown hair. It was noted that he had his own initials tattooed on his left forearm. He gave his age as 18 years and two months and his religion as Church of England. Promotions came fast, and Fred was promoted corporal on 24 February 1873, lance sergeant on 1 April 1876, and sergeant on 6 July of the same year. He had received a second class certificate of education on 1 March 1876.

In 1876 the 2nd Battalion, 3rd Regiment, received orders for active service in South Africa, and he and his unit set sail from Dublin aboard the troopship *St Lawrence*. The passage was an uncomfortable affair, and on 8 November 1876, the ship struck a reef about 90 miles north of Cape Town. They were forced to abandon ship before it sank, with no loss of life, but nine mountain guns, 50 tons of gunpowder and a £1,000 worth of government rations went down with her. Some newspapers listed Sergeant Millne as having been 'lost', so he held the dubious honour of being one of the very few men to read his own obituary after the shipwreck.

On the outbreak of the Zulu War, the 3rd Buffs were attached to the 1st Column, under Colonel Pearson, 3rd Buffs, which was to cross the river border at the Lower Drift. However, Sergeant Millne probably became attached to Lieutenant Newnham-Davis's unit of mounted infantry which was detached from the battalion on scouting and reconnaissance duties, and he must have remained at Rorke's Drift when the unit moved on to iSandlwana, maintaining the ponts and waiting for a party of Royal Engineers to arrive.

In his official report Lieutenant Chard stated:

I desire here to mention for approval the offer of these pont guards, Daniels and Sergeant Milne, of the 3rd Buffs, who, with their comrades, volunteered to moor the ponts out in the middle of the stream, and there to defend them from the decks, with a few men to assist.

However, as Reverend Smith stated: 'Our defensive force was too small for any to be spared, and these men subsequently did good service within the fort.'

Lieutenant Chard also requested Sergeant Millne to post himself in the storehouse, where he was to protect two caskets of rum, with strict orders to shoot any man who tried to touch them. A trooper of the Natal Carbineers named J. P. Symons stated:

The men spoke very highly of Chard, and another man named Millne. He ought to get the Victoria Cross. For when the men were distracted with thirst and parched with dust from the thatch and smoke, they went to breach a cask of rum, but this man stood upon it and threatened to shoot any man who touched it.

The 2nd Battalion, East Kent Regiment, formed part of the British square which inflicted the final crushing defeat of the Zulu Army at Ulundi on 4 July 1879. For his service Sergeant Millne received the South Africa Medal with 1879 clasp. Fred was promoted to colour sergeant on 1 October 1879, but he reverted to sergeant at his own request in 1882, being promoted back to colour sergeant on 11 January 1883. He served at Singapore and Hong Kong, where he won $40,000 on the lottery. He purchased his discharge on 15 December 1883, and gained employment as an instructor with the Shanghai Municipal Police.

On returning to England, Fred lived with his aunt-cum-step-mother, Louisa, and her family, at 1 Camden Villas in Sebastopol Road, Edmonton, London; which placed him in an emotional dilemma when he became involved with his own cousin and half-sister, Catherine, who was thirteen years his younger, and they married at Edmonton Parish Church, on 2 April 1889.

He entered into a business partnership with Stephen White as joint proprietors of a grocery store in Dale Road, Matlock. It is listed in Kelly's 1891 directory as 'White and Millne, wholesale and retail family grocers and tea dealers, wine and spirit merchants, and mineral water manufacturers.' They had a daughter named Catherine in 1890, and the 1891 census shows Frederick and his family living at 'The Beehive'. It is uncertain what happened to the business, which only lasted for two years, but it seems that the parting of Frederick and Stephen White was not amicable, and nothing was left of Fred's winnings.

Fred moved to Manchester in 1893, where he gained employment as assistant labour master at the Crumpsall workhouse, before becoming the caretaker at Birley Street Board School in Hulme. The family lodged at the school for a while, where George Frederick, was born in 1893. Four girls were also born in Manchester but three of them died very young, the only survivor being Ada Rorke, her second Christian name reflecting the fact that she was born on 22 January 1902.

In 1905 he made the interesting statement:

Firing was heard in the Rorke's Drift camp on the morning of 22 January, and about eleven o'clock a party of native women and children with a few decrepit old men, came to the river bank and wanted to be put across, 'As Cetshwayo had killed all the white men.

At the outbreak of the Great War in 1914, Fred, then aged 60, volunteered for active service with several training battalions of the Lancashire Fusiliers, retaining his old rank of colour sergeant, and he had rose to regimental sergeant major with the Devonshire Regiment, the unit from which he took his discharge at the age of 65. His son also served in the Great War.

In retirement Fred Millne he became the caretaker at the Princess Road School at Moss Side in Manchester, where he was described as 'A sturdy gentleman with a small pointed beard.'

He died of pneumonia at his home, 5 Lofas Street, Moss Side, on 5 June 1924, aged 71, and he was buried in an unmarked grave at the Southern Cemetery, Manchester (non-Conformist, section H, grave 483). His campaign medal and a commemorative bible which had belonged to him were sold at a Sotheby's auction in 1990, and on 8 July 2001, a service of commemoration and re-dedication was held at his grave.

Father's birth certificate
London Evening Standard for 17 April 1891
Manchester Evening Chronicle for 2 December 1905
Manchester Evening News for 9 June 1924

Michael Minehan was a survivor of the defence.

He was born in 1845, at Castlehaven, near Castletownsend in County Cork, Ireland. He had joined the West Coast Artillery Militia on 9 May 1864, and left his job as a groom to enlist into the regular army at Bandon in County Cork, on 14 October 1864. As 1527 Private Minehan he was posted to the 2nd Battalion, 24th Regiment, being described as just under five feet ten inches tall, with a fair complexion, blue eyes and dark brown hair. He served in India from

12 October 1866 to 3 January 1873, having been granted two pence a day good conduct pay by the time he re-engaged at Secunderabad on 7 October 1871, to serve 21 years. He forfeited a penny of his good conduct pay, but he was receiving three pence a day by 18 February 1875. He was admitted to hospital in April 1875, after being injured in a fight.

He received orders for active service in South Africa, and sailed to the Cape in February 1878, taking part in the Cape Frontier War. He forfeited a penny of his good conduct pay in July 1878, and another penny while he was stationed at Rorke's Drift on 9 January 1879, being present during the defence of the garrison. It was reported that Private Minehan was posted in the kraal to the east of the defences which was not so well lit up by the light of the burning hospital. A Zulu crawled under the straw and grabbed him by the leg, and Minehan retaliated by prodding the straw with his bayonet, and one of the thrusts killed the warrior. For his service he received the South Africa Medal with 1877-8-9 clasp.

Captain Penn-Symons was with the force which relieved the garrison on 23 January, and Minehan, unable to speak properly from exhaustion, had taken him to the kraal to show him the body of the Zulu and related his story. In his memoirs Penn-Symons stated: 'Minehan was a great pal of mine; he was right-hand man, front rank of B Company, who knew his drill well and had often kept me straight.'

He served at Gibraltar in 1880, and in India, where his good conduct pay was restored to three pence a day on 9 January 1881. A testimonial regarding Private Minehan was written by Major Bromhead in India on 24 March 1884. He received treatment for cholera on 2 April 1884, and on being examined by a medical board he was invalided to England on 30 April 1884. He was examined by a medical board at Netley Hospital, and discharged as unfit for further service on 2 September 1884. His character was described as good, clean and temperate, and he gave his next-of-kin as his sister, M. Regan of Castletown.

Michael Minehan died on 26 May 1891, and lies buried in the churchyard at Castletownsend. A wrought iron marker stating that he was 'one of the gallant defenders of Rorke's Drift', was placed at the grave site, but a document in the regimental archive dated 1997 states that the church was derelict and the marker had rusted and broken in two. His South Africa Medal was sold at auction in 2016.

Mkungo native who died in the hospital during the defence.

During the skirmish at Sihayo's Kraal on the second day of the invasion, a native of Mkungo's tribe had his thigh split by a rifle bullet. He was placed in a small room at the south-west corner of the hospital.

Eventually, the Zulus concentrated their attack on the hospital building. Private Henry Hook stated:

> But it was the hospital they assaulted most fiercely. I had charge, with a man that we called 'Old King Cole' [Private Thomas Cole] of a small room with only one patient in it... He went outside and was instantly killed by the Zulus; so that I was left alone with the patient–a native whose leg was broken, and who kept crying out, 'Take my bandage off, so that I can come!' But it was impossible to do anything but fight, and I blazed away as hard as I could... Fire and dense choking smoke forced me to get out of my own room and go into the other. It was impossible to take the native patient with me, and I had to leave him to an awful fate. But his death was, at any rate, a merciful one. I heard the Zulus asking him questions; and he tried to tear off his bandages and escape.

Reverend George Smith recorded:

> The native of Mkungo's tribe, who had been shot through the thigh at Sihayo's kraal, was lying unable to move. He said that he was not afraid of the Zulus but wanted a gun. When the end room in which he lay was forced, Private Hook heard the Zulus talking with him; next day his charred remains were found amongst the ruins.

Surgeon James Reynolds stated that he was under treatment for a compound fracture of the femur.

It has to be pointed out that Private Hook did not actually witness him being killed by the Zulus. When they were 'asking him questions' they may have been trying to gain intelligence, and he may have been trying to tear off his bandages to escape from the 'fire and dense choking smoke'. Therefore, as he could not move, he either suffocated from the smoke or was a victim of the flames.

His body was placed in the kraal next to the storehouse and his remains are probably in that area to this day.

Hook VC, Sergeant Henry, *How They Held Rorke's Drift: Survivors' Tales of Great Events* from the *Royal Magazine*, February 1905.

Smith, Reverend George: Account dated 3 February 1879, published in the *Royal Army Chaplains' Department Journal* for July 1936–Royal Army Chaplains' Department Museum at Aldershot.

Thomas Moffatt was a survivor of the defence.

He was born on 5 December 1855, at High Street in Runcorn, the son of Thomas Moffat (with one 't'), and his wife, Catherine (formerly Rowley). A son named Thomas had been born previously, but he died early in 1855 and the new baby was named after him and baptised at home immediately after his birth. Thomas senior had worked for the Manchester Ship Canal Company, and died of consumption at Back Brunswick Street in Runcorn, on 31 January 1858, and after moving to Mill Street in Runcorn, Catherine died of tuberculosis on 5 July 1869, leaving Thomas as a teenage orphan. Thomas junior had also worked for the Manchester Ship Canal Company with his father.

He joined the army at Liverpool on 30 November 1876, and as 968 Private Moffatt, he was posted to the 2nd Battalion, 24th Regiment. He received orders for active service in South Africa, and sailed to the Cape in February 1878, taking part in the Cape Frontier War, and during the Zulu War he was present at the defence of Rorke's Drift. For his service he received the South Africa Medal with 1877-8-9 clasp. In the company re-shuffle caused by the losses at iSandlwana, he was transferred to G company, on 29 January 1879.

He served at Gibraltar in 1880, and in India, from where he returned to England on 27 January 1883. He was discharged to the army reserve on 19 July 1883.

He found accommodation at Plant's lodging house, at 9 Mill Street in Runcorn, and employment as a dock worker with the Bridgewater Canal Company on the Runcorn Waterways. It was reported in 1889 that he had an argument with a fellow lodger named Michael Rowley, during which he stabbed Rowley with a kitchen knife. He was charged of 'felonious wounding' but Rowley withdrew his accusation and Thomas was acquitted.

When the teenage daughter of his landlord, Martha Plant, moved to Widnes, Thomas also moved to the town, where he found lodgings at 55 James Street, and they kept in touch. They married on 6 December 1892, at St Mary's Parish Church in Widnes, and they made their home at 2 Back Brunswick Street in Runcorn, and Thomas worked as a rope gatherer on the canal, later moving to Mersey Street in Mount Pleasant, Runcorn. By 1900 Thomas had become a dock labourer.

They had ten children. Catherine was born at 2 Back Brunswich Street on 8 August 1895; the next eight were born at Mount Pleasant. Thomas Joseph on 5 August 1897; Eliza on 1 July 1900; John on 5 February 1903; Mary on 2 April 1904; Francis on 28 September 1906; James on 26 February 1909; Edward on 13 October 1911; Nora on 24 May 1916. The tenth and last child was William, who was born on 17 February 1919, after they had moved to 9 Brunswick Street, Runcorn, and Thomas was described as a lock-tender. They went on to have 29 grandchildren.

King George V opened the new bridge between Runcorn and Widnes in 1925, and Thomas Moffatt and fellow Rorke's Drift man, Thomas Taylor, were presented to the King, along with 'Todger' Jones VC. Thomas suffered from nightmares about the events at Rorke's Drift, and in his later years cataracts impaired his vision. He was often seen about town talking to Todger Jones.

Tom died of myocardial degeneration and arterial sclerosis, on 18 November 1936, aged 80, and he was buried with military honours in Runcorn Cemetery (section 13, grave 138), where Thomas Taylor was already laid to rest. His devoted dog, Toby, died a week later. Martha died at 9 Brunswick Street on 21 June 1941, and was buried with Thomas.

In 1999 a renovation and re-dedication service was held at his graveside, and the grave of Thomas Taylor. The service included a troupe of Zulu dancers in regalia. The memorial stone refers to him as Thomas J., but there is no reference to him having a middle name in any of the official documentation listed below. His eldest son is referred to on the memorial as Joseph, but his full name was Thomas

Joseph, and there seems to have been a mix up with the names. In 2020 a blue plaque was unveiled in the street where he was born, which was attended by members of his family, and later that year his campaign medal was sold at auction.

Birth certificate–Runcorn FC045721
Father's death certificate–Runcorn FC959465
Mother's death certificate–Runcorn – FC959466
Marriage certificate–Widnes MXC236566
Catharine birth certificate–Runcorn FC720665
Thomas Joseph birth certificate–Runcorn FC720745
Eliza birth certificate–Runcorn FC720740
John birth certificate–Runcorn FC720741
Mary birth certificate–Runcorn FC720742
Francis birth certificate–Runcorn FC720743
James death certificate–Runcorn FC720744
Edward birth certificate–Runcorn FC959449
Nora birth certificate–Runcorn FC959451
William birth certificate–Runcorn FC959450
Death certificate–Runcorn FC720902
Martha's death certificate–Runcorn FC720903
Runcorn Examiner for 16 February 1889
Liverpool Echo for 10 November 1927 and 19 November 1936
Western Mail for 20 November 1936

Augustus Morris was a survivor of the defence.

He was born a Roman Catholic in Dublin in 1857. In 1871 he was living with his family at 44 Louis Street in Liverpool. He left his job as a labourer to enlist at Liverpool on 3 March 1877, and as 1342 Private A. Morris he was posted to the 2nd Battalion, 24th Regiment, at Brecon. He was described as being five feet seven inches tall, with a fair complexion, dark-grey eyes and red hair.

He and his older brother, Frederick, received orders for active service in South Africa, and sailed to the Cape in February 1878. He took part in the Cape Frontier War, and during the Zulu War he and Frederick were present at the defence of Rorke's Drift. For his service he received the South Africa Medal with 1877-8-9 clasp. He was appointed lance corporal on 5 February 1879, and he was awarded one penny a day good conduct pay from 6 March 1879. He reverted to private on 24 October 1879.

He served at Gibraltar in 1880, and in India, where he gained a fourth class certificate of education in September 1881, his good conduct pay was increased to two pence a day from 6 March 1883, and he was permitted to extend his service to ten years on 4 September 1883.

His brother, Frederick died of disease in India in 1883. He served in Burma to 7 December 1887, being appointed lance corporal on 12 June 1886. He received the Indian General Service Medal, 1854, with Burma 1885-87 clasp. He transferred to the first class army reserve as a lance corporal on 18 December 1887, and discharged from the army on 5 March 1889, his character being described as 'very good' and his habits 'temperate'.

His next-of-kin was given as Mrs Hughes, sister, of Oliver Street in Bootle, Liverpool.

Augustus died on 3 November 1914. A death certificate in the Regimental Archive records the internment of Augustus Morris, on 6 November 1914, aged 52, of 6 Johnstone Street, Bootle, Liverpool, at Kirkdale Cemetery (C of E, section 9, public grave 119). His sister may have lived in Olivia Street, Bootle, where close by up to 1889 lived Augustus Morris, coppersmith, of 11 Stewart Grove.

Frederick Morris was a survivor of the defence.

He was born a Roman Catholic in Dublin in 1855, the older brother of fellow Rorke's Drift man, Augustus Morris. He enlisted in Liverpool on 4 December 1876, and as 529 Private F. Morris he was posted to the 2nd Battalion, 24th Regiment, at Brecon.

He and Augustus received orders for active service in South Africa, and sailed to the Cape in February 1878. He took part in the Cape Frontier War, and during the Zulu War the two brothers were present at the defence of Rorke's Drift. For his service he received the South Africa Medal with 1877-8-9 clasp, which is now regimental property, and the Address from the Mayor of Durban in January 1880.

He served at Gibraltar in 1880, and in India. Private Frederick Morris died of disease at Secunderabad, India, on 26 September 1883, aged 26, having never returned home.

Thomas Morrison was a survivor of the defence.

He was born in Armagh, County Armagh, Ireland, and he enlisted on 8 March 1877, probably at the same time as John Murphy at Tredegar in Monmouthshire. As 1371 Private Morrison, he was posted to the 2nd Battalion, 24th Regiment at Brecon, on 11 May 1877.

He received orders for active service in South Africa, and sailed to the Cape in February 1878. He took part in the Cape Frontier War, and during the Zulu War he was present at the defence of Rorke's Drift. He made a monthly remittance to a Mrs Shillcock in March 1879. For his service he received the South Africa Medal with 1877-8-9 clasp.

He served at Gibraltar in 1880, and in India, from where he returned to England on 26 April 1883.

What is said to have been his campaign medal was offered for auction in 2019.

James 'John' Murphy was a survivor of the defence.

He is believed to have been born at Abergavenny in Monmouthshire, and left his job as a railway guard to enlist at Tredegar as 662 Private John Murphy on 22 November 1875, being posted to the 2nd/24th Regiment on 6 January 1875.

He received orders for active service in South Africa, and sailed to the Cape in February 1878. He was confined and sentenced to receive 25 lashes, on 11 February 1878, while on board ship in transit to the Cape. He took part in the Cape Frontier War, and during the Zulu War he was present at the defence of Rorke's Drift. For his service he received the South Africa Medal with 1877-8-9 clasp.

He served at Gibraltar from 12 February to 11 August 1880, being posted to India on the following day. His service continued with the South Wales Borderers, but he did not transfer. He served at the Brecon depot from 1 April to 30 September 1882, and transferred to the 1st South Wales Borderers on 11 November 1882. He returned to England from India, 28 October 1883. He discharged from army service on 3 November 1887.

He married Alice Lilian Mary Ann Thrash (also known as Margaret) at the Cardiff Registry Office, on 23 December 1905.

On the outbreak of the Great War he re-enlisted into the South

Wales Borderers on 29 September 1914, his description being recorded as aged 42, height 5 feet 8 inches, chest 38 inches, hazel eyes, black hair and a fresh complexion. He was a Roman Catholic, and his next-of-kin was Mrs Murphy of 30 Bell Street in Barry. He was posted to the Brecon depot on 3 October 1914, having been promoted corporal on that date. He became sergeant on 6 November 1914, when he was posted to the 9th Battalion, South Wales Borderers. He was discharged on 14 May 1916, as being no longer physically fit for war service. He received the British War Medal, 1914-20, and the Victory Medal, 1918.

John lived at 81 Witham Street in Newport. He died of senile myocarditis on 28 July 1927, aged 70, and is buried in a grave paid for by his wife, at St Woollos Cemetery in Newport; where John Lyons had been laid to rest and Alfred Saxty would later be buried. A plaque was placed at his grave, and new headstones were erected at the graves of John J. Lyons and Alfred Saxty in 1996.

N

William Neville was a survivor of the defence.

He was born on 12 May 1858, at Broom Street in Ince-in-Makerfield, Wigan. He was the last child of six born to William Neville, a spindle maker at an iron forge, and his wife Jane (formerly White). He was baptised at All Saint's Parish Church in Wigan, on 2 July 1858, where fellow Rorke's Drift man, John Smith, had also been baptised. His father died in December 1861, and his mother re-married in 1864, becoming Mrs Richard Anderton, her new husband being the son of a doctor. At the aged of 12, William became a coal miner's labourer working on the coal face, and the 1871 census records him as living with his sister Jane, and her husband Richard at 35 Broom Street in Wigan.

He enlisted at Liverpool on 23 February 1877, at the same time as fellow Rorke's Drift man, John Thomas, and as 1279 Private Neville, he was posted to the 2nd Battalion, 24th Regiment at Brecon. He was just over five feet five inches tall, with a fresh complexion, hazel eyes and brown hair. His religion was Church of England.

He received orders for active service in South Africa, and sailed to

the Cape in February 1878. He took part in the Cape Frontier War, and during the Zulu War he was present at the defence of Rorke's Drift. For his service he received the South Africa Medal with 1877-8-9 clasp.

He served at Gibraltar in 1880, and in India, where he was granted one penny a day good conduct pay from 6 November 1880. A week after his service continued with the South Wales Borderers on 1 July 1881, he began to show the first signs of being a troublesome soldier when he forfeited his good conduct pay, and he arrived home from India on 28 May 1883. He joined the first class army reserve, and was passed around several districts, presumably still making life difficult for his superiors. He joined the 20th Regimental District (Bury), on 21 June 1883, being transferred to the 40th District (Warrington), on 24 August 1883. He returned to the 20th District on 7 February 1884, before returning to the depot at Brecon on 1 April 1884.

On 1 June 1884, he married Sarah Elizabeth Graham at Christ Church, Ince-in-Makerfield, Wigan, and they lived at 28 Broom Street, Ince. They had had five sons. William was born in 1885, James in 1887, Thomas in 1890, John in 1891 and Ernest in 1894.

On the morning of 28 November 1885, a woman named Phoebe Benyon was walking to work along the Leeds-Liverpool Canal at Ince, when she was attacked by a man, who manhandled her and stole threepence. Local newspapers reported the assault as a 'Dastardly Outrage'. William Neville, described as a miner, appeared in court at Wigan on 4 December charged with committing highway robbery and attempted criminal assault in connection with this incident. The woman identified him, but William denied the charges and produced witnesses who said he was at home at the time of the crime. He twice went to Court at the Liverpool Assizes to face the charges, where, on the first occasion the jury failed to reach a verdict, and on the second he was acquitted. However, it seems that the authorities were determined to blame someone for the crime, and the victim eventually produced a witness of her own, who stated he had seen William running from the scene of the crime. He was ordered to appear before the Liverpool Assizes for a third time on 19 May 1886. Local newspapers reported that he had been 'Convicted At Last', and he was sentenced to 12 months in prison with hard labour. He was released from Walton Prison in Liverpool, on 18 May 1887, and his army service continued from the following day.

William Neville was discharged on 25 February 1889, his character being described as 'bad' and his habits 'intemperate'. His next-of-kin was given as Mrs Anderson (mother), of Longbroom Street in Ince. He died of heart failure at his home, 52a Broom Street in Ince-in-Makerfield, Wigan, on 28 August 1895, aged 37, and he was buried in public grave (C of E - section C/grave 478), of the Urban District Cemetery at Ince-in-Makerfield, Wigan. There is no memorial stone at his grave.

Birth certificate–Hindley, Wigan CN284375
Marriage certificate–Ince, Wigan Y569854
Death certificate–Hindley, Wigan HC990968

Edward Nicholas was killed in action at Rorke's Drift.

He was born in 1857. He enlisted in Newport on 4 October 1875, stating his age as 18, and as 625 Private Nicholas he was posted to the 1st Battalion, 24th Regiment. He was sent with a draft of reinforcements from the battalion on 2 August 1877, for active service in South Africa, taking part in the Cape Frontier War.

He may have originally been one of the men of G Company: 'who had been to the rear with prisoners...' but he was present at the defence of Rorke's Drift, where he was killed in action by a bullet through the head. He was buried in the cemetery at Rorke's Drift and his name is inscribed on the monument. His effects were recorded for claim by his next-of-kin. For his service he received the South Africa Medal with 1877-8-9 clasp, which is now regimental property. His name is variably spelt wrong on regimental records with errors such as E. Nicholls and W. Nicholas.

Robert Norris was a survivor of the defence.

He was born in Liverpool in February 1858. The only child named Robert Norris baptised in Liverpool from July 1857 to July 1860 was at St David's Church in Brownlow Hill, Liverpool, on 11 September 1859. He was the son of a brass founder named Edward and his wife, Margaret, of Henry Street in Liverpool, but they had moved by the time of the 1861 census.

Robert had worked as a labourer until the age of 19, when he enlisted from the 2nd Lancashire Militia at Liverpool on 21 February 1877, and as 1257 Private Norris he was posted to the 2nd Battalion, 24th Regiment, a month later. He was described as just over five feet seven inches tall, with a fresh complexion, grey eyes and dark-brown hair. His religion was Church of England. He was admitted to hospital in 1877 to be treated for syphilis.

He received orders for active service in South Africa, and sailed to the Cape in February 1878. He took part in the Cape Frontier War, and during the Zulu War he was present at the defence of Rorke's Drift. For his service he received the South Africa Medal with 1877-8-9 clasp.

He served in Gibraltar in 1880, and in India, where he was admitted to hospital in 1881 to be treated for syphilis, the treatment being repeated three times in 1882. His good conduct pay was increased to two pence a day from 22 February 1883 and he returned home from India on 30 May 1883. He transferred to first class army reserve at Warrington, 28 June 1883, moving to Brecon on 25 May 1884.

As 1933 Private Norris, he joined the 1st Battalion, Royal Sussex Regiment, on 5 May 1885, regaining his two pence a day good conduct pay. He later resigned, but re-engaged on 28 June 1885, to complete 12 years' service. He gained a fourth class certificate of education on 24 March 1886, and a third class certificate of education on 14 October 1886, and he was promoted corporal on 17 December 1886. However, on 27 July 1887, he was allowed to resign and revert to private at his own request because he considered himself to be unfit for NCO duties. He was allowed to retain his good conduct pay, and he re-engaged to complete 21 years' service on 29 February 1888. On 25 July 1888, even though he had indicated a lack of confidence in his own abilities, he transferred to the Corps of Military Police.

On 13 June 1889, he was examined by a Medical Board at the Curragh Camp in Ireland, and was found to be suffering from venereal disease of the heart. He was discharged as unfit for further service on 16 July 1889, his character being described as temperate and steady, but he obviously returned to civilian life in very bad health. His next-of-kin was given as J. Norris, uncle, 15 Hinds Street in Edge Hill, Liverpool. His South Africa Medal was sold at auction in 2021.

O

William Osborne was a survivor of the defence.

He was born on 20 February 1858, and according to newspaper reports in 1927 he was born at Duke Street in Blaenavon, Monmouthshire; the son of Thomas Osborne, who was employed at the Blaenavon Company Mill. Apparently, he started working at the Blaenavon Iron Works at the age of five.

'When quite a youngster' he enlisted for the army at Pontypool in Monmouthshire, on 28 November 1877, and as 1480 Private Osborne, he was posted to the 2nd Battalion, 24th Regiment.

He received orders for active service in South Africa, and sailed to the Cape in February 1878. He took part in the Cape Frontier War, and during the Zulu War he was present at the defence of Rorke's Drift. He made a monthly remittance to Mrs Osborne in January 1879, and for his service he received the South Africa Medal with 1877-8-9 clasp. He served at Gibraltar in 1880, and in India, from where he returned to England in October 1883.

He worked underground at the local coal mine, and lived with his wife at 79 Cambrian Row in Blaenavon, where he died on 21 February 1931, aged 73. He was buried with military honours at St Peter's Churchyard in Blaenavon. In recent years members of his family have been trying to locate his exact grave site so they can commemorate his name. However, the site and area is now a World Heritage site because of its part in the Industrial Revolution.

Free Press of Monmouth for 21 January 1927
Western Mail for 21 February 1931
Wales Online for 15 October 2014

P

Samuel Parry was a survivor of the defence.

He was born in about 1861, one of eight children to George and Matilda Parry, in the Bedwelty District of Sirhowy near Tredegar, Monmouthshire. He had served in the Monmouthshire Militia at

Pontypool when he enlisted for the regular army at Monmouth, on 23 May 1877, and as 1399 Private Parry he was posted to the 1st Battalion, 24th Regiment, at Brecon. He was described as aged 18, was just under five feet six inches tall, with a 34 inch chest, a fresh complexion, light-brown hair and grey eyes, and his religion was Church of England. His home address was 13 George Street in Blaenavon. He transferred to the 2nd Battalion, and on receiving orders for active service in South Africa he sailed to the Cape in February 1878. He took part in the Cape Frontier War, being confined in cells from 28 September to 4 October 1878. During the Zulu War he was present at the defence of Rorke's Drift, and for his service he received the South Africa Medal with 1877-8-9 clasp.

He transferred to C Company, and was admitted to hospital at Pinetown with fever on 3 January 1880, being examined later that month and recommended for return to England. He served at Gibraltar from 12 February to 17 March 1880, and on returning home he was admitted to Netley Hospital, where he was found to have chronic rheumatism which had originally manifested at Rorke's Drift, and it was attributed to the climate and service as his regiment underwent exposure. It was stated that the disability need not be permanent and eventually he ought to be able to earn a livelihood and his pension appeal was rejected. He was discharged as unfit for further service on 25 May 1880, being described as aged 23 years, and his conduct as fair and temperate.

His intended place of residence was Birmingham. It is believed he was living with his widowed mother and blind brother at Long Acre in Aston, Birmingham, at the time of his death, which occurred during the June quarter of 1898, aged 37. He was buried at Witton Cemetery in Birmingham, where fellow defender, Robert Cole was buried at about the same time, and Joseph Windridge would be buried four years later. In 2015 new memorials dedicated to Sam, Robert and Joseph were placed at the cemetery.

Thomas Parry was a survivor of the defence.

He was born on 2 July 1853, in the village of Swainshill Bank in Stretton Sugwas west of Hereford (now in the West Midlands). He was the son of Thomas Parry, and his wife, Elizabeth (formerly Nicholls, nee Lewis), who was born in Hereford. He had an older sister named Ellen, and at least two younger sisters named Elizabeth and Mary Ann, all born in Hereford. Thomas eventually moved to Merthyr Tydfil to work as the head gardener at the Castle Hotel and Gardens.

Thomas junior enlisted into the army and as 572 Private Parry he was posted to the 2nd Battalion, 24th Regiment, on 6 April 1875, and served at Aldershot and Dover. He was confined to cells for three days in October 1876, and forfeited pay. He was on furlough from 15 February to 14 March 1877, and he transferred to D Company of the 1st Battalion on 13 June 1877. He was sent to South Africa with reinforcements, taking part in the Cape Frontier War, and during the Zulu War he was present at the defence of Rorke's Drift. For his service he received the South Africa Medal with 1877-8-9 clasp.

He wrote a letter to his parents from Helpmekaar on 14 February 1879, which was published in the *Western Mail* on 16 April 1879.

Dear Father and Mother;

I now take the first opportunity of writing to you that I have had for the last week or two. We have been very busy, the few of us that is left of the 2-24th Regiment...

They then made their way down to Rorke's Drift, where I was with a company of the 2-24th. We gave them such a warming there that they won't forget for some time to come. They kept coming at us all night, but gave it up as a bad job. We killed 400 of them, and lost 10 and 9 wounded.

The way I came to be with them down there, and not at the camp, was that one of my horses got lame and I had to stop with him, or else you would not have heard from me any more.

My master got shot [Pulleine at iSandlwana], and then ripped up. He had my horse shot under first then he got someone else's. It was a lucky job for me that his horse got lame. I dare say that there is a full account in the papers by this time.

We had our colours lost, but it was brought into camp two days ago... We expect to have a big fight next Monday (17 February). We are about 2,000 strong here and on a fort, but the Zulu King tells us that if we don't shift out of this country he will eat us all up. So, dear father and mother, I must conclude with best love, and remain your affectionate son:

Tom.

The following appeared in the *Merthyr Express* on 12 April 1879:

> This week Mr Thomas Parry, gardener at the Castle Hotel, who had a son in the 24th Foot at Natal, and had given him up as dead, was overjoyed at the receipt of a letter from the young man reporting himself alive and well, and explaining his providential escape.
>
> In a letter published in the *Merthyr Express* for 19 April 1879, Private Thomas Stephens, 2nd Battalion, 24th Regiment, a defender of Rorke's Drift, suggests that Thomas was not a defender on the strength that he could not see his name on Lieutenant Chard's list of defenders. Several men who were later confirmed defenders were also not on the list. It is likely that a strong bond developed between the men of B Company after the defence, which would explain why Stephens made the strong objection, but Thomas was serving with the 1st Battalion, and Private David Jenkins, one of the other names not on the list was also serving with the 1st Battalion. 'Absence of proof is not proof of absence.'

He was promoted to corporal on 1 June 1879, but he was in confinement from 8 to 10 August 1879 and reduced to private. He was posted to England, being reported absent from 4-7 November 1879, for which he was imprisoned from 25 November to 23 December 1879. He transferred to the first class army reserve at Cardiff on 31 May 1880, then to Brecon on 25 May 1884.

He rejoined the colours and was posted to the 2nd Battalion, Royal Sussex Regiment depot at Chichester, on 14 March 1885. He was posted to Egypt on 12 May 1885, serving at Alsiout and Aabbassaiyeh. He returned to England on 5 January 1886, and was transferred back to the first class army reserve. He was posted to the 35th Regimental District at Chichester, on 20 January 1886, from where he was discharged with good character on 2 April 1887.

On the outbreak of the Great War he tried to re-enlist into the Army Service Corps at Aldershot on 11 September 1915, giving his age as 46. However, on 6 December he was discharged as unfit due to his true age being 60. His address was 19 Corporation Road in

Pendown, Merthyr Tydfil, and his trade was a groom. He was stated to have had 'Ellen' tattooed on his left forearm.

Thomas died of chronic bronchitis at 44 Thomas Street in Merthyr Tydfil, on 13 September 1922, aged 69, his home address being 10 Mill Street in Quakers Yard, Merthyr Tydfil. He was buried at Cefn Cemetery in Merthyr Tydfil (grave J/17) consecrated section.

Herefordshire Times for 12 April 1879
Merthyr Express for 12 April and 19 April 1879
Western Mail for 16 April 1879

William Partridge was a survivor of the defence.

He was born on 27 June 1858, in Broad Street, Ross-on-Wye, Herefordshire, the oldest child of four to William Partridge, a sawyer and carpenter, and his wife, Sarah (formerly Williams). They moved back to their native Monmouthshire.

Having served with the Monmouthshire Militia, William enlisted for the regular army at Monmouth, on 5 June 1877, and as 1410 Private Partridge, he was posted to G Company, 2nd Battalion, 24th Regiment, being described as just over five feet six inches tall, with a fresh complexion, grey eyes and brown hair. His religion was Church of England.

He received orders for active service in South Africa, and sailed to the Cape in February 1878. He took part in the Cape Frontier War, being appointed lance corporal on 1 August 1878, but he reverted back to private on 1 December 1878. It was during this campaign that he was batman to Colour Sergeant Bourne, who stated in his account:

> One day I heard a man named Wall ask my batman 'if the kid was in', a day or two later I asked Partridge who 'the kid' was, and received the answer 'why, you are of course!'

During the Zulu War he was present at the defence of Rorke's Drift. For his service he received the South Africa Medal with 1877-8-9 clasp.

He served at Gibraltar, from where he embarked on 23 February 1880, to return home. An injury assessment board held at the Royal

Hospital in Chelsea, in November 1881, confirmed that he was suffering from chronic rheumatism, which would materially affect his ability to earn an income. His condition was attributed to having been brought about by climate and exposure during the Zulu War, and he was awarded a pension of seven pence a day for 12 months. He was discharged as unfit for further service at Devonport on 10 November 1881. He gave his intended place of residence as Llangstone, Newport, Monmouthshire, the home of his father, William, who by this time was the local Parish Clerk.

He married Mary Letitia 'Polly' Reeves, on 13 November 1880, at the Brecon Register Office. Polly was the sister-in-law of William Allan VC. They had six children; Sarah Eleanor, known as 'Nellie', was born in 1882, William Henry was born in 1885, Elizabeth was born in 1889, Lily was born in 1891, but she only lived for a few days, Beswick was born in 1894 and Jessie was born in 1899. They lived at 46 Lancaster Street in Blaina, where William found employment as a stoker. At the time of the Great War he and William Henry were working at the same pit, before William junior enlisted for service with the Royal Warwickshire Regiment.

William died on 16 April 1930, aged 71, the cause of death being myocardial degeneration. He was buried in Blaenau Cemetery, Gwent (section 7, grave 349).

Birth certificate–Ross, Hereford Y569854
Marriage certificate–Brecknock WMXZ106477
Herefordshire Life for June 2008–*Our Hero of Rorke's Drift*
Monmouthshire County Life for Early Spring 2008–*Zulu! A Look at the Life of One Rorke's Drift Hero*

Thomas Payton was a survivor of the defence.

He was aged 23 when he enlisted at Cross Lane Barracks in Salford, on 12 July 1874, and as 372 Private Payton he was posted to the 24th Regiment on 11 October 1874, and joined the 1st Battalion in South Africa. He was stationed at East London in 1877, and received numerous fines for drunkenness throughout 1877. He served in the Cape Frontier War, and in the Zulu War. It was stated in newspapers at the time the unit returned home: 'Among the men of the 1st Battalion of the 24th who disembarked were Sergeant

Wilson, Lance-Corporal Roy, and Privates Desmond, Payton and Jenkins, who had been to the rear with prisoners...' and he was present at the defence of Rorke's Drift. For his service he received the South Africa Medal with 1877-8-9 clasp.

He returned to England with his battalion on 2 October 1879, being transferred to the first class army reserve at Gosport on 2 January 1880. His intended place of residence was 7 Planet Street, off Cross Street, Stafford; where he is believed to have died.

William Pearce was a survivor of the defence.

Information concerning William Pearce is scarce. He was described as the servant to Doctor Reynolds during the action at Rorke's Drift, and his name appears on the roll of defenders compiled by John Chard. He is known to have been in his late twenties at the time, and he came from the West Country.

Samuel Pitt was a survivor of the defence.

He was born on 20 October 1855, at Portskewett in Monmouthshire, the oldest of six children to Jesse Pitt, a land drainer, and his wife, Jane (formerly King).

The red-haired young man left his home at New Buildings in Trisha, St Brides Minor, Glamorgan, on 9 February 1877, to enlist in Cardiff, and as 1186 Private Pitt he was posted to the 2nd Battalion, 24th Regiment.

He received orders for active service in South Africa, and sailed to the Cape in February 1878. He took part in the Cape Frontier War, and during the Zulu War he was present at the defence of Rorke's Drift.

He stated:

Then we pounded away for all we were worth, raining bullets amongst them, but on they came, not fearing death. They were sharp enough, however, to take advantage of every bit of cover they could. By nine o'clock, when darkness had set in, they got to close quarters, and were gripping our bayonets through the spaces left between the bags for firing. It was 'touch and go' at that time, and how they were kept out was miraculous. The

Zulus held up their dead comrades for us to fire at, the idea, I think, being to get us to expend our ammunition.

For his service he received the South Africa Medal with 1877-8-9 clasp. He made a remittance of one pound to his widowed father in March 1879. He served at Gibraltar in 1880, where the one penny a day good conduct pay he had at some time forfeited was restored. He returned to England from India on 26 May 1883, and was transferred to the army reserve on 21 June 1883.

While he was living at Werndew, Aberkenfig, he married a Londoner named Mary Venn on 23 July 1883, at Bridgend Register Office, and they lived at Coytrahen in Llangynwyd, Bridgend, and Samuel became a miner at Wyndham Colliery. They had six children. Mary Ann was born in 1884 (died aged two), Charles Henry in 1886, Elizabeth Ann in 1889, Kezia in 1891, Jesse in 1894, Wyndham in 1896. The family moved to Cildendy, Llangynwyd in 1889, and Samuel became a gamekeeper on the Coytrahen Estate.

He received his final discharge from the first class army reserve, at Aberkenfig, on 9 December 1889. By 1896 they had moved to 9 Frowen Terrace in Tynewydd, Llangeinor in Ogmore Vale, and Samuel returned to the pit. His wife died of typhoid fever in 1897. By 1901 Samuel had moved the family to 3, Perycal Buildings in St Bride's Minor, where he frequented the White Lion public house, and in 1909 he was president of the team when they won the Bridgend and District Bagatelle Championships. He was also a life member at the Royal British Legion. The *Western Mail* published a narrative on 11 May 1914 in which Samuel spoke of his experiences at Rorke's Drift.

By 1918 he was living at 47 Wyndham Street in Ogmore Vale, and on 16 March that year he was working as a coal hewer when he married Rosina David, at the Bridgend Register Office. They lived at 13 Carmen Street, Caerau, Maesteg, where Samuel died of acute myocardia, and cardiac failure, on 21 November 1926, aged 71, and he was buried at the Church of St David, Bettws, Newport (row 3, plot 29a).

Birth certificate–Shirenewton, Monmouth WCN028734
Marriage certificate (first)–Bridgend, Glamorgan
Marriage certificate (second) Bridgend, Glamorgan

Western Mail for 11 May 1914

R

James Henry Reynolds was awarded the Victoria Cross for valour at Rorke's Drift.

He was born at Kingstown (now Dun Laughaire), Ireland, on 3 February 1844, the son of Laurence Reynolds, a merchant and Justice of the Peace, of Dalyston House, Granard, County Longford, where he had been born in 1843. He had an older brother named Thomas James. James was educated at Castle Knock, and at Trinity College, Dublin, from where he graduated Bachelor of Medicine and Bachelor of Surgery in 1867.

Prior to the Crimean War medical officers and orderlies were 'regimental', in that medical officers were appointed to each regiment and it was his duty to provide a hospital and keep an eye on the continuing health of the troops in the regiment not just at the theatre of war. However, during the Crimean campaign the Medical Staff Corps was established, which became the Army Hospital Corps (men only) in the following year, and later was officered from the Army Medical Department.

Doctor Reynolds entered the Medical Staff Corps as assistant surgeon, on 31 March 1868, and in this capacity he was appointed to the 36th (Herefordshire) Regiment on 24 March 1869. He received a commendation for his efficient service during an outbreak of cholera in the regiment in India.

In 1873 a co-ordinated medical service was set up, and a qualifying doctor needed to be single, aged over 21, and much more trained and qualified. Having been placed on the Medical Staff in 1870, Doctor Reynolds was appointed surgeon in the Army Medical Service in 1873.

When the 1st Battalion, 24th Regiment, sailed to South Africa in 1874, he went with them as part of the medical team. He took part in the campaign in Griqualand West in 1875, and during the Ninth Cape Frontier War, he was stationed at the Impetu depot with the 24th Regiment when the garrison was besieged for several weeks until relief came in January 1878. He was appointed for service with the

British troops preparing for hostilities against the Zulus, and on 22 January 1879 he was on medical duties at Rorke's Drift. He was helped by a servant named William Pearce.

His account of the action at Rorke's Drift was published as an appendix to the Report of the Army Medical Department in 1878, in which he concluded: 'I do not think it possible that men could have behaved better than did the 2/24th and the Army Hospital Corps (three), who were particularly forward during the whole attack.'

His award of Victoria Cross was announced in the *London Gazette* of 17 June 1879, which stated:

For conspicuous bravery during the attack at Rorke's Drift on the 22 and 23 January 1879, which he exhibited in his constant attention to the wounded under fire, and in his voluntarily conveying ammunition from the store to the defenders of the Hospital, whereby he exposed himself to a cross fire from the enemy both in going and returning.

He was promoted to surgeon major, dated 23 January 1879. He remained at Rorke's Drift after the battle, and Henry Harford wrote:

I shall not easily forget one particular night when Doctor Reynolds and I met in the dark having literally been washed out of our sleeping place, and mooched about, endeavouring to find a more sheltered spot. Suddenly we hit on the idea of lying down under the eaves of B Company's (storehouse) roof, so coiled ourselves up in our soaking-wet blankets, thanking our stars that at all events there would be no river running under us, when presently swish came about half a ton of water clean on top of us–B Company were emptying their tarpaulin!

According to the Records of Service Ledger of the 1st/24th Regiment, Doctor Reynolds received his Victoria Cross from Colonel Richard Glyn of the 24th Regiment during a parade of the troops at Pinetown on 26 August 1879; along with Lieutenant Edward Browne of the 24th Regiment for gallantry at Khambula on 29 March 1879.

He was at the decisive battle of Ulundi to witness the defeat of the Zulus, and he arrived back in England onboard the *Eagle* on 2 October 1879. For his service he was awarded the South Africa

Medal with 1877-8-9 clasp. In July 1879, he was awarded the British Medical Association's gold medal, and he was elected Honorary Fellow of the Royal College of Physicians, Ireland, and Honorary Doctor of Law, Dublin. On 17 October 1879, he and John Chard were guests of honour at a dinner held at the Wanderers Club, Pall Mall, London, 'In recognition of their splendid defence of Rorke's Drift.'

In 1880 he was appointed senior medical officer for the expedition to aid Captain Charles Boycott during the Irish Land War, and while stationed at Richmond Barracks in Dublin he married Elizabeth Mary McCormick, the daughter of a medical doctor named George McCormick, at Glenealy Church in County Wicklow, on 22 September 1880. They lived at 5 Usher's Island in Dublin.

A son named George Cormac was born on 3 August 1881. He was accidentally shot and killed while serving as a private with the Loyal North Lancashire Regiment on 14 January 1916. Percival was born on 9 January 1884. He was killed in action while serving as a private with the Royal Dublin Fusiliers on 13 November 1916. Henry Laurence was born on 30 June 1885. He served as a private with several units during the First World War. He survived the conflict, but died of tuberculosis in Liverpool in 1935.

His wife was aged only 30 when she died on 8 December 1886. In 1891 he was living at Cheriton Cliffs, St Paul's Parish, Sandgate, at Hythe in Kent, with four children, George, Percy, Henry and Lily, who had all been born in Ireland. He also had a daughter named Elizabeth.

Doctor Reynolds was promoted to lieutenant colonel on 1 April 1887 and to brigade surgeon lieutenant colonel on 25 December 1892. He retired on 8 January 1896, and while on the retired list he was employed as senior medical officer at the Royal Army Clothing Factory at Pimlico in London. He retired this post in May 1905. According to the *Naval and Military Magazine* for 1899, he was at that time medical officer for the 1st Cadet Battalion, King's Royal Rifle Corps.

On 1903 he was described as:

...spare, a well-dressed gentleman, with silver hair, spectacles, and soft modulated voice, who smokes his cigarette at the club, and discusses the topics of the town with a pleasant relish of life...

A keen sportsman, he was a member of the Army and Navy Club from 1890 until his death. On 9 November 1929, he and John Fielding were guests of honour as the two senior Victoria Cross holders at a dinner hosted by the Prince of Wales in the Royal Gallery at the House of Lords.

The 1901 census records him as living alone at 156 Cambridge Street in Belgravia, London, and he was living at the Rubens Hotel in Westminster, when he became ill and was admitted to the Empire Nursing Home in Victoria, London. He died of pleurisy and influenza on 4 March 1932, aged 88, and he was buried in St Mary's Roman Catholic Cemetery at Kensal Rise in London. The granite cross memorial which marks his grave became blackened and had subsided badly, so it was cleaned and re-set in 1991. His medals are with the Royal Army Medical Corps Museum in Aldershot.

At the time of the death of Doctor Reynolds, Walter G. Spencer sent some personal recollections of him which were published in the *British Medical Journal*:

When Colonel Reynolds was in charge of the Pimlico Clothing Department he frequently sent workers to Westminster Hospital for treatment, and later he came to me about his health, the last time at the beginning of 1929. Then a cancer, for which a grave operation would previously have been called for, disappeared in about ten days under radium. Colonel Reynolds was thus able to walk at the head of the VCs at the thanksgiving ceremony and to be present at the dinner in the House of Lords. Our conversations often returned to Rorke's Drift, and from notes I jotted down I have picked-out a few of his reminiscences which I have not noticed in print.

There were 36 patients in the hospital, most in different stages of typhoid fever. No preparations had been made for the defence of the station. Reynolds was senior officer, having been already six years in South Africa; Bromhead and Chard were young subalterns just come out from England; Dalton, an army non-commissioned officer, who had re-joined, had had experience in methods of defence employed by the Boers. When fugitives from iSandlwana reached Rorke's Drift it was first proposed to evacuated the place, but Reynolds declared that to be impossible. Even if the convoy could cross the river the ascent of the opposite bank was so long and steep that the Zulus would certainly catch it up. It was Dalton who arranged the defence with mealie bags.

When the Zulus came into view there appeared horsemen in scarlet and the cry was that the cavalry were returning; but Reynolds pointed out that the riders were not rising in their saddles but sat on the horses as the natives did. Coming nearer, the Zulu impi drew up and ceremoniously took snuff, heralding a charge to the uttermost. A few Zulus got into the garden and into the hospital before two patients in bed could be got within the laager, and a third lost his head, took a wrong turning, and was also killed. The remaining 33 cases were saved and survived the subsequent stench.

A number of items which Surgeon Reynolds had used at Rorke's Drift were auctioned at Spinks in 2001. They included two Gladstone bags engraved with his initials, a travelling wooden medicine chest containing unused ointment tubes and glass bottles, and two leather pocket cases containing the surgical instruments he used in the field. The lot included his revolver, an 18th Century pocket watch he had been given by his grandfather, a silver medal which had been presented to him by the Royal Welsh Fusiliers and dress miniatures of his Victoria Cross and South Africa campaign medal.

91-year-old Cecilia Cheetham recalled her grandfather, Surgeon Reynolds, during an interview at the Soldiers of Gloucestershire Museum in 2004.

WO32/7793–Medical services
VC Magazine for 30 April 1903
British Medical Journal for 19 March 1932

Edward Robinson was a survivor of the defence.

He was born in 1853, at St Patrick's in Dublin. He enlisted at Bow Street Police Court in London on 23 February 1877, and as 1286 Private Robinson he was posted to the 2nd Battalion, 24th Regiment, at Brecon. He was described as being five feet nine inches tall, with a fresh complexion, grey eyes, and brown hair. His religion was Church of England.

He received orders for active service in South Africa, and sailed to the Cape in February 1878, where he took part in the Cape Frontier War. He was charged with 'disgraceful conduct in losing a pair of boots' and was imprisoned for three months from 27 April 1878. During the Zulu War he was present at the defence of Rorke's Drift. For his service he received the South Africa Medal with 1877-8-9 clasp.

He served at Gibraltar in 1880, and in India, from where he returned on 25 May 1883, having gained a penny a day good conduct pay and a third class certificate of education. He transferred to the first class army reserve on 21 June 1883, and discharged from Brecon on 25 February 1889. His conduct was described as 'very bad, latterly good.' He stated that his next-of-kin was his brother.

Charles John Robson was a survivor of the defence.

He was born on 7 January 1855, at 7 Ebury Mews in Belgravia, London, the son of George Robson, a coachman, and his first wife, Ann (formerly Dieper). He had five older sisters. In 1871 they lived at 16 Bloomsbury Street in Westminster, and his father was working as an ostler (stableman).

Charles left his job working with his father as a groom, and enlisted into the Corps of Royal Engineers at Bow Street Police Court, on 30 April 1873, suggesting that he chose a stretch with Her Majesty's army, as opposed to a stretch at Her Majesty's pleasure. He was described as being five feet five inches tall, and weighing nine stone seven pounds. He had a fresh complexion, grey eyes and brown hair. He had several scars on his neck and between his shoulder blades and his muscular development was average. 12046 Driver Robson was sent to Aldershot, being posted to B Troop (Equipment) Royal Engineers Train. He spent three days in jail at Aldershot in January 1874, for a misdemeanour which is unrecorded, and would be the only blemish on his army career, and he was in hospital on several occasions suffering with a variety of ailments. In October 1874 his mother fell down a flight of stairs which left her paralysed, and she died a month later.

When Lieutenant John Chard joined the company on 18 April

1876, Charles was detailed as his batman and groom. He received good conduct pay of one penny a day from 13 September 1876. On 2 December 1878, he and his officer accompanied the 5th Company as they boarded the SS *Walmer Castle* bound for active service South Africa. They arrived in Durban on 4 January 1879, to be greeted by a torrential downpour in which they had to unload hundreds of tons of stores and equipment. Lieutenant Chard and Driver Robson, a corporal and three sappers, were ordered to go up to Rorke's Drift post to repair the pontoon bridge across the Buffalo River. A small mule train was organised on which the men and their equipment were loaded. Chard rode on horseback with Charles on his spare mount.

On the morning of 22 January the engineers rode to iSandlwana, where they saw Zulus on the distant hills. Charles and his officer rode back to Rorke's Drift, leaving the other men behind, and they were all killed in action. During the defence he placed himself behind the stone kraal at the eastern end of the defences where he could fire at the Zulus who were trying to ransack the engineer's wagon. He told Chard that during the fighting: 'I was protecting our things.'

Charles and Chard remained at Rorke's Drift for several weeks to work on a more permanent fortification of the garrison. On 4 July 1879, they were in the British square at the battle of Ulundi, for the final devastating defeat of the Zulus. Following the cessation of hostilities the 5th Company moved to Saint Paul's Mission, where they were occupied in building another fortified position. They embarked for home aboard the SS *Eagle* and arrived in Portsmouth on 2 October. They were met as heroes, and Charles accompanied his officer on many official engagements, including a trip to Balmoral for an audience with Queen Victoria.

The Royal Engineers Journal for 1 November 1879, recorded:

Major Chard was accompanied by his military servant in full regimentals and the appearance of this soldierly young fellow bearing an armful of Zulu assegais and other trophies of the campaign excited much interest.

It is believed that some of these war trophies were presented to Queen Victoria. Such items can be seen in the Swiss Cottage, an outbuilding at Osborne House on the Isle of Wight. There are three shields, and information on site states that they were taken from royal kraals around Ulundi on 4 July 1879, and presented to the sovereign. However, it is also thought that they were brought back by officers of the 13th Light Infantry.

He transferred to the 7th Field Company at Chatham in February 1880. However, when the 7th Company left for Natal in 1881, he decided to leave the army and discharge to the reserve from the 11th Field Company on 20 June 1881. However, in September 1881, he began a new job at the Chatham barracks as a civilian groom and general servant to Captain C. H. Gordon, Royal Engineers. He accompanied his officer to Cork, and when his officer returned to Chatham in July 1882 they parted company. He was re-called to the Colours on 2 August 1882, and posted to Aldershot as 'batman' to Lieutenant Maude. He received two pence good conduct pay from that date, and on 13 November 1882, he re-engaged to serve a further 12 years. He received his final discharge on 30 April 1894.

Charles met Jane Elizabeth Farrand in Aldershot, and they married at Hale Parish Church in Surrey, on 13 May 1883. John Chard VC attended the wedding. He and Jane both gave their address as Heath End in Hale, and by 1891 they had moved to 8 Perowne Street in Aldershot, and it was there on 22 June 1891, that their only child, Annie Lilian, was born. The family moved to Orchard Road in Dorking, and by 1901 they had moved to Ceres Road in Plumstead, before settling at 43 Swingate Street in Plumstead, where he kept a chicken house, grew a grapevine and enjoyed smoking his variety of pipes. Charles and Jane worked in the Royal Arsenal during the Great War, and in 1917 Annie, then Mrs Peter Ewart, gave them a grandson, Edwin Peter, who remembered his 'kind, solidly-built' grandfather with great respect.

Charles Robson died on 19 July 1933, at St Nicholas Hospital in Plumstead, the cause of death being 'cerebral embolism'. He was aged 78, and he had been married to Jane for 50 years. He was buried in an unmarked common grave in Woolwich Old Cemetery. A hand-carved wooden marker plaque was placed at the grave site on 22 January 1993, and in 1999 a more permanent memorial plaque was placed at the grave by the Royal Engineers Association. His South Africa Medal, along with the holy bible presented to him by The Ladies' Rorke's Drift Testimonial Fund, were sold at auction in 2017.

Birth certificate (Belgravia)
London census 1851-1921
Dix, Noonan, Webb Catalogue (now Noonans of Mayfair) for 2
March 2017
Service records (WO97)
Stevenson, Lee: *The Noble Sapper on the Box: Charles Robson RE. The
Royal Engineers Journal,* August 1995
Marriage certificate (Surrey)
Death certificate (Plumstead)

William Roy was awarded the Distinguished Conduct Medal for
gallantry during the defence.

He was born in November 1854 at Portmoak, Scotlandwell, near
Kinross, his religion being Church of England. He was the youngest
of five sons of James Roy, a ploughman, of Orwell near Kinross, and
his wife, Elisabeth (formerly Buchan), who came from Kent. Their
eldest son, also named William, had died in infancy before the second
William was born. By 1861 they had moved to Gospetay,
Strathmiglo, Fife, where their only daughter was born, and by the
mid-1860s they lived at 316 Hawkhill, Dundee.

William left his job as a baker at the Grassmarket in Edinburgh, to
enlisted into the 32nd (Cornwall) Light Infantry, on 8 August 1870, at
Edinburgh Castle. He was described as five feet five and a half inches
tall, with a fresh complexion, red hair and brown eyes. He weighed
eight stone-eight pounds, with a chest of 33 inches, and good
muscular development. 1933 Private Roy arrived in South Africa with
his unit on 16 June 1871. He was admitted to hospital at Fort Napier
in Pietermaritzburg, with a head wound he suffered in a fall, when
drunk. He then arrived at Mauritius on 18 November 1871, and
served for two years and nine months. He contracted malaria and was
admitted to hospital for treatment on eight occasions between 12
March 1872 and 9 May 1874. He returned to South Africa on 27
August 1874, where he was admitted to hospital several times for
treatment of tonsillitis and primary syphilis. During his service with
the 32nd Regiment he twice deserted for periods of 14 months and
four months. He transferred to the 1st Battalion, 24th Regiment, on 4
December 1877, regimental number 1522, and served in the Cape
Frontier War, and during the Zulu War he was present at the defence

of Rorke's Drift.

It was stated in newspapers at the time the unit returned home: 'Among the men of the 1st Battalion of the 24th who disembarked were Sergeant Wilson, Lance-Corporal Roy, and Privates Desmond, Payton and Jenkins, who had been to the rear with prisoners...', but in a letter home he stated that he was a patient in the hospital at Rorke's Drift suffering with a sore throat, and while he was defending a window at the back of the building he was unaware that the Zulus had broken in at the front. 'My rifle got disabled so I fixed my bayonet and charged out of the house. There were thirty Zulus chasing us but the men in the fort shot them before they could harm us.' Major Chard particularly mentions Private Roy in both his official account and the one he submitted to Queen Victoria a year later. For his conduct in the battle he was mentioned in dispatches and was awarded the Distinguished Conduct Medal, dated 31 October 1879, which he received from Queen Victoria at Windsor Castle on 9 December 1879. He also received the South Africa Medal with 1877-8-9 clasp.

In her diary for 9 December 1879, Queen Victoria wrote from Windsor Castle concerning distributing gallantry medals:

Private Roy, who likewise behaved most admirably at Rorke's Drift, having, when an invalid himself, got up and helped in removing the sick from the hospital under fire from the Zulus.

He transferred to the 2nd Battalion on 13 August 1879, being promoted lance corporal on 22 September 1879, and corporal on 24 November 1879. However, a medical examination held at Haslar Hospital in Gosport, on 2 October 1879, found him to be suffering from 'opacity of the cornea resulting in impairment of vision—the result of syphilis.' He was declared unfit for further service and discharged on 7 December 1880. His discharge papers state that his conduct was 'irregular' and his character was 'indifferent and intemperate'. However, his latterly habits were regular and his conduct good and temperate.

An injury assessment board held at the Royal Hospital, Chelsea, confirmed his condition, although it was considered that he could contribute to his own keep, and he was awarded a pension of seven pence a day for a year. The document states that he was five feet nine and a half inches tall, suggesting that he had grown four inches since he signed on. Being promoted corporal and having gained a third class certificate of education and one good conduct badge, it would seem that he had just started to perform his duties as a good soldier when his eyesight failed him.

His intended place of residence was the Post Office in Gosport, but the 1881 census records that he was living with his parents at 316 Hawkhill, Liff and Benbie, Dundee, being described as a twenty-six year old labourer. On 27 October 1882, he married Cecilia Butcher, a domestic servant, of 11 Southerly Street, Dundee, at Brook Street, Broughty Ferry, Monitieth, Dundee. She was the youngest daughter of William Butcher (deceased), the local railway station master, and his wife, Mary (formerly Nicol). William is described as a railway worker.

On the invitation of an older brother, John, who had emigrated to Australia, William boarded the bounty ship SS *Roslyn Castle* at Plymouth, and set sail for Sydney, where he arrived on 1 March 1883. Cecilia followed after him aboard the SS *Pericles*, as a single woman in her maiden name of Butcher, arriving in Sydney on Christmas Eve, 24 December 1883. However, by 1887 William was: '...in very sad circumstances, almost blind and helpless', and he was described as 'an invalided inmate of a New South Wales benevolent institution.' On 27 October 1887, a Grand Military Concert under the patronage of Lord Carrington, Governor and Commander-in-Chief, and attended by the Lord Mayor, was held at the Sydney Exhibition Centre, which raised £120 for his benefit.

William had been living in an asylum when he died on 30 May 1890, of paralysis and arterial decay 'after years of painful illness', at the home of his brother, John, at 182 Hunter Street, Parramatta, near Sydney, aged 35. He was buried in the Mays Hill Baptist Cemetery, Parramatta, 'two of his old comrades from Sydney being among the little band of mourners.'

Death certificate–New South Wales
Dundee Courier for 8 March 1879
Sydney Daily Telegraph for 25 May 1887

James Ruck was a survivor of the defence.

He was born on 15 April 1858. He attested for 25 Brigade on 18 January 1877, and as Private Ruck he was posted to E Company, 2nd Battalion, 24th Regiment, at Brecon. He was promoted corporal on 12 January 1878.

He received orders for active service in South Africa, and sailed to the Cape in February 1878. He took part in the Cape Frontier War, being reduced to private on 17 July 1878. During the Zulu War he was present at the defence of Rorke's Drift. He was promoted to lance corporal on the day after the defence, and transferred to G Company on 31 January 1879. He was promoted to corporal on 30 April 1879, but reduced to private.

For his service he received the South Africa Medal with 1877-8-9 clasp. He was promoted to corporal on 15 May 1881, while in India, but reduced to private, and was placed on the unattached list while serving at Madras, on 28 November 1886, and joined the Madras Public Works Department, rising to the rank of commissary and honorary captain in the Indian Army.

They had a daughter named Bessie Alice, born on 1 October 1894, who died on 14 October 1930, aged 36; and Marjorie Richmond, born on 24 July 1909, who died on 8 April 1927, aged 17. They are both buried at Quinton Cemetery in Halesowen near Birmingham.

James retired in 1913, and brought his family to live in Birmingham. He died on 10 February 1927, in his 69th year, and he was buried at Quinton Cemetery.

S

Edward Savage was a survivor of the defence.

He was born as Edmund Savage on 19 April 1858, at Water's Court in Newport, Monmouthshire, and he was baptised at St Mary's Church, Stow Hill in Newport. He was the third child of four to Irish-born parents, Timothy Savage, a mason's labourer, and his wife, Ellen (formerly Flinn). By 1860 they had moved to 12 Granville Street, St Woollos, Newport, and his father was killed while working as a wharf labourer in 1864. By 1871 the family had moved to 18

Canal Parade in St Woollos.

He had previously served in the Royal Monmouthshire Militia, when he enlisted for the regular army at Cardiff on 8 February 1877, and as 1185 Private Savage he was posted to the 1st Battalion, 24th Regiment, later transferring to the 2nd Battalion. He was five feet four and a half inches tall, with a fresh complexion, blue eyes and light brown hair. His religion was recorded as Roman Catholic, and he had a tattoo on his right arm. His home address was given as 54 George Street in Newport. He was hospitalised at Dover and Chatham several times during 1877.

He received orders for active service in South Africa, and sailed to the Cape in February 1878. He took part in the Cape Frontier War, after which he was hospitalised in September and then confined in cells in November. During the Zulu War he was present at the defence of Rorke's Drift.

He was in the hospital at Rorke's Drift on 22 January suffering with a knee injury, and he was a patient in the hospital during the defence of the garrison. His account appeared in newspapers in Brecon and Manchester in July 1879, which stated:

> Savage describes the warning given to the unfortunate inmates of the hospital. Seeing the danger drawing nearer, though suffering from an injured knee, he jumped out of the window into the fort. He assisted in the defence, lying on his side and taking aim at the Zulus through an opening in the biscuit boxes. In the night time, when under fire, Savage heard a fellow soldier of the name of Fagan, cry out for water, and managed to crawl along to help his disabled comrade-in-arms, who died before daylight the next morning. Savage says he never spent such a miserable night in all his life. There was a momentary danger of being shot dead, and the likelihood of perishing from cold and hunger. He had no recollection of ever having gone through such hardships as whilst an invalid at Rorke's Drift.

For his service he received the South Africa Medal with 1877-8-9 clasp.

Edward was transferred to G Company on 29 January 1879, and he remained at Rorke's Drift for 12 weeks, before transferring to E company on 3 April 1879. He was hospitalised in Pietermaritzburg for recurring fever, and on being recommended for a change of climate, he returned to England on 26 June 1879, and was admitted to Netley Military Hospital. He was posted to the 1st Battalion, 24th Regiment, at Gosport, on 24 February 1880, and to Colchester in the following November, being hospitalised on several occasions suffering with syphilis. He was posted to Salford near Manchester on 29 August 1882, and spent more time in hospital at Chester, from 29 November to 8 December 1882, being treated for inflammation of the glands. He was discharged to the first class army reserve at Brecon on 9 February 1883, and gave his intended place of residence as 11 Halkett Street in Cardiff. His character was described as fair.

He married Johanna McCarthy on 26 March 1883, at St Marie's School Chapel in Canton, Riverside, Cardiff, and they lived in 7 Edward Street in Canton. Sadly, his wife died of tuberculosis in 1886. He married Mary Thomas, a widow with two daughters, Sarah Ann and Emma Jane, at the Cardiff Register Office, on 28 June 1887, and they lived at 137 Wellington Street in Canton, where Edward was employed as a road labourer for the local council. They had four children. Edward John was born in 1888, William in 1889, Timothy George in 1891, and Beatrice Maud in 1892.

Edward was discharged from the first class reserve to the D list reserves on 11 February 1889. However, his health went into decline, and he was admitted to the Bridgend County Asylum at Angelton, Bridgend, on 13 May 1892, and he was given his final discharge on 20 June 1892.

He died in the Bridgend Asylum, on 30 January 1893, aged 32, the cause of death being given as general paralysis. He was buried with his first wife at St Cathay's Cemetery in Cardiff, in an unmarked common grave number R464. A new black marble memorial stone was unveiled at his grave in 2011.

Manchester Weekly Post for 17 July 1879

Alfred Saxty was a survivor of the defence.

He was born as Albert Saxty on 11 March 1859, at Minety, near Chippenham in Wiltshire. He was the third son and fourth child of five to Thomas John Saxty, a policeman on the Great Western

Railway, and his wife, Grace Thomas (maiden name Collett). His siblings were named Ann, William, John and Sarah Emma, in order of age. The family moved to Buckland Dinham in Somerset in 1864, where Thomas continued to work for the Great Western Railway. All five children were educated at the Buckland Dinham School, and Albert left school to start work at the age of ten.

His older brother, John, joined the army, and Albert enlisted on 12 September 1876, as 849 Private 'Alfred' Saxty. He was posted to the 2nd Battalion, 24th Regiment, at Brecon, being described as five feet seven and a half inches tall, with a fresh complexion, blue eyes and light-brown hair. His religion was Roman Catholic.

Army life seems to have suited him and promotion was quick. He was appointed lance corporal in April 1877, and he reached the rank of lance sergeant on 1 February 1878, the day he embarked on the Himalaya for active service in South Africa. He took part in the Cape Frontier War, reverting to corporal on 11 July 1878, and he gaining a second class certificate of education. During the Zulu War he was present at the defence of Rorke's Drift. He was promoted to sergeant on 23 January 1879, and for his service he received the South Africa Medal with 1877-8-9 clasp.

He served at Gibraltar in 1880, and had to undergo medical treatment on board HMS *Orantes* while on the way to India, which was followed-up as soon as he arrived in Secunderabad. Soon after his father died in 1881, he was found to be drunk on piquet duty on 6 May 1881, and after being confined in cells he was tried by District Court Martial and sentenced to 56 days imprisonment with hard labour. He was reduced to private, fined one pound, his pay was stopped and he lost all his good conduct pay. He was released on 13 July 1881, and despite his misdemeanour his superiors saw something in him as his good conduct pay was restored on the day of his release, and he had reached the rank of sergeant by 2 December 1885. He served in Burma from May 1886 to January 1887, for which he received the Indian General Service Medal, 1854-95, with Burma 1885-7 clasp.

He re-engaged on 4 October 1887, and as 2595 Sergeant Saxty he was posted to the 1st Battalion, Bedfordshire Regiment, for such term as would complete 21 years' service. He transferred to the 2nd Battalion on 1 August 1888. He transferred to the 2nd Battalion, Royal Inniskilling Fusiliers, on 14 August 1891, as 3760 Sergeant

JAMES W. BANCROFT

Saxty.

He married in the church of St Stephen at Ootacamund in Rangoon in his given name of Albert Saxty, on 30 December 1885, his new wife being 17-year-old Maria Copeland. Sadly, Maria died in Thayetmayo, Rangoon, on 10 December 1886, aged 19, of puerperal septicaemia.

Sergeant Saxty's service record states that he married Mary Maud Cole, in Wellington on 1 Aug 1888. They had four children. Wilfred St Clare was born in 1890, Mabel Bridget Grace in 1892, Robert Lionel Anthony in 1893, and Leo Desmond Cole in 1894.

He was tried and convicted for an unrecorded misdemeanour in September 1894, being sentenced to be reduced to the rank of corporal and to forfeit his good conduct pay. The sentence was remitted by the General Officer Commanding Rangoon on 2 October 1894, but within a month he was tried and sentenced to be reduced to the rank of corporal, and to forfeit his good conduct pay. He was discharged at his own request in Burma on 28 February 1894.

His mother died in 1896, and Albert began work on the railways in Burma, but a few years later he left home and did not return, leaving all his possessions, including his medals. He was officially pronounced dead seven years later, and his wife re-married and had a daughter, Alma Leslie born in 1908.

He re-appeared on 12 June 1930, when he was admitted to the Royal Hospital in Chelsea, which was not far from his wife, who had returned to England to live with her daughter in Kensington. In about October 1930 Alfred applied for replacements for his lost medals, and they were issued under Authority Chelsea, Rep/68/GEN/5160. He reverted to outpatients at his own request on 4 October 1933, and left the Royal Hospital to live with his sister at 1 Blewitt Street in Newport, Wales.

He attended the ceremony for the 'Laying up of the Colours' in Brecon Cathedral in 1934, and he attended the Northern Command Tattoo in Gateshead in the same year.

His death certificate records that Albert died of myocarditis and senility while visiting a friend named Lewis Norman at 131 Stow Hill in Newport, on 11 July 1936, aged 76. He was buried with full military honours at Saint Woollos Cemetery in Newport (RCD block 32, grave 127); where John J. Lyons and John Murphy had already been laid to rest. New headstones were placed at his grave, and that of John J. Lyons, along with a plaque on the grave of John Murphy in 1996. His replacement medals were sold at auction in 2023

Marriage certificate of parents–Batheaston AA935670
Birth certificate–Malmesbury East FC846505
Marriage certificate to his first wife–Rangoon SAM005649
Death certificate of his first wife–Thayetmayo SA067109
Death certificate–Newport West HD048426
Swindon Advertiser for 10 March 2009

Carl Scammel was wounded in action during the defence.
He served with the 2nd Battalion of the Natal Native Contingent

John Scanlon was killed in action at Rorke's Drift.
He was born in County Sligo, Ireland, attested for 25 Brigade on 16 January 1877, and as 1051 Private Scanlon he was posted to A Company, 2nd Battalion, 24th Regiment, on 11 May 1877. He received orders for active service in South Africa, and sailed to the Cape in February 1878.
He took part in the Cape Frontier War, and during the Zulu War he had been a patient in the hospital when he was killed in action by a Zulu slug at the defence at Rorke's Drift. He is buried in the cemetery at Rorke's Drift and his name is inscribed on the monument. His effects were claimed by his mother. For his service he received the South Africa Medal with 1877-8-9 clasp.

Ferdinand Christian Schiess was awarded the Victoria Cross for valour at Rorke's Drift.
According to the Canon William Lummis VC files held at the National Army Museum, he was usually known as Frederich, and he was born at Bergedorf, Canton Berne, Switzerland, on 7 April 1856, the son of Niclaus Schiess, who worked as a stone cutter, and his wife Anna (formerly Ruchti). His father was known locally as 'Bernese Schiess'. Their parents having died while they were young, Ferdnand, and his sister, Anna Marie, were brought-up at the Municipal Orphanage at Herisau in Canton Apenzell.

'Friederich', as he became known, left the orphanage at the age of 15. The Franco-Prussian War began in 1870, so he joined General Bourbaki's French Legions. In 1877 he boarded the *Adele* at Hamburg bound for South Africa, arriving at East London on 21 August 1877. He was a strong, stocky young man, and was able to find work as a general labourer.

He served with distinction as a volunteer in the Cape Frontier War, and when colonial forces were being mustered for the campaign against the Zulus, Colonel Anthony Durnford of the Royal Engineers appointed him a corporal in the 2nd Battalion, 3rd Regiment, Natal Native Contingent, under Commandant Robert Lonsdale.

Commandant George Hamilton-Browne, an Irish colonial adventurer of the 3rd Natal Native Contingent, which was Schiess's unit, stated:

(They were) a motley crowd, a few of them old soldiers and ex-clerks, the majority of them runaway sailors, ex-navvies, and East London boatmen. They were an awfully tough crowd, but they looked a hard-fighting lot and though their language was strong, and they were evidently very rough, they looked very ready...

This unit was intended to be used as scouts for the advancing British Army. On the outbreak of hostilities there had been no time to train the men in the use of firearms, and due to loyalty fears expressed by some Natal colonists no guns were issued to the ordinary natives. Only the African officers and ten NCO's from each company received Enfield percussion rifles. All other ranks were required to carry their traditional weapons of spears and shields. They had no uniform and remained dressed in their traditional native attire. The only item which distinguished them from Zulu warriors was a red rag, known as a pugree, wrapped around their forehead.

Lieutenant Chard reported:

Corporal Schiess, Natal Native Contingent, who was a patient in the Hospital with a wound in the foot, which caused him great pain, behaved with the greatest coolness and gallantry throughout the attack, and at this time (the retreat to the biscuit boxes) creeping out a short distance along the wall we had abandoned, and slowly raised himself, to get a shot at some of the enemy who had been particularly annoying, his hat was blown off by a shot from a Zulu on the other side of the wall. He immediately jumped up, bayoneted the Zulu, and shot a second, and bayoneted a third who came to their assistance, and then returned to his place.

Reverend Smith stated:

One fellow fired at Corporal Schiess of the Natal Native Contingent, the charge blowing his hat off. He instantly jumped upon the parapet and bayonetted the man, regained his place and shot another, and then, repeating his former exploit, climbed upon the sacks and bayonetted a third. A bullet struck him on the instep early in the fight, but he would not allow that his wound was sufficient reason for leaving his post, yet he has suffered most acutely from it since.

Private Hitch noted:

There was a certain space of about nine yards where the barricade was uncompleted. It was, of course, the weakest link in the chain, and the Zulus were not long in discovering this fact. In this position eight of us, Bromhead, Nichols (Nicholson) Fagan, Cole, Dalton, Schiess, Williams and myself—made a stand, and it was here, I think, that the hardest work was done.

Henry Harford stated:

Some of the men of the 24th told me that he fought like a tiger. At one time, when some Zulus actually managed to clutch hold of his bayonet, he got it out of their hands, and springing over the parapet bayoneted some six or seven straight away.

Captain William Penn-Symons recorded:

Corporal Schiess, they said, 'fought like a tiger.' He could not restrain himself, but more than once dashed over the barricade, bayoneted a Zulu, and got back in again.

Surgeon Reynolds was a first-hand witness to the fighting at the compound in front of the hospital veranda when it was at its fiercest, and later stated: 'It would be difficult to pick out the heroes from our garrison, but Corporal Schiess of the Natal Native Contingent (a Swede by birth) came under my notice as the most deserving of praise and recommendation.'

Eventually, Major Chard was asked to provide a statement concerning Schiess's bravery, which he did in a letter dated 22 October 1879. The letter formed the basis of his Victoria Cross citation:

I have the honour in accordance with instructions from the Field Marshal, Commander-in-Chief, to forward for your approval this my application for the decoration of the Victoria Cross on behalf of Corporal Schiess, late Natal Native Contingent, in recognition of his gallant conduct on 22nd-23rd Jany last at Rorke's Drift.

This man, who had been wounded in the attack on Sihayo's Kraal a few days before, was a patient at Rorke's Drift on the 22nd Jany 1879, and in spite of his wound (in the foot) he particularly attracted my notice by his activity and devoted gallantry throughout the defence. Amongst many acts of his I may mention one I myself witnessed—after we had retired to our inner line of defence. The Zulus occupied the wall of mealie bags we had abandoned. Corporal Schiess without any order, crept out along this wall a few feet, to dislodge one in particular of the enemy who was shooting better than usual; on his raising himself to get a shot, the Zulu who was close to him on the other side of the wall, fired knocking off his hat. Cpl Schiess immediately jumped on the wall and bayoneted the Zulu, and in less time than I take to write it, shot a second and bayoneted a third, and then came back to the cover of the inner defence again.

Corporal Schiess became the first man serving with South African forces under British command to be awarded the Victoria Cross, when his VC citation, the last for the defence of Rorke's Drift, appeared in the *London Gazette* of 29 November 1879:

> For conspicuous gallantry in the defence of Rorke's Drift post on the night of 22 January 1879, when, in spite of his having been wounded in the foot a few days previously, greatly distinguished himself when the Garrison were repulsing, with the bayonet, a series of desperate assaults made by the Zulus, and displayed great activity and devoted gallantry throughout the defence.

Frederich suffered most acutely from his wounded foot after the defence, but he served throughout the Zulu War, and he was with the British square at Ulundi on 4 July 1879, to witness the final defeat of the Zulu Army. For his services in the campaign he also received the South Africa Medal with 1877-8-9 clasp.

He received his Victoria Cross from Sir Garnet Wolseley at a special parade of the troops in garrison in Pietermaritzburg, on 3 February 1880.

When the Natal Native Contingent was disbanded he joined C Troop of Baker's Horse on 24 January 1880, for service in the Basuto Gun War, and he discharged on 12 April 1881. Jesse Mayor served in A Troop of the same unit. When he left Baker's Horse he went back to civilian life and gained employment in the telegraph office at Durban.

In 1881 he was described by a fellow trooper with Baker's Horse:

> But we had a good man in charge, Corporal Schiess VC, one of the Rorke's Drift heroes. He is a nice fellow, and we are the best of friends. He was born in the Alps and is a Swiss. He is a dead shot.

He then went to Allahabad in India, where he gained employment in a jeweller's shop and was a volunteer serving with the East Indian Railway. A report in the 'Military Intelligence' column concerning the *Homeward Mail from the East* dated 10 January 1884, states:

> The Duke of Connaught at Allahabad–On arrival of the special train at Allahabad on 1 December with their Royal Highnesses the Duke and Duchess of Connaught (after being presented to

the nobilities of the Station), the Duke proceeded to inspect the guard of honour composed of a very strong muster of the E I R Volunteers (East Indian Railway). Glancing over the men his quick eye detected one little fellow, Volunteer F C Schiess VC, in the ranks, on whose breast hung the Victoria Cross. With that readiness and good feeling so general with the members of the Royal Family, he at once stepped up to him and kindly with interest enquired where and how had he earned the distinguished decoration. The gallant little fellow answered: 'At Rorke's Drift in South Africa,' such being actually the case. Unfortunately, poor Schiess, having his rifle at the present, was unable to grasp the ready hand extended to him by the Duke.

By the latter months of 1884 he was unemployed and had become destitute. He spent most of his time writing neat and eligible letters desperately trying to gain some kind of Government work in Natal, the colony he had fought so bravely to defend. Towards the end of the year he was found in tragic circumstances on the streets of Cape Town suffering from the effects of exposure to the elements and malnutrition. The Royal Navy offered him a trip to England on the *Serapis*, the cost of his rations being paid for by a public fund. Sadly, his health deteriorated and he died onboard ship off the coast of Angola, West Africa. He was only 28-years-old. The ship's log recorded:

> Sunday, 14 December 1884, 10:20am. Departed this life Mr F C Schiess VC, aged 28. 5:10pm. Stopped. Committed to the deep the remains of the late Mr Schiess VC. 5:15pm Proceeded. He was buried about 1,376 kilometres north-east of St Helena in the South Atlantic Ocean. (Latitude 13.00 south– Longitude 07.24 west).

His Victoria Cross is believed to have been found on his person, and according to the National Army Museum in London it arrived there from the Ministry of Defence in about 1958. They also suggested that it would probably have been taken to the predecessors of the Ministry of Defence after being taken from him. The whereabouts of his South Africa Medal are not known. He may well have sold it, or even thrown it away because of its association with the country he had helped to defend and could not offer him work of any kind. The fact that he held on to his Victoria Cross when in such desperate circumstances is another indication of his gallantry. He received a five minute burial service.

There is a bronze plaque dedicated to him at the Rorke's Drift Memorial Museum in Natal; a plaque dedicated to him at the home of the VC Trust at Ashworth Barracks in Doncaster; and he is one of the men awarded the Victoria Cross who has no known grave and is commemorated on a plaque at the Union Jack Club in London.

A strange note appears at the back of a page in Captain Penn-Symons' report held at the Brecon Museum, which states:

I saw Corp Schiess in Nov 1891, in Allahabad, India. He had been working in a jeweller's shop, and was just going to Australia. Being afraid to lose his Victoria Cross, he has sent it on ahead by registered post to his destination.

However, it would seem that Penn-Symons made a hurried note and the date should have been November 1883; Penn-Symons was in India in 1883, and Schiess never went to Australia.

The 'Personalia' column in the *Natal Witness* for 2 November 1899, states:

Cpl Schiess, Natal Native Forces, was at Rorke's Drift in January 1879. P. G. Crow asks 'Where is he now?

A response two days later says: 'A correspondent writes that he remembers reading years ago both in the *Witness* and the *Advertiser* of Corporal Schiess (of Rorke's Drift fame) dying in India destitute.'

A further reply two days afterwards says:

A correspondent writes: I see information is asked on the whereabouts of the late Corporal Schiess. Immediately after the Zulu War he joined the Telegraph Service as a linesman and was stationed at Durban. He left after being decorated with the VC. He went through the Basuto War later, and returned to Durban invalided and destitute. He was (if memory serves me correctly) sent to England in one of HM transports and died either at Netley or Haslar Hospital. The Hon. Mr Jameson was,

I think, the means of his being sent home. I have a good photo given me by Schiess. Should anyone care for a copy I will get it re-taken.

Lincoln, Rutland and Stamford Mercury for 15 April 1881
Natal Witness for 5 February 1880, and 2, 4 and 6 November 1899

Arthur John Sears was a survivor of the defence.

He was born on 29 January 1854, at Harmondsworth, near Sunbury-on-Thames in Middlesex, where his family had been established for hundreds of years. He was the sixth son of seven in a family of eight children, born to John Sears, an agricultural labourer (head gardener), and his wife, Ann (formerly Ives), who had married in Hounslow, Middlesex, on 5 December 1841, and settled in a house called 'Greensleeves' in Sunbury. Soon after Arthur's birth the family moved to Nursery Road in Sunbury, and by 1861 they lived at a house called 'The Ceson' in Sunbury.

Arthur's siblings were all born at Sunbury—Charles was born on 27 March 1842, Henry was baptised on 5 May 1844, William was baptised on 6 September 1846, John was baptised on 10 September 1848, Joseph was baptised on 22 September 1850 (he died during the September quarter of 1852), a second Joseph was baptised on 23 March 1856 and Clara Ann was baptised on 13 June 1858.

Arthur and two of his brothers, Henry and Joseph chose the army life, and Arthur enlisted at Little Warley in Essex, on 14 February 1873. He was described as being five feet nine inches tall, with grey eyes and light-brown hair. His muscular development was good, and his religion was Church of England. As 2404 Private Sears, he was posted to A Company, 2nd Battalion, 24th Regiment. Henry and Joseph also joined the 24th Regiment. He was detached to the School of Military Music at Kneller Hall in 1874-75, and in 1878 he was appointed bandsman.

He received orders for active service in South Africa and sailed to the Cape with his battalion in February 1878. He took part in the Cape Frontier War, and during the Zulu War he was present at the defence of Rorke's Drift. For his service he received the South Africa Medal with 1877-8-9 clasp. Sadly, as 279 Private Sears of the 1st/24th, his brother, Henry, is believed to have been killed in action at iSandlwana on 22 January 1879.

He married Emma Park, the daughter of John Park, a deceased Royal Artillery officer, at St John's Episcopalian Church in Secunderabad, on 14 August 1882. His brother Joseph was a witness at the wedding. They had seven children–Mildred Clara was born on 14 September 1883 (Secunderabad), Arthur John on 12 September 1885 (Madras), Alice Emma on 4 January 1889 (Ambala), Charles Thomas in the June quarter of 1895 (Brentford), Florence in the December quarter of 1897 (Kensington), Walter Edward in the June quarter of 1900 (Kensington) and Cyril Leslie in the December quarter of 1903 (Fulham).

He obtained a third class certificate of education, and was promoted corporal on 6 March 1883, and sergeant on 1 May 1884. He re-engaged in Madras on 30 January 1885, for such term as would complete 21 years' service. He was posted to Rangoon in Burma on 9 May1886, and from there to Tongou on the 2 November 1886. He was appointed sergeant-drummer on 1 June 1888. He returned to India in 1889, being stationed at Bareilly and Allahabad, and in October 1893 they boarded HMS *Serapis* for the journey to England. He discharged on 14 February 1894, having been awarded the Burma Medal with 1887-89 clasp, and the Long Service, Good Conduct Medal. He was granted a weekly pension of 11 shillings.

His father was buried at Sunbury Cemetery on 23 February 1901, and his mother was buried in the same cemetery on 26 January 1903, although they are not in the same grave, and the graves are unmarked.

Arthur began working for the Royal Parks Department as PK24 (Park keeper) at Kensington in June 1895, but he left the Royal Parks Department for health reasons in 1905. He died on 15 December 1906, at 85 Stephendale Road, Fulham, London, aged 51, having been suffering from tubercular phthisis. He was buried in Fulham Cemetery (section C18, grave 6A). Emma died in 1914 and is buried with Arthur, and John Waters is buried in the same cemetery. His medals were pawned on the King's Road in Fulham to raise money to look after the family. His Long Service, Good Conduct medal was sold at auction in 2002.

Marriage certificate–Secunderabad SAM005630
Death certificate–South Fulham–HC832540
Bracknell Times for 13 January 1972

George Shearman was a survivor of the defence.

He was born on 5 November 1847, at Hayes in Middlesex, and lived at St Margaret's in Twickenham, Middlesex.

He enlisted at the Westminster Police Court, London, on 4 November 1864, and as 1618 Private Shearman he was posted to the 1st Battalion, 24th Regiment. He was five feet five and a half inches tall, with a fresh complexion, grey eyes and brown hair. He transferred to the 2nd Battalion on 31 January 1865. He served in India from 16 June 1865, where he attained 18 years of age on 5 November 1865. He was awarded a penny a day good conduct pay, on 7 March 1871, and obtained a third class certificate of education. He re-engaged at Secunderabad to complete 21 years' service on 6 July 1872. He returned home on 2 January 1873, being promoted corporal on 2 June 1874. He was tried for being drunk on 11 July 1874, and imprisoned until 27 February 1875, being reduced to private, lost his good conduct pay, and was deprived of a day's pay. He retrieved himself, as his good conduct pay was restored in 1876, and he was promoted lance corporal on 17 February 1877. However, he was reduced to private and forfeited his good conduct pay in September 1877.

He received orders for active service in South Africa, and sailed to the Cape in February 1878. He took part in the Cape Frontier War, and during the Zulu War he was present at the defence of Rorke's Drift. He was appointed lance corporal on 5 February 1879, but reverted to private in the following November. For his service he was awarded the South Africa Medal with 1877-8-9 clasp.

He served at Gibraltar in 1880, and his good conduct pay was restored on 2 August 1880, just prior to sailing for service in India. He was promoted and demoted, and gained and forfeited good conduct pay several times, and was imprisoned for being drunk on duty while serving in India. However, he reached the rank of sergeant on 15 August 1885, and by this time he had obtained a second class certificate of education, gained his first good conduct badge, and was allowed to continue his service beyond 21 years. He returned home from Burma on 17 November 1886. He was confined for absence on 19 November 1886, and at his trial on 30 November he was reduced to corporal and forfeited his good conduct badge. He discharged at Gosport on 14 December 1886.

John Shergold was a survivor of the defence.

He was born on 11 November 1839, at 2 Exeter Buildings in Chelsea, the oldest child of five to a shoemaker named James Shergold, and his wife Rosina (formerly Wartnaby). They moved around several London districts, and his siblings were Rosina Jane, born at 2 Exeter Buildings in Chelsea, on 15 May 1841; Ann, born at Gellow Court, New Street in Brompton, on 14 May 1848; Richard Thomas, born at 5 Palace Place in Fulham, on 18 April 1855; Susan Mary Teresa, born at 7 Oakham Street in Chelsea, on 5 April 1858. They fostered a sixth child, a baby named Charles, who had been born in Brompton on 15 April 1860.

His father died of chronic gastritis at Ebury House, Roberts' Buildings in Pimlico, on 5 May 1865; and his mother died of bronchitis, in Wandsworth, on Christmas Day, 25 December 1872.

John left home and travelled to Coventry, where he enlisted on 28 February 1858, and as 914 Private Shergold he was posted to the 2nd Battalion, 24th Regiment, at Aldershot. He was five feet four inches tall, with a fresh complexion, hazel eyes, and brown hair, and he had a 31 inch chest.

He was imprisoned for what must have been a serious offence on 2 May 1859, before spending 46 days in hospital in Aldershot later that year being treated for syphilis, this being the first of many treatments for one complaint or another during his army career. He was stationed in Cork from 7 January 1860, and arrived at Mauritius on 23 May 1860, where he was hospitalised suffering with cholera on 27 January 1862, and he was in hospital several times at Mauritius suffering from the effects of gonorrhoea. He forfeited his good conduct pay, which was reinstated on 14 December 1864. He arrived in Rangoon on 10 November 1864, where at various times he was hospitalised with fever, an infected cut, bronchitis and a swelling on his heel. His good conduct pay was increased to two pence on 4 March 1867, and he re-engaged at Rangoon on 26 March 1868, for such term as would complete 21 years' service. He arrived in India on 16 February 1869, where he was hospitalised for gonorrhoea for 15 days, and after forfeiting his good conduct pay it was reinstated at two pence on 12 February 1872. He arrived back at the Warley depot on 4 January 1873. His good conduct pay was increased to three pence a day at Aldershot on 19 December 1873, which increased to four pence per day while he was at Dover on 4 March 1876. He was posted to Chatham in 1877, where he was back in hospital being treated for a sprain.

He married Emily Birch on 6 September 1873, at the Church of St Philip in Battersea, and they had a son named William John, who was born at 43 Heath Road in Clapham, on 3 February 1880.

On receiving orders for active service in South Africa, his wife sailed to the Cape with him in February 1878. He took part in the Cape Frontier War, and during the Zulu War he was present at the defence of Rorke's Drift. For his service he received the South Africa Medal with 1877-8-9 clasp.

He was hospitalised with debility and rheumatism on 9 November 1879, brought about by service and conditions. A medical board recommended he should be sent to Netley Military Hospital, later confirming that he was suffering from chronic rheumatism. John left hospital on 6 April 1880, and on the same day he discharged from the army as 'weakly and worn out' and 'unfit for further service.' He was described as being five feet five and three-quarter inches tall, and he was awarded a pension of one shilling and two pence per day.

He and his family are believed to have lived at 44 Gladstone Street in Battersea, and John found employment as a railway carriage cleaner. However, he fell at work and suffered a head injury, for which he was taken to St George's Hospital where he died of his injuries on 18 February 1884, aged 44. The cause of death was given as:

> Abscess in the brain from injury to the head. Fell accidentally from a buffer when at work at Victoria Train Station of the London, Brighton, and South Coast Railway Company. 3 Weeks.

After a service at Battersea Church, he was buried in an unmarked common grave at Brompton Cemetery in west London, and the burial records give his address as 17 Landseer Street in Battersea. At my last inspection the grave remains unmarked and overgrown.

Birth certificate–St Luke, Chelsea CN367442
Marriage certificate–St Phillips, Battersea–GO11469
Rosina Jane birth certificate–St Luke, Chelsea CN367443
Ann birth certificate–Brompton BXCC428508

Susan Mary Teresa birth certificate–Chelsea FC486266
Richard Thomas birth certificate–Kensington, Fulham BXCC458760
William John birth certificate–Clapham, Wandsworth BXCC458730
Charles birth certificate–Brompton BXCC458931
Father's death certificate–Belgrave DYB495656
Mother's death certificate–Belgrave DYB495942
Death certificate–St George, Hanover Square–GO11469
Brompton Cemetery Burial Records
Friends of Brompton Cemetery

Reverend George Smith was a survivor of the defence.

He was born at Docking in Norfolk, on 8 January 1845, the son of William and Frances Smith, and he was at college in Canterbury, before going to South Africa as a lay missionary in 1870. He was ordained Deacon in 1871, and Priest in 1872. He was a tall man with a great red beard, and he was appointed to St John's Parish, based at the Estcourt Mission in Natal, where he became well-known as a hard-working man. He served as a volunteer during the Langalibalele Rebellion, and in 1878 he was appointed acting chaplain to the volunteers. It was in this capacity that he took part in the Zulu War.

On 22 January 1879, he was going about his duties at Rorke's Drift when it was reported that there was possible action at iSandlwana, so, in the company of Surgeon Reynolds and the Reverend Witt, he decided to go on a reconnaissance to the top of the Oscarberg Hill to try to get a clearer view of what was happening. They saw a number of colonials returning from enemy territory on the Zululand side of the river, so Surgeon Reynolds went back to the mission station in case they required medical assistance. The two clerics watched a large number of natives moving slowly up from the Natal bank of the river at such a leisurely pace that they believed them to be colonial troops. However, the increasing force was within rifle range when they saw that the two men on horseback leading them were not Europeans, but had black faces. When they realised that the oncoming mass was a Zulu impi, they climbed hastily back down the hill to report the danger to the officers.

During the ferocious Zulu onslaughts he spent his time moving along the barricade, handing out cartridges from his hat, as well as reproving the curses of the hard-fighting soldiers and stopping to give spiritual consolation to the wounded.

Colonel Harford was with the Column which arrived at Rorke's Drift on the morning of 23 January, and stated:

> The part which the Reverend Smith played in the defence, and the splendid example he set throughout that terrible night, ought to have earned for him the VC. I noticed that directly Mr Smith showed himself, he received an ovation from the men.

He served throughout the Zulu War, his deeds and reputation earning him the nickname 'Ammunition Smith', and he was in the British square at Ulundi to witness the final defeat of the Zulus. He visited the devastated battlefield at iSandlwana, and said many prayers for the soldiers who had been massacred, and held a short service at the bodies of Lieutenants Coghill and Melvill, who had lost their lives while trying to save the Queen's colour of their battalion from falling into enemy hands, and would many years later be awarded the Victoria Cross. In November 1879, he was one of several clergymen who visited the site, with the view to establish a mission church in remembrance of the dead. This became the Zululand Memorial Church.

His report of the action at Rorke's Drift dated 3 February 1879 was published in the *Royal Army Chaplains' Department Journal* for July 1936.

After a period at home, the Reverend Smith served under Sir Garnet Wolseley in his north-east Africa campaigns from 1882 to 1887. He took part in the battle of Tel-el-Kebir in Egypt on 13 September 1882, and in the battle of El Teb in the Sudan on 29 February 1884, when the British defeated a mass army of fanatical Dervish warriors. For his service he received the Queen's Medal for Egypt and the Khedives Bronze Star.

He was second class chaplain at various military stations at home and abroad from 1887 until gaining an appointment as first class chaplain on 16 February 1900, including a spell of duty as chaplain at Fulwood Garrison Church in Preston, from about 1897 to 1903. He retired in 1905.

It would seem that he was a well-known character, with many friends, who knew him as 'Daddy Smith', because of his great bushy beard. He was visited in Preston by Colonel Chard, and the Reverend

Smith went to see Chard in Somerset. Both meetings were during the last months of Chard's life, and his former comrade may have wanted his spiritual consolation.

He chose to take a room at the Sumners Hotel, across the road from the barrack gates, where the manager remembered him as being very popular in the hotel, and staff made sure their 'favourite guest' was always looked after. It has been said that the famous painting of the defence of Rorke's Drift by Alphonse de Neuville once hung in the hotel, which was of particular interest because the names of several of the defenders had been written in by George Smith himself. On his retirement in 1905 he continued to reside at the hotel, although he visited South Africa and Australia frequently and was away a considerable time.

As a note of interest, in 1910 some ghostly figures were said to have been seen in the barracks, and Reverend Smith became so interested in the matter that he said prayers in the rooms and even got in touch with the Psychical Society in London.

In 1918 he became ill with bronchial trouble, and after being confined to his hotel room for six months, he died during the night of 26/27 November 1918, aged 63. His death was only a few days after the armistice which ended the Great War, so his funeral was a small military parade, and among the floral tributes was one from the officers of the South Wales Borderers–'In Memory of Rorke's Drift.' He was buried in the New Hall Lane Cemetery, and a monument was erected in memory of one of the heroes of Rorke's Drift–'Who was a brave and modest Christian gentleman.'

In July 2009, bible and ammunition box representations were placed among a floral tribute to George Smith at Miller Park in Preston, along with helmets commemorating the eleven VCs gained in the battle.

George Henry Smith was a survivor of the defence.

He was born on 26 January 1840, at Bird Cage Fields in Stamford Hill, north London, the sixth child of seven to George Smith, a dairyman's labourer, and his wife, Susannah (formerly Willshire). The family moved to Moore's Field Cottages in Stamford Hill, and by 1851 they had moved to 6, South Row in Stamford Hill.

He enlisted in the Royal London Militia on 14 April 1860, before joining the regular army on 29 May 1860, at Worship Street Police Court in Finsbury, and as 1387 Private G. Smith he was posted to the 2nd Battalion, 24th Regiment. He was five feet four inches tall, with a sallow complexion, grey eyes and brown hair. He had small pox marks, and a bald spot on the back of the head from a burn. He arrived at Cork on 31 May 1860, where he was awarded a penny a day good conduct pay on 30 May 1863. He arrived on the sugar island of Mauritius on 6 November 1863, where he spent some time in hospital suffering from severe constipation caused by intestinal obstruction, and later inflammation of the testicle caused by an injury. He was sent to Port Blair on the Andaman Islands, India, where he was admitted to hospital in December 1865, being treated for dysentery, and he was re-admitted to hospital early in 1866, again being treated for inflammation of the testicle caused by an injury. He was twice admitted to hospital in Rangoon suffering from boils and then with a fever. He re-engaged on 10 January 1868, to complete 21 years, and his good conduct pay increased to two pence a day from 30 May 1868. He arrived in Port Blair, India, on the 22 June, and in the following September he was hospitalised with a swelling of the groin caused by a sprain. He was admitted to hospital again on 3 October being treated for fever.

He forfeited one penny of his good conduct pay on 4 December 1868. He was posted to Madras on 27 January 1869, and by 5 March he had moved to Secunderabad, where he was hospitalised with tonsillitis, followed by a couple of bouts of enteric fever, attributed to a defective malaria injection. George was to have several more bouts of fever. He was promoted to corporal on 4 August 1871, he obtained a third class certificate of education on 15 April 1872, and he began receiving good conduct pay at the rate of three pence a day from 30 May 1872. He was posted to England and arrived at the Warley depot on 4 January 1873, before being posted to the new depot at Brecon on 1 April 1873. He completed the course at the Hythe School of Musketry on 31 December 1873. He was hospitalised at Brecon in 1874 suffering from inflammation of the eye caused by a common cold. He was promoted to lance sergeant on 1 April 1876.

George married Fanny Martin of Brecon, on 13 June 1877, at the Wesleyan Chapel in Brecon, and they lived in Free Street, Brecon. They had five children. Louisa was born in 1878, Elizabeth in 1881,

Llewellyn George in 1882, Arthur Joseph in 1886, and Daisy in 1889. Llewellyn was killed in action during the Great War in 1917.

George was promoted to sergeant on 1 February 1878, the day he embarked for active service in South Africa. He took part in the Cape Frontier War, after which he was once again admitted to hospital with fever, and no sooner had the fever been dealt with than on the same day he began to suffer from another bout of orchitis, being discharged as fit for duty on 29 November 1878.

During the Zulu War he was present at the defence of Rorke's Drift, from where he wrote a letter to his wife on 24 January in which he stated:

I am thankful that I have been saved from the cruel slaughter and bloodshed that we had all gone through the last four days. The Zulus got hold of four boys of the 1st/24th band and cut them up in bits, and destroyed everything they could get their hands on. After destroying all they could they made for Rorke's Drift, and at about 2.30pm the same day we were attacked by about 3,000 of them, and had to build up a fort... how we ever escaped I can hardly tell you. I myself had given up all hopes of escaping. We have counted the number of Zulus that were shot by my company, and they were over 800, so that they dearly paid for what they killed of our men. I cannot tell you a quarter of the horrors that have taken place. My dear wife, I trust you will feel thankful to God for having preserved my life. My company was very highly praised for the noble stand they made in keeping the place, and the cool manner in which they defended it.

On 4 February 1879, George was transferred to A company on 4 February 1879, in the re-shuffle which followed the massacre at iSandlwana. For his service he was awarded the South Africa Medal with 1877-8-9 clasp.

He served at Gibraltar in 1880, and just four days after arriving in India in August 1880, he was hospitalised suffering yet another bout of fever caused by climate, and two days after his discharge he was re-admitted suffering with orchitis. He was re-admitted for the same complaint three days later. The authorities finally realised that he had a weak constitution and he was invalided home on 11 March 1881.

He began to suffer with a condition which was diagnosed as hoops disease, and he was admitted to Netley Hospital in June 1881. In spite of this he was permitted to serve beyond 21 years by authority dated 22 August 1881. He transferred to the Permanent Staff, 3rd (Volunteer) Battalion, South Wales Borderers, at Devonport, on 28 December 1881. He remained in Brecon until 24 September 1882, when he was posted to the Provisional Battalion, Colchester, and from 30 May 1883 he received five pence Good Conduct Pay.

George was discharged from the 3rd South Wales Borderers Staff on 31 July 1883. His character on discharge was described as good, clean and temperate, and his conduct was very good. He was awarded a pension of one shilling and ten pence a day, and gave his intended place of residence as c/o Sarah Martin, 79 Lombard Street, London. He had earned five good conduct badges, and received the Long Service Good Conduct Medal, and the Meritorious Service Medal.

By the turn of the century he was living at 15 Roman Road in Islington, where he was employed as an estate agent's assistant. George Smith died of a cerebral haemorrhage at his home, 31 Grafton Road in Islington, on 20 January 1925, aged 85, and he was buried with several other people in public grave number Z27 16834 at the Islington and St Pancras Cemetery in East Finchley. William Dicks died later in the same year and was buried in the same cemetery. The area was described as a nature reserve, which was densely overgrown. A headstone bearing the name Albert John Smith has been found there, but he is one of the other people buried in the grave and he is not related to George.

Birth certificate–Stamford Hill, Hackney BXCC692651
Marriage certificate–Brecknock
Death certificate–Tufnell, Islington DYB611253
Brecon County Times for 29 March 1879

John Smith was slightly wounded during the defence.

He was born on 28 December 1851, at Wood's Houses, Chapel Lane in All Saint's Parish, Wigan, and he was baptised at All Saint's parish church on 28 February 1852, where fellow Rorke's Drift man, William Neville, had also been baptised.

He was the son of John Smith, and his second wife Mary

(formerly Hallam). His father was a cotton spinner, and they had married in Bolton on 6 December 1846. A daughter named Ann was born in the year after their marriage.

At the time of the 1851 census the family had moved to Kay's Cottages at Ince-in-Makerfield, Wigan, where John worked for the Lancashire and Yorkshire Railway. However, he was working as a brakes man when he fell from a train engine onto the line and was run over by some carriages and crushed to death at Trinity Street Station in Bolton on 3 April 1856. A report on his inquest was published in the *Bolton Chronicle* two days after his death.

Mary and her two children left the family home in Wigan and returned to Bolton, where most of the Smith family had settled, and they rented a house at 1 Shepherd Street, Little Bolton, before moving to lodgings in Waterloo Street in Little Bolton. At the time of the 1861 census they lived at Cellar Stott Court in Bolton, where Mary was a cotton reeler, and Ann was a steam loom weaver. Ann died of kidney failure brought on by bright's disease on 16 December 1867.

Having joined the 7th Royal Lancashire Militia, John decided to enlist into the regular army which he did at Ashton-under-Lyne, on Christmas Eve, 1876, and as 1005 Private Smith he was posted to the 2nd Battalion, 24th Regiment. He was five feet seven and a half inches tall, with a chest measurement of 36 inches. He had a fresh complexion, blue eyes and brown hair, with a scar on his right forefinger, a scar on his forehead and on his chin. He had only been able to put his mark on the papers.

He received orders for active service in South Africa and sailed to the Cape in February 1878. He took part in the Cape Frontier War, and during the Zulu War he was present at the defence of Rorke's Drift, where he received an assegai thrust in the abdomen, the only man fighting at the barricades to receive a spear wound.

He was granted one penny a day good conduct pay from 14 April 1879, and on 8 July 1879, he received treatment in hospital at Pietermaritzburg for a minor sprain, the result of an accident. He was examined on 8 August and was recommended for a change of climate. He was sent home, and arrived at Netley Hospital in Southampton, on 20 September 1879, being discharged as fit for duty on 10 October. He was posted to Brecon, where he was admitted to hospital in December 1879, being treated for a sprained ankle. He was discharged on 15 February 1880, being recommended for further treatment. He received the South Africa Medal with 1877-8-9 clasp.

John was discharged to the first class reserves, Bury District, on 21 July 1880, having served three years and 178 days, and he gave his intended place of residence as Bury, Lancashire. A note on his service papers stated that he had:

> ...an outstanding claim for compensation for kit lost at iSandlwana, Zululand; ditto for shirt and trousers issued for fatigue work at Fort Melville, Rorke's Drift; ditto for tunic left by order in squad bay at Pietermaritzburg when ordered to the front in 1878.

He possibly found it difficult to settle into civilian life, as less than eight months later he re-enlisted for the 46th Brigade General Depot Duties, on 1 March 1881, and as 2333 Private Smith, he was sent to join the 2nd Battalion, 97th (Royal West Kent) Regiment. Four days later he boarded a ship with his new regiment and was once again on his way to South Africa, where a Boer uprising was causing major problems for the British forces.

He was on the march in Natal on 10 March 1881 when he was lifting something heavy and a hernia in his groin ruptured. He was admitted to hospital for treatment on 26 May, where he remained until 31 August, being re-admitted on 10 September 1881, for the same problem, remaining there until 6 October, at which point he was shipped back to Dublin and hospitalised on 21 March 1882. He was examined by a medical board on 8 June 1882, and declared unfit for further service due to an inguinal hernia. No further injuries other than those recorded when he joined the army were noted on his papers.

John was discharged from the army in Dublin on 25 June 1882, with a pension of six pence a day, and his papers state that during his service with both regiments he had three entries in the regimental defaulter's book, but had never been tried by court marshal. He gave his intended place of residence as Wigan, Lancashire.

He was married to Heather, and he worked as a hawker. He committed suicide at Heather Railway Station in Leicestershire at the age of 53. He was buried in an unmarked grave at Ashby-de-la-Zouch Cemetery on 11 July 1899 (cemetery 2, grave 763).

The *Leicester Chronicle* for 15 July 1899 published the following:

The Leicestershire coroner held an inquest on Saturday on a Rorke's Drift hero named John Smith, an army pensioner, who committed suicide under shocking circumstances. He first attempted suicide by cutting his throat. He was charged and bound over, but afterwards he lay down in front of a train and was shockingly mutilated.

His South Africa Medal was sold at auction in 2002, and a service of rededication for a new memorial stone was held at his grave in 2023.

Birth certificate–Wigan 389702-3
Bolton Chronicle for 5 April 1856
Leicester Chronicle for 15 July 1899
Marriage certificate of parents–Bolton AB374819

Thomas Stevens was a survivor of the defence.

He was born in 1854, at St John's in Exeter. He left his job as a bricklayer to enlist into the army at Brecon, on 9 March 1876, and as 777 Private Stevens he was posted to the 2nd Battalion, 24th Regiment. He was described as five feet five and a half inches tall, with a dark complexion, brown eyes and black hair. His religion was Church of England. Having been promoted lance corporal on 20 January 1877, he obtained a third class certificate of education on 18 July 1877, and was promoted corporal on 12 August 1877. However, he was tried for being absent on 19 January 1878, and was reduced to private.

He received orders for active service in South Africa and sailed with his battalion to the Cape in February 1878. He took part in the Cape Frontier War, and during the Zulu War he was present at the defence of Rorke's Drift. For his service he received the South Africa Medal with 1877-8-9 clasp.

It seems that he read the list of those present at the defence of Rorke's Drift compiled by Lieutenant Chard, and noticing that there was no man named Parry on the list, which prompted him to write to the *Merthyr Express* on 19 April 1879:

Sir, By a paragraph headed 'The Zulu War—Providential Escape of a Merthyr Soldier' which appeared in your paper of April 12th, a copy of which I received from my relatives, I was much surprised to learn that a soldier named Parry, of the 24th Regiment, had taken part (according to his own statement) in the defence of the post at Rorke's Drift on the 22nd January last, after the disaster which took place at Isandhlwana on that day.

Now, Sir, as I belong to B. Company 2nd Battalion 24th Regiment, and was present with same during the defence referred to, and as I do not care to read of men who were not present or even participated in any way in that memorable affair, misleading their friends and others by mis-representings, I think I shall be doing justice to yourself and readers, as also to real defenders in question, if I mention that no soldier or other person of the name of Parry was present at Rorke's Drift on that occasion. If you desire I will gladly forward a correct list of all who were actually concerned therein. I beg to Sir, your humble and respectful servant,

Thomas Stephens—Private, 2-24th Regiment, Natal.

However, it is my view that, although the names of Thomas Parry and Samuel Parry were not on the Chard list, they were present at the defence of Rorke's Drift. It is interesting to think if the families of both men ever met to discuss it.

He was granted one penny a day good conduct pay while he was in Gibraltar, on 28 April 1880, but this was forfeited on 12 September 1881, while he was serving in India. He returned to Brecon on 25 November 1881, being transferred to the first class army reserve on 17 March 1882. He was recalled to the South Wales Borderers on 2 August 1882, and re-transferred to the army reserve at Salford on 28 August 1882.

He married Ellen Calvert at Merthyr Tydfil, on 1 September 1883, and received his final discharge on 16 March 1888, giving his next-of-kin as his father, Robert Stevens, Robin Hood Inn at Dowlais in Glamorganshire.

Cardiff Times and South Wales Weekly News for 29 May 1879
Merthyr Express for 29 March and 19 April 1879

William Tasker was a survivor of the defence.

He was born in 1846, at St Martin's Parish in Birmingham. He left his job as a buffer to enlist at Sheffield on 25 September 1866, and as 1812 Private Tasker he was posted to the 2nd Battalion, 24th Regiment. He was just over five feet ten inches tall, with a fair complexion, grey eyes and fair hair. He served in India from 4 November 1867, gaining and forfeiting good conduct pay until it was restored on 27 June 1872. He returned home on 3 January 1873, and re-engaged to complete 21 years' service on the following 20 August. However, he deserted on 10 March 1874, and on re-joining two weeks later he was imprisoned from 30 March to 10 May 1874, forfeited good conduct pay and former services towards good conduct and pension, for conviction of desertion. However, he was appointed lance corporal on 13 August 1875, and his good conduct pay was restored on 12 March 1877. He was caught drunk on picquet duty on 26 May 1877, for which he was reduced to private and forfeited good conduct pay, and he was imprisoned for 28 days with hard labour from 2 June 1877, being released after 20 days.

He received orders for active service in South Africa and sailed with his battalion to the Cape in February 1878. He took part in the Cape Frontier War, and during the Zulu War he was present at the defence of Rorke's Drift, where he was wounded when a splinter from a Zulu slug which glanced his forehead and broke the skin. For his service he received the South Africa Medal with 1877-8-9 clasp.

His good conduct pay was restored on 1 January 1880. He served at Gibraltar in 1880, and in India, where his good conduct pay was increased to two pence a day from 15 January 1882, He returned home on 27 January 1883, and his previously forfeited service towards good conduct pay and pension was restored on 4 July that year.

He married Elizabeth Ridney at the Brecon Register Office, on 29 September 1883. His good conduct pay was increased to three pence a day on 15 January 1884. He was prematurely discharged for the benefit of the public service, on 31 January 1885, his character being described as clean, good and temperate.

He suffered a heart attack, collapsed and died in the street at Bordesley Green in Birmingham, on 7 July 1898, and he was buried in an unmarked grave at Yardley Cemetery in Birmingham.

Frederick Taylor was a survivor of the defence.

He was born at Mangotsfield near Bristol, in about 1858, and he had previously served in the Royal Monmouth Militia when he enlisted for the regular army at Newport, Monmouthshire, on 9 December 1876, and as 973 Private F. Taylor he was posted to the 2nd Battalion, 24th Regiment.

He received orders for active service in South Africa and sailed with his battalion to the Cape in February 1878. He took part in the Cape Frontier War, and during the Zulu War he was present at the defence of Rorke's Drift. For his service he received the South Africa Medal with 1877-8-9 clasp.

Sadly, Frederick died of disease at Pinetown in Natal, on 30 November 1879, and his medal was issued to his next-of-kin on 29 September 1881.

James Taylor was a survivor of the defence.

He was born on 24 March 1855, at Lane Side in the village of Meltham near Huddersfield, and he was baptised at St Bartholemew's Church in Meltham on 16 April 1855. He was the son of William Dyson Taylor (1835-1877) and his wife Sarah (formerly Kenyon– 1921), both natives of Meltham, who had married in Almondbury, Huddersfield, on 21 December 1854. They had a daughter named Annie, born in 1857, and a son named Hiram, born in 1860.

William was described as 'well-educated' and worked as a clerk/cashier at Jonas Brook and Brothers, a cotton thread manufacturers in Huddersfield, and later moved across the Pennines with the company to take up employment at their Manchester premises on Fountain Street. They lived at 33 Parkfield Road in Moss Bank, Rusholme.

William suffered an unfortunate fall from grace when he was convicted of several accounts of embezzlement at Manchester Police Court, on 17 August 1871, and was sentenced to twelve months hard labour. He was known to have got into 'financial worries' at the time of his death in 1877.

Possibly because of the upheaval within the family after his father was sent to prison, James enlisted into the army at the Cross Lane Infantry Barracks in Salford, on 13 March 1874, aged apparently 19. He was just over five feet eight inches tall, with a fresh complexion, blue eyes and brown hair, and he had a small scar on his forehead. His religion was Church of England. As 92 Private Taylor he was posted to E Company, 2nd Battalion, 24th Regiment. His next-of-kin was given as his mother, although his father was still alive at that time.

His army records suggest that his education helped him, but he seems to have found it difficult to adjust to army life. He was appointed corporal on 3 March 1875, but he was confined for drunkenness on 27 May that year and was reduced to private. He was appointed corporal on 4 August 1876, and was granted one penny a day good conduct pay from 27 March 1877. He was promoted lance sergeant on 26 October 1877, but reverted to corporal in the following month.

He received orders for active service in South Africa, and sailed with his battalion to the Cape in February 1878. He took part in the Cape Frontier War, being promoted lance sergeant on 11 July 1878, and during the Zulu War he was present at the defence of Rorke's Drift. He was promoted sergeant on 23 January 1879. For his service he was awarded the South Africa Medal with 1877-8-9 clasp.

He served at Gibraltar in 1880, where he was confined in cells on 17 March 1880, and three days later he was tried by Regimental Court Martial, and reduced to private. He served at Bombay in India, where his good conduct pay was increased to two pence a day from 20 March 1883. He was promoted lance sergeant on 3 September 1884, but he was deprived of this rank on 19 February 1885. He was tried by Regimental Court Martial on 22 September 1885, and sentenced to 21 days imprisonment with hard labour, being reduced to private and forfeiting one good conduct badge. However, the sentence was later remitted.

He lived for a short period at 1 Summer Villas in Urmston (now in Trafford, Manchester), before he re-engaged at Madras on 23 November 1885, to complete 21 years' service.

He went with the battalion to Burma on 9 May 1886, being granted three pence a day good conduct pay from 19 September 1888, and for his service he received the Indian General Service Medal with Burma 1887-89 clasp. He returned to India on 10 November 1888, where he remained until 17 November 1893. He had reached the rank of orderly room sergeant from 5 June 1891, and he was granted four pence a day good conduct pay from 1 March

1892. He also gained a second class certificate of education. He discharged on 8 March 1894, his conduct being described as good, and his habits regular.

On 2 February 1900, at Stretford in Manchester, he married Eva Sophia Clive Mallalieu, who was 18 years younger than him, having been born at Chorlton-on-Medlock (not to be confused with Chorlton-cum-Hardy, which is a sub-district of Stretford), on 7 April 1873.

He lived with his wife, Sarah, and two children at 33 Parkfield Road in Rusholme, Manchester, for about twenty years. His daughter, also named Sarah, went to live at St Asaph in Denbighshire, and in 1915 he took his family to live in the village of Trefnant near Denbigh, making their home at 'Siop Bach', and James returned to his previous occupation as a clerk, with the firm of Richard Evans.

James died on 15 November 1919, from a malignant disease of the throat and exhaustion, aged 64, and he was buried with military honours in an unmarked grave at Holy Trinity Church in Trefnant. A new headstone was placed at his grave in 2019 with a service of re-dedication. His South Africa campaign medal is with the Regimental Museum at Brecon.

Birth certificate (Meltham, County of York)
Burials in Holy Trinity Church, Trefnant
Death certificate (St Asaph, Denbigh)
England and Wales Criminal Registry, 1791-1892
Huddersfield Chronicle for 12, 17 June and 8 July 1871
Huddersfield Weekly Examiner for 19 and 26 August 1871
Wales census 1911 (RG14/339/57/ (79)

Thomas Edward Taylor was a survivor of the defence.

He was born on 9 September 1856, in the Hatton Village Cottages, at Hatton near Warrington, the son of Thomas Taylor, an agricultural labourer, and his wife, Ellen (formerly Andrews).

He enlisted at Liverpool on 11 November 1876, and as 889 Private Taylor, he was posted to the 2nd Battalion, 24th Regiment. He was described as being five feet seven and a half inches tall, with a chest measurement of thirty four and a half inches. He had brown hair, and his religion was Church of England.

He received orders for active service in South Africa, and sailed with his battalion to the Cape in February 1878. He took part in the Cape Frontier War, and during the Zulu War he was present at the defence of Rorke's Drift. For his service he was awarded the South Africa Medal with 1877-8-9 clasp. He served at Gibraltar in 1880, and in India, being credited with home service from 27 January 1883. In 1879 he lived at Wrea Green in Lancashire.

He married Lucy Maddock at Daresbury Church (the Lewis Carroll Church), on 29 December 1884, and they lived at St George's Cottages in Weston, Runcorn, where Tom gained employment as a stone quarry labourer at the Weston Quarry. They had seven children. Sarah C. was born in 1886; Thomas Bradshaw in 1887; Florence Louisa in 1889; John Percy in 1892 (drowned aged 15); Margaret Elizabeth in 1894; Elsie Maude in 1898; and Lucy Lillian in 1901 (died aged three). In 1891 they lived at Quarry Bank Lea in Weston, and in 1901 at Bankes Row in Weston.

King George V opened the new bridge between Runcorn and Widnes in 1925, when he and fellow Rorke's Drift man, Thomas Moffatt, were presented to the King, along with 'Todger' Jones VC.

Lucy died in 1903, and Tom died of bronchitis and heart failure on 17 April 1926, aged 69, at 5 St John's Cottages in Weston. He was buried in Runcorn Cemetery (section 5/363), where Thomas Moffatt would later be laid to rest.

In 1999 a renovation and re-dedication service was held at his graveside, and that of Thomas Moffatt, which included a troupe of Zulu dancers in regalia. His medal and the illuminated address presented to him by the Mayor of Durban remain with the family. In 2019 a blue plaque was placed near his former home at St John's Cottages by Runcorn Heritage.

Preston Pilot for 26 March 1879

John Thomas was a survivor of the defence.

He was born as Peter Sawyer on 31 May 1850, at Banks Cottages in Bootle-cum-Linacre, Liverpool. He was the oldest child of four born to Samuel Sawyer (born at Ormskirk on 10 April 1819), and his wife, Elizabeth (formerly Collier), who already had three children, and they had married at Maghull in Liverpool on 12 October 1847.

By 1861 the family had moved to Brickfields, Great Crosby, Liverpool. At the age of eleven Peter joined his father and brother working as labourers in Brickfields. However, by 1869 both his parents were dead, and having to fend for himself, he took lodgings at Haigh's Cottage in Waterloo Park, Liverpool.

He joined the 2nd Royal Lancashire Militia (Duke of Lancaster's Own Rifles), before enlisting for the regular army at Liverpool, on 23 February 1877. Another recruit enlisting at the same place and on the same day was fellow Rorke's Drift man William Neville. He used a false name, and as 1280 Private John Thomas, he was described as five feet five and three-quarter inches tall, with a sallow complexion, dark blue eyes and brown hair. His religion was Roman Catholic.

He received orders for active service in South Africa and sailed with his battalion to the Cape in February 1878. He took part in the Cape Frontier War, being hospitalised with pneumonia on 29 June 1878. He was transferred to Natal where he was re-admitted to hospital, the cause of his illness being 'exposure in service.' During the Zulu War he was present at the defence of Rorke's Drift. He was awarded one penny a day good conduct pay on 26 February 1879, and on 15 May of that year he was promoted to lance corporal. For his service he received the South Africa Medal with 1877-8-9 clasp.

He served at Gibraltar, where on 5 June 1880 he forfeited his good conduct pay, and in India, where his good conduct pay was restored on 5 June 1881, but he forfeited it again in the following month. He appeared before the Cantonment Magistrate in Secunderabad on 26 May 1882, to sign a document stating that he had enlisted under a false name. However, the pay and muster rolls continued to state his name as John Thomas up to the date of his discharge. His good conduct pay was restored again on 4 July 1882. Arriving in England on 30 May 1883, he received his final discharge at Gosport, and was posted to the 1st class reserve on 28 June 1883. His character was described as good and his habits as temperate. His intended place of residence was the post office at Devizes, c/o Mrs Bryant, Melksham, Wiltshire.

He married Annie Louisa Kelsey at the Portsea Register Office, on 5 July 1883, giving an address as Smith's Lane in Portsea. His father's Christian name was given as Solomon on the marriage certificate. However, they travelled to Peter's home city and lived at 3 Sweden Street in Great Crosby, Liverpool, where he obtained employment as a bricklayer's labourer. By 1901 they had moved to 78 Sweden Street in Great Crosby, and shortly afterwards to 21 Sweden Street.

Peter died of cardiac thrombosis at 21 Sweden Street in Waterloo, Liverpool, on 16 May 1903, aged 52, and he was buried in an unmarked communal grave at Kirkdale Cemetery in Liverpool (section 16, grave 166). His wife died in 1916 and is buried with him.

A wreath from 'Peter Sawyer' was sent to the funeral of Rorke's Drift man, George Edward Orchard in 1940, which has caused some confusion. It was sent by his cousin, also Peter Sawyer, who had gone to live in Canada in 1904. The late defender of Rorke's Drift could not send a tribute himself so his cousin had decided to pay a final respect to his fellow defender on his behalf.

It would seem that Peter Sawyer of Canada kept contact in some way, perhaps with the regimental association, because in 1939 Patrick Hayes wrote a newspaper article which suggests that he thought the Peter Sawyer in Canada was his fellow defender.

Birth certificate–Walton, West Derby FD088792
Marriage certificate–Portsea Island, Portsmouth–TJ375419
Death certificate–Crosby, West Derby–HD047157

John Thompson was a survivor of the defence.

He attested for 25 Brigade at Brecon on 3 May 1877, and as 1394 Private Thompson he was posted to the 2nd Battalion, 24th Regiment, on 16 January 1878.

He received orders for active service in South Africa, and sailed to the Cape in February 1878. He took part in the Cape Frontier War, and during the Zulu War he was present at the defence of Rorke's Drift. He was appointed lance corporal on 5 March 1879, being reduced to private on 6 December that year. For his service he received the South Africa Medal with 1877-8-9 clasp.

He served at Gibraltar in 1880, and returned to England from India in October 1883. He discharged at Gosport on 31 October 1883, and he was given a travel warrant to Newport in Wales.

Michael Tobin was a survivor of the defence.

He was born in 1856, at Windgap in County Kilkenny, Ireland, his father being shown as named Michael. He enlisted at Monmouth on 6 November 1876, and as 879 Private M Tobin, he was posted to the 2nd Battalion, 24th Regiment at Brecon. He was five feet nine and a half inches tall, with a fresh complexion, grey eyes and brown hair. His religion was Roman Catholic.

He received orders for active service in South Africa, and sailed to the Cape in February 1878. He took part in the Cape Frontier War, being granted good conduct pay on 7 November 1878. During the Zulu War he was present at the defence of Rorke's Drift. For his service he received the South Africa Medal with 1877-8-9 clasp.

He was found drunk on guard duty on 4 July 1879, the day the Zulus were defeated at Ulundi. He was sentenced to receive 50 lashes, which was later remitted, but he forfeited his good conduct pay, and was imprisoned until 8 July 1879. He was released in Gibraltar on 30 June 1880, his good conduct pay being restored on 8 July 1880. He arrived in India on 11 August 1880, where his good conduct pay was increased to two pence from 12 November 1882. He returned home on 27 January 1883, and discharged from Brecon on 23 March 1883.

His intended place of residence was Nine Mile House in Tipperary. He married Margaret Mohan at his home town of Windgap, in February 1886.

He entered the first class army reserve on 11 November 1888, and took his final discharge from section D on 10 November 1892.

Patrick Tobin was a survivor of the defence.

A Patrick Tobin was born at Ardagh in County Limerick on 7 August 1857, and his father's name was given as James.

Patrick enlisted for 25 Brigade at Newport in Monmouthshire, on 17 September 1875, and as 641 Private P. Tobin, he was posted to the 2nd Battalion, 24th Regiment, on 21 March 1877.

He received orders for active service in South Africa, and sailed to the Cape in February 1878. He took part in the Cape Frontier War, and during the Zulu War he was present at the defence of Rorke's Drift. For his service he received the South Africa Medal with 1877-8-9 clasp.

He appears to have been appointed lance corporal in 1880, while in Gibraltar, but incorrectly named Michael Tobin, and he may have been appointed corporal in India in April 1881, again incorrectly named, the muster rolls appear to confuse him with 2698 Lance Corporal John Tobin. He returned home from India on 28 October 1881.

William John Todd was a survivor of the defence.

He was born in Liverpool in about 1857, possibly with the surname of Tod. His family are believed to have come from Moffat near Dumfries in Scotland. He enlisted on 2 March 1877, and as 281 Private Todd he was posted to the 2nd Battalion, 24th Regiment.

He received orders for active service in South Africa, and sailed to the Cape in February 1878. He took part in the Cape Frontier War, and during the Zulu War he was present at the defence of Rorke's Drift. For his service he received the South Africa Medal with 1877-8-9 clasp.

He served at Gibraltar in 1880, and returned home from India on 26 April 1883. His intended place of residence was with his uncle in Liverpool.

Robert Tongue was a survivor of the defence.

He was born on 3 June 1857, at Ruddington in Nottinghamshire. He was the child of John Tongue, and his second wife, Elizabeth (formerly Powdrill). His father had a son from his first marriage. John Tongue died within five years, and Elizabeth re-married and had three more children before she died in 1877.

Having previously served with the Nottingham Militia, he left his job as a framework knitter and enlisted for the regular army on 26 February 1877, and as 1315 Private Tongue, he was posted to the 2nd Battalion, 24th Regiment, at Brecon, giving his half-brother, Thomas, as his next-of-kin. He was five feet seven inches tall, with a fresh complexion, grey eyes and brown hair. His religion was Wesleyan.

He received orders for active service in South Africa, and sailed to the Cape in February 1878. He took part in the Cape Frontier War, and during the Zulu War he was present at the defence of Rorke's Drift. For his service he received the South Africa Medal with 1877-8-9 clasp.

He received good conduct pay from 1 March 1879, and obtained a fourth class certificate of education. He was in hospital several times for minor ailments during his service with the colours. He served at Gibraltar in 1880, and in India, where his good conduct pay was increased to two pence a day on 1 March 1883, and from where he returned home on 29 May 1883.

He married Mary Wright at Ruddington Parish Church on 27 June 1884, and they took a house at Church Street in Ruddington. They had nine children. Florence Elizabeth was born on 16 August 1884, Beatrice Rebecca on 11 September 1885, Edith Ellen on 23 February 1887, Ethel Maty on 10 May 1889, and Agnes on 3 April 1891, but these first five daughters had all died of child-related diseases before the age of ten. Evelyn was born on 9 August 1894, and the first son, John George, was born 20 March 1896. Mary Elizabeth was born on 13 September 1898 and Jesse Arthur in 1904.

Robert began working as a road repair man until he went into declining health. During the Great War he and his wife welcomed many Commonwealth soldiers into their home at Wilford Road in Ruddington, and wrote letters of encouragement to them while they were on active service.

Robert died on 29 January 1918, aged 60, and he was buried in an unmarked grave at Shaw Street Cemetery in Ruddington. His son, John George, was killed in action soon after his death.

Fellow defenders James Marshall and Caleb Wood were later buried in the same cemetery. A headstone was erected at his grave during a dedication ceremony in 2004.

Birth certificate (Wilford, Nottingham–CM541506)

Henry Turner was a survivor of the defence.

He was born at Ball Bridge, County Dublin, Ireland, in 1851. He enlisted at Aldershot on 27 March 1874, being described as aged 24, and he was six feet one inch tall, with a fresh complexion, light hazel eyes and brown hair. His trade was given as a bricklayer, later described as a mason, and his religion was Church of England. He was medically examined on the following day, when his birth place was recorded on the medical history sheet as Killeatty, County Wexford, Ireland, and he was found to have a scar on his right cheek from a decaying tooth.

As 104 Private Turner he was posted to the 2nd Battalion, 24th Regiment, on 30 March 1874, before transferring to H Company, 1st Battalion on 26 November that year. He was granted a penny a day good conduct pay from 30 March 1876, and gained a first class certificate of education. He served for nine months on the island of St Helena. When on picquet duty in 1876 he was struck over the left ear by a black bottle, the scar being evident. Since that time he suffered with epilepsy at long intervals, the first attack being at Simonstown, Cape Colony in 1876.

He served in the Cape Frontier War, and in the Zulu War. His epilepsy caused him to have bouts of loss of memory so it was probably for this reason that he was one of the store-keepers at Rorke's Drift. For his service he was awarded the South Africa Medal with 1877-8-9 clasp.

He suffered an attack of epilepsy on 17 June 1879, and he was admitted into hospital at Pietermaritzburg on 9 July 1879, when a medical board declared him unfit for further service. He suffered an epileptic fit on the ship bringing him home to England, and he had a further attack before being examined at Netley Hospital on 29 January 1880, where it was considered that his disability was permanent and that he may not be able to struggle for a precarious livelihood. He was discharged as unfit for further service on 9 February 1880, and his character was described as good and temperate. An injury assessment board held at the Royal Hospital in Chelsea on 25 May 1880 confirmed that he was suffering from epilepsy and he had no memory. He was awarded a pension of a shilling a day, which was amended to a permanent award of six pence a day on 11 July 1882. His intended place of residence was at Borough in Surrey.

In May 1883, he was working as a labourer on Sherbourne Farm at Albury near Guildford, for Captain Archibald Hamilton Mathison (1851-1922), 2nd Royal Surrey Militia, and living in lodgings with a fellow worker named William Carter. He was sent to a field to collect some stones, and was found lying dead by his employer late that afternoon. It was stated that he was 'A very fine man, over six feet tall... a steady, sober man, and was 32 years of age.' He was found to be badly affected with congestion of the lungs, to which his death was attributed, and the verdict was 'Death from natural causes.'

An Australian newspaper entitled *The Bulletin*, dated 22 September

1883, stated that Henry:

> ...was wounded at Rorke's Drift, and there got a bullet wound in the head, a grim legacy, from the effects of which he died. On the poor fellows death the 'hat' had to be sent round to avoid a pauper's grave...

He was possibly buried at St James' Churchyard in Shere.

Death certificate entry
Bulletin dated 22 September 1883
General County Advertiser dated 12 May 1883
Reigate and Redhill Reporter dated 12 May 1883
Southern Weekly News for 26 May 1883
Surrey Advertiser and County Times for 14 May 1883
Surrey Mirror, Reigate and Redhill Reporter, and General County Advertiser for 12 May 1883

W

John Wall was a survivor of the defence.

He was born in 1859, at St James's Parish in Deptford, Kent. He had served with the West Kent Light Infantry Militia, before he enlisted for the regular army at Chatham on 1 December 1877, and as 1497 Private Wall, he was posted to the 2nd Battalion, 24th Regiment. He was just over five feet five inches tall, with a fresh complexion, blue eyes and brown hair.

He received orders for active service in South Africa, and sailed to the Cape in February 1878. Colour-Sergeant Bourne stated: 'One day I heard a man named Wall ask my batman 'if the kid was in.' This being a reference to the fact that Bourne was a senior ranking NCO at the age of only 23. He took part in the Cape Frontier War, and on 19 October 1878, he was sentenced to 21 days in prison with hard labour. During the Zulu War he was present at the defence of Rorke's Drift. For his service he received the South Africa Medal with 1877-8-9 clasp, which was returned to the Mint on 7 November 1882.

He served in Gibraltar in 1880, and in India, where he was in hospital at Secunderabad from 4 May to 12 August 1881. He was treated for dyspepsia, the diagnosis later being changed to mania. He returned home, and was admitted to Netley Hospital on 25 November 1881, being treated for mania, attributed to intemperance. His condition had not improved, and it was considered that he was unable to contribute to his own support. He was discharged from the army at Netley on 27 December 1881, after a disturbing military career in which his name appeared in the defaulters book on ten occasions, he was twice convicted by court martial, and his character was described as 'bad and dirty'. An Injury Assessment Board held at the Royal Hospital in Chelsea on the day of his discharge had no sympathy for him when it confirmed the original findings but rejected a pension award. His intended place of residence was the Lunatic Asylum at Barming Heath in Maidstone, Kent.

John Waters was a survivor of the defence.

He was born on Christmas Eve, 24 December 1839, at 9 Carnaby Street, London, and he was Christened at St James Church on 16 February 1840. He was the second child of four to William Waters, a coach builder, and his wife, Ann (formerly Smith), who had married at St James, Westminster, on 5 December 1836. His siblings were all born at St James, Westminster—Mary Ann on 18 August 1837; Thomas on 8 December 1845.

By the time of the 1851 census, the family had moved to 16 Silver Street, Golden Square, Westminster. In 1861 his father was a ship's mate working on the vessel *Industry* moored near Exeter, while John remained in London working as a clerk.

On 7 March 1858, he enlisted at Westminster, and as 447 Private Waters he was posted to the 1st Battalion, 24th Regiment, at Chatham. He was described as being five feet five inches tall, with a fresh complexion, hazel eyes and brown hair. His place of birth was given as Lichfield, Staffordshire. The 1861 census shows Private John Waters in barracks at 1st Depot Battalion, Chatham. He was awarded good conduct pay of one penny a day on 3 May 1864, and this was increased to two pence a year later. From 31 March to 3 August 1865, the battalion was stationed at Curragh Camp in Ireland, and from August 1865 to February 1866 at Begger's Bush in Dublin, returning from there in February to receive their new colours at Curragh Camp, where they remained until August 1866. During August and September 1866, the battalion were garrisoned at Belfast and Londonderry. They sailed for Malta in February 1865, where they were garrisoned at Fort Verdala until February 1868. While in Malta he re-engaged to complete 21 years' service, on 9 September 1867. In February 1868, the battalion moved to Floriana Barracks in Malta, and from 23 September 1869 to 29 February 1872, they were garrisoned at Fort Ricasoli. John was promoted to corporal on 10 October 1871, and on 5 March 1872, the battalion was posted to Gibraltar. In September 1874, he was charged with 'neglect of duty', being tried and confined from 16 to 26 September of that year, with loss of one penny of his good conduct pay.

On 28 November 1874, the 1st Battalion was posted to South Africa for active service in the Cape Frontier War, and from 1 April to 30 June 1877, he was stationed at the Wynberg Musketry Camp in Cape Colony. When hostilities with the Zulus began and the 1st Battalion crossed into enemy territory, John was left behind at Rorke's Drift as a special orderly to Surgeon Reynolds in the hospital, and he was present at the defence of Rorke's Drift. John's own account of events was published on 13 June 1879, in *The Cambrian* newspaper.

Major Chard reported that John had told him that, having escaped the burning hospital, he found himself lying in a position with Zulus all around him. It was too late to retreat so he slowly made his way to the cookhouse and, standing up in the chimney, blackened his hands and face with soot, he remained there until morning when he emerged from his hiding place. On coming out into the open he was nearly shot when one of the men on the wall raised his rifle to fire, but Waters cried out in time to save himself. Private Waters had been severely wounded: 'a bullet having entered the arm six inches from the shoulder joint and lodging.' The ball was cut out 12 hours later by Surgeon Reynolds, and he kept it as a souvenir. The official report of his injury stated:

During the fight he was hit in the right shoulder. The bullet entered the deltoid muscle about its lower third anteriorly, and lodged opposite the surgical neck of the humerus postiorly, where it had been cut out. On probing this wound no bone was felt, and after the usual sloughing it healed.

He arrived at Pietermaritzburg on 14 July 1879, where he was found to be unfit for further service. He returned to England and *The Stroud News and Gloucestershire Advertiser* for 13 June 1879, carried a report which stated:

> The bullet with which Waters was wounded passed into his shoulder, and made its exit at his elbow, and the missile is now saved and prized by him as a memorable memento of the struggle in which he took part... The wounded men arriving home from the affair at Rorke's Drift assert that the Zulu did not throw their assegais, but waited until they had chance of getting within stabbing distance, and then used them with deadly effect.

John was officially discharged from the army at Netley on 27 October 1879. He had earned four good conduct badges, was entered in the regimental defaulter's book six times, twice being court martialled, and his conduct during his service was described as: 'very good'. He received the South Africa Medal with 1877-8-9 clasp, on 15 October 1880. The medal was originally inscribed G Waters, which was later changed to J. Waters. His pension was eighteen pence a day for the first six months, then it was reduced to eight pence. From 31 January 1882, he received a permanent pension of ten pence a day. The address he gave for his intended place of residence was 12 Courtfield Gardens in South Kensington, London, which was the home of a wealthy landowner, where his sister, Mary Ann, lived and worked as a house servant.

His papers state that he was discharged: 'From length of service and age 39, and wound, his capacity to earn a living will be in a considerable degree impaired.'–However, within weeks of his discharge he became a messenger for the War Office, while lodging with the family of one of his co-workers, John Delve, at 8 Britten Street, London. By 1881 he had a home of his own at 8 Little Windmill Street, St James.

He married Bridget McNally, on 2 October 1881, at St Peter's Church in the parish of St James. Bridget's address was given as 5 Cambridge Street, and by 1882 they had moved to 84 Burnthwaite

Road, Fulham, and John remained in the employment of the War Office.

On 17 November 1883, after only two years of marriage, John died of pneumonia at his home, aged 43. He was buried in Fulham Cemetery on 24 November (section E16, grave 11). Arthur Sears was buried in the same cemetery in 1906. John's South Africa Medal with 1877-8-9 clasp was sold at auction in 2020. It had some damage to the edge, which was probably caused by the initial change.

Birth certificate–St James, Golden Square FC747273
Marriage certificate–St James MXC705423
Death certificate–Fulham HD 025069
Daily Telegraph for 11 June 1879

Alfred Whetton was a survivor of the defence.

He was born on 24 May 1841, at St Luke's Parish in Islington, London. He joined the army at Westminster on 24 March 1859, and as 977 Private Whetton, he was posted to the 2nd Battalion, 24th Regiment. He was five feet five and a half inches tall, with a fresh complexion, hazel eyes and brown hair. Only a month after enlistment he went absent without leave on 27-28 April 1859. He was tried on 2 May 1859, and was in confinement until 23 May 1859, the day on which he attained 18 years of age, and the sentence was remitted. He served at Mauritius, and was granted good conduct pay on 24 May 1862, which had risen to three pence by 24 May 1871. He re-engaged at Secunderabad in India on 15 April 1869, to complete 21 years' service.

He received orders for active service in South Africa, and sailed to the Cape in February 1878. He took part in the Cape Frontier War, where his good conduct pay was increased to four pence a day from 24 May 1878, and during the Zulu War he was present at the defence of Rorke's Drift. For his service he received the South Africa Medal with 1877-8-9 clasp.

He served at Gibraltar, where his good conduct pay was increased to five pence a day from 24 May 1880, and three days later he claimed his discharge on completion of his second term of limited service. His character was described as very good, he was in possession of five good conduct badges, and he received the Long

Service Good Conduct Medal with a gratuity of five pounds. His intended place of residence was 5 Tower Hamlets Road in Newham, London. He died at Shoreditch in London, on 6 April 1891, aged 50.

William Wilcox was a survivor of the defence.

He was born on 17 August 1860, at Higher Welsford in Hartland, Devon. He was the sixth child of seven born to Richard Wilcox, an agricultural labourer, and his wife, Ann (formerly Harris), who had married at Bideford in 1842. His siblings were all born in the Bideford registration district. They were: Mary Jane, born in 1845; Sarah Jane, born on1847; John, born in 1850; Richard, born in 1853; Charles, born in 1857, and Thomas, born in1863. Sadly, Ann and her baby died in childbirth in 1866.

William had left home by 1871 to take up employment as a general servant at Hescoth Farm.

He enlisted for the army at Cardiff on 9 February 1877, and as 1187 Private Wilcox he was posted to the 2nd Battalion, 24th Regiment, at Dover. He was five feet seven and a half inches tall, with a sallow complexion, hazel eyes, and dark hair, and his religion was given as Roman Catholic (though he later married in the Church of England). It is known that William was a servant for one of the regiment's officers.

He received orders for active service in South Africa, and sailed to the Cape in February 1878, being hospitalised with pneumonia from 15 to 28 February. He took part in the Cape Frontier War, and during the Zulu War he was present at the defence of Rorke's Drift. For his service he received the South Africa Medal with 1877-8-9 clasp.

He received good conduct pay from 10 February 1879, but he was tried for desertion and theft of government property and sentenced to imprisonment from 25 November to 30 December 1879, all former service towards pensions and his good conduct pay being forfeited. He was in prison in Pinetown charged with 'disgraceful conduct' when the battalion embarked for Gibraltar, and he was shipped back to England to serve the remainder of his sentence in Forton Military Prison at Alverstoke in Hampshire, from where he was released on 27 September 1881. He was posted to the 1st Battalion at Colchester, and then to Salford on 29 August 1882, and it was from there that he was discharged to the 1st class reserve on 10

February 1883, giving his intended place of residence as New Oldfield Road in Salford. He received his final discharge on 9 February 1889.

On his return to Devon he found that his father had re-married. He obtained employment as an agricultural labourer, and by 1891 he was working at Docton Farm, having developed a passion for any kind of engine. His father died in 1893.

He married Lily Vanstone, on 27 February 1892, at the Bideford Register Office, and they rented a home in Limebridge in Hartland, where their only child, Maud Mary, was born on 4 August 1892. By 1901 they were living at Limebridge Cottages. Lily died in 1917, and William gave up his home and moved into a caravan at Brightly Quarry.

William died in the caravan at Newbridge in Dolton, north Devon, on 29 May 1925, aged 64. The cause of death was given as 'valvular disease of the heart and mitral incompetence', and he was buried in Dolton Churchyard.

Local newspapers reported:

A very tall man, he drove Mr James S Haynes's 'Excelsior' traction engine for years, and in 1915 had charge of the vertical boiler and steam winch used to haul the 'Flora' salvage up Milford Cliff and across the valley. Since then he has driven a steam roller Littleham way, and lately lived in a van at Brightly Quarry in Dalton.

Birth certificate–Hartland, Bideford CN052957
Marriage certificate–Bideford TJ374386
Maud Mary birth certificate–Hartland, Bideford CN052958
Death certificate–Winklagh, Torrington HD090358

John Williams was a survivor of the defence, but not of the Zulu War.

He was born at Cadoxton near Neath in Glamorganshire. He had previously served with the Glamorgan Artillery when he left his job as a collier to enlist into the regular army on 28 November 1876, at Pontypool, and as 934 Private Williams he was posted to E Company, 2nd Battalion, 24th Regiment.

He received orders for active service in South Africa, and sailed to the Cape in February 1878. He took part in the Cape Frontier War, and during the Zulu War he was present at the defence of Rorke's Drift. He died of disease at Rorke's Drift on 5 February 1879, and he is buried in the cemetery there. His name is inscribed on the monument, and for his service he received the South Africa Medal with 1877-8-9 clasp, issued on 29 March 1881.

John Williams was awarded the Victoria Cross for valour at Rorke's Drift.

He was born as John Fielding in Merthyr Road in Abergavenny, Monmouthshire, on 25 September 1857. He was the second son of nine in the family of ten children to Michael Fielding, and his wife, Margaret (formerly Godsil). His parents were both born at Cork in Ireland in 1836. The family settled at 3 Penywain Cottages, Llantarnam, Cwmbran, when John was five. His father was a gardener, and John went to work as a labourer at the Patent Nut and Bolt Factory in Newport in 1865.

He entered the Royal Monmouth Militia in 1877, but when he decided to join the regular army his family disapproved and tried to stop him, so he used the name John Williams to enlist into the 24th Regiment at Monmouth, on 22 May 1877, along with Joseph Williams from Newport, who was killed in action fighting alongside John in the hospital at Rorke's Drift. 1395 Private John Williams was posted to the 2nd Battalion at Dover. He was just less than five feet six inches tall, with a fresh complexion, blue eyes and light-brown hair. His religion was Church of England.

He received orders for active service in South Africa, and sailed to the Cape in February 1878. He was charged at King William's Town on 20 April 1878, with quitting barracks improperly, admonished. He took part in the Cape Frontier War, and during the Zulu War he was present at the defence of Rorke's Drift. The official citation for the award of Victoria Cross to Private John Williams appeared in the *London Gazette* for 2 May 1879:

These two men together [he and Private Henry Hook] one man working while the other fought and held the enemy at bay with his bayonet, broke through three more partitions, and were thus enabled to bring eight patients through a small window into the inner line of defence.

He was granted good conduct pay from 23 May 1879, but the trauma of the events at Rorke's Drift seem to have affected him badly, and he was charged with being absent from duty at Pietermaritzburg on 25 October 1879, for which he was severely reprimanded (admonished).

He went to Gibraltar, where he was charged with being drunk on 13 February 1880, returning to barracks at 4:30 pm, admonished.

He received his Victoria Cross from Major General Anderson at the Almeda Parade Ground in Gibraltar, on 1 March 1880.

He arrived in India on 12 August 1880, and six days later he was charged at Secunderabad with being in bed at 7:00 am, against orders. He was charged at Secunderabad for committing a nuisance in the water room on 1 May 1882, being confined to barracks for five days. His good conduct pay was increased to two pence a day from 23 May 1883, and he obtained a fourth class certificate of education. He returned from India on 30 November 1883.

He transferred to the first class army reserve at Brecon, on 13 December 1888, his character being described as very good, and his intended place of residence was 3 Stercus Row in Cwmbran, Monmouthshire, his next-of-kin being his father, of 4 Abbey Row in Llantarnam. He was at some time a sergeant with the 3rd Volunteer Battalion of the South Wales Borderers. He attested for general service infantry at Newport on 23 May 1889, and discharged on termination of his engagement on 22 May 1893, becoming attached to the civilian staff at Brecon Barracks.

He attended the Cardiff exhibition in 1896, where it was said of him:

There's a 'Victoria Cross' man at the Cardiff Exhibition. His name is John Williams; he hails from Cwmbran, and he is 38 years of age. But his hair is prematurely grey, and his features are lined and furrowed, as a result of the terrible experiences he went through on behalf of his country during the Zulu War. He is in Mr R P Culley's employ...

He went back to work at the Nut and Bolt Factory, and he met

Elizabeth Murphy, who already had a daughter, named Annie. They married at St Alban's Catholic Church in Pontypool, on 15 April 1884, and together they had three sons and two daughters. The 1891 and 1901 census shows them living at 43 Morgan John Street in Llantarnam, Cwmbran, and the 1911 census shows them living at 146 Pritchard Terrace in Llantarnam.

He was appointed recruiting officer at the barracks during the Great War, where he suffered a double tragedy. His wife died on 29 May 1914, and later that year he received the tragic news that their eldest son, Tom, had been killed in action at Mons while serving with the South Wales Borderers.

On 9 November 1917, John was one of the Brecon depot who attended the celebration to mark the award of Victoria Cross to Captain Angus Buchanan, South Wales Borderers, held at Coleford in the Forest of Dean. He was present at the garden party held by King George V and Queen Mary at Buckingham Palace, on 26 June 1920, to commemorate all holders of the Victoria Cross, and he attended a VC dinner in the House of Lords, on 9 November 1929, which was hosted by the Prince of Wales. He was one of 25 Zulu War veterans who attended The Old Comrades Club of the 24th Foot reunion at the Victoria Barracks in Portsmouth on 30/31 March 1929, along with Thomas Driscoll, Henry Gallagher, John Jobbins and Henry Martin; and newspapers stated: 'He declared that he would gladly join the army again if he were a young man.'

Described as 'a rather tall, charming man', he retired from his employment at the Brecon Barracks on 20 May 1920, and left the Nut and Bolt Factory in 1922. In later life he led a quiet life at his home in Llantarnam Road in Cwmbran, and he eventually went to live with his married daughter, Margaret, at 28 Cocker Avenue in Cwmbran.

On 24 November 1932, the last surviving Zulu War VC was visiting his daughter, Elizabeth, at Tycoch in Cwmbran, and while he was there he suffered heart failure and died in the early hours of 25 November 1932. He was aged 75. His funeral cortege was half-a-mile long, including a place of honour for survivors of the Zulu War, and there were floral tributes from the families of Fred Hitch and Harry Hook. He was buried with military honours provided by the South Wales Borderers, who erected a memorial at his grave in St Michael of All Angels Churchyard in Llantarnam. A memorial service and parade was held at his grave to celebrate the unveiling of a new memorial stone.

Cardiff Evening Express for 6 June 1896

Joseph Williams was killed in action during the fight for the hospital.

He enlisted at Monmouth on 23 May 1877, and as 1398 Private J. Williams, he was posted to the 2nd Battalion, 24th Regiment.

He received orders for active service in South Africa and sailed to the Cape with his battalion in February 1878. He took part in the Cape Frontier War, and during the Zulu War he was present at the defence of Rorke's Drift, where he was killed in action defending the hospital. He and Private John Williams were posted in a far corner room of the building in charge of three patients, which had no communication with the interior. When the Zulus made a fierce assault on the hospital, they managed to keep the enemy away from an exterior door by shooting through loopholes, and through panels in the flimsy door. When they ran out of bullets the Zulus closed and smashed their way in, and Joseph and two patients were dragged away and slaughtered. Reverend Smith stated:

> Private Joseph Williams fired from a small window at the far end of the hospital. Next morning fourteen warriors were found dead beneath it, besides others along his line of fire. When their ammunition was expended, he and his companions kept the door with their bayonets, but an entrance was subsequently forced and, he, poor fellow was seized by the hands, dragged out and killed before the eyes of the others.

He was buried in the cemetery at Rorke's Drift and his name is inscribed on the monument. His effects were recorded for claim by his father. For his service he received the South Africa Medal with 1877-8-9 clasp.

In 1924 a Mr R. Jenkins of Newport stated that Joseph was a playmate of his. They grew up together, and both worked at the Dos Works. They were motherless at an early age. His gallantry was recognised by Queen Victoria, who sent a letter of condolence to his father, accompanied by a sum of money to compensate him for the loss of so gallant a son.

The Dos Works was the Cordes (Dos Works), a large nail manufacturer which had been established in 1835, and remained open until 1961.

South Wales Argus for 29 January 1924

Thomas Williams was mortally wounded at Rorke's Drift.

He attested for 25 Brigade on 6 March 1877, and as 1328 Private T. Williams he was posted to the 2nd Battalion, 24th Regiment, on 3 December 1877. Thomas took to the army well and promotions came quick. He was appointed lance corporal on 8 January 1878, and corporal on 1 February 1878, the day he embarked for active service in South Africa, and he was appointed lance sergeant while serving in the Cape Frontier War. In the Zulu War he was mortally wounded during the defence of Rorke's Drift. It was stated: 'There were two mortally wounded men to attend to and Doctor Reynolds did all he could to save them, but did not succeed.' He was buried in the cemetery at Rorke's Drift and his name appears on the monument. For his service he received the South Africa Medal with 1877-8-9 clasp.

Edward Wilson was a survivor of the defence.

He was born on 28 October 1855, at Peshawar in India, the son of Colour Sergeant Thomas Wilson and his wife, Annelin.

He had purchased his discharge from the 3rd East Surrey Militia, when he joined the regular army at Kingston-upon-Thames in Surrey on 27 January 1874. He was five and a half feet tall, with a fresh complexion, hazel eyes, and brown hair, and he had two moles on his neck. His religion was Church of England. As 56 Private Wilson he was posted to the 1st Battalion, 24th Regiment, at Brecon, on 31 January 1874. He was promoted corporal on 5 July 1875, and was granted good conduct pay on 28 February 1876. He was appointed lance sergeant on 16 May 1877; and sergeant on 12 January 1878.

He served in the Cape Frontier War, and in the Zulu War. It was stated in newspapers at the time the unit returned home on 2

October 1879:

Among the men of the 1st Battalion of the 24th who disembarked were Sergeant Wilson, Lance-Corporal Roy, and Privates Desmond, Payton and Jenkins, who had been to the rear with prisoners...

For his service he was awarded the South Africa Medal with 1877-8-9 clasp.

He became colour sergeant on 22 November 1879, and he obtained a second class certificate of education, and his service continued with the South Wales Borderers. However, his career took a knock-back when he was confined in cells on 15 August 1881, and was tried by district court martial on 27 of that month; being reduced to corporal and forfeiting a penny a day of his good conduct pay from the date of his initial confinement.

On 1 July 1882 he transferred to the 1st Battalion, where his career started to improve again. He qualified for a second good conduct badge on 28 August 1882; was appointed lance sergeant on 12 December 1882; and sergeant on 10 February 1883. He was posted to the permanent staff of the 3rd (Militia) Battalion of the South Wales Borderers on 31 March 1884, on the authority of the Adjutant General's Office; and on 23 January 1886 he became entitled to a third good conduct badge. He re-engaged for the South Wales Borderers at Brecon on 23 January 1886, for such term as shall complete a total of 21 years' service. He at last gained promotion to his old rank of colour sergeant on 1 January 1888.

However, on 18 January 1889 he was permitted to revert to the rank of sergeant in order to escape trial by court martial, and he was posted back to the 1st Battalion on 12 February 1889. He continued as sergeant until his discharge on 16 February 1890. His service of just over 17 years was allowed to count towards his pension.

Edward died of hypotrophy of the heart (heart failure) at the Cambridge Military Hospital, on 19 February 1891, aged 36, and he was buried in the Aldershot Military Cemetery; where Daniel Sheehan (James Graham) was buried eight years later.

John Wilson was a survivor of the defence.

He was born as James B. Welson at Hay-on-Wye in Herefordshire, in about 1848. He died in South Africa.

Melbourne Argus for 21 April 1897 carried an article under the title The Defence of Rorke's Drift by an Old Soldier. The identity of this man is not known but the details provided in the narrative suggest that it may have been Corporal John Wilson. He states that he was a former soldier with the Royal Engineers, and that he knew Colonel Anthony Durnford.

Joseph Lenford Windridge was a survivor of the defence.

He was born on 14 May 1842, at 10 Keppel Street in Southwark, Surrey (now Greater London). He was the eldest child of four to Daniel Windridge, a hatter, and his wife, Martha (formerly Clark). The family had moved to Newington in Surrey, by 1845, and in the following year they moved to Daniel's home town of Atherstone in Warwickshire.

Joseph left his employment as a compositor at the Birmingham Mercury newspaper, to enlist into the army on 26 January 1859, and as 735 Private Windridge he was posted to the 2nd Battalion, 24th Regiment. He gave his age as 18, which was something that many young men did at the time to bluff their way into the military. He was just over five feet six inches tall, with a fresh complexion, hazel eyes and brown hair. He gave his home address as Granville Street in Birmingham.

He served at Mauritius from 23 May 1860 to October 1865, where he seems to have made good progress. He was granted good conduct pay on 31 January 1862, being promoted corporal on 6 May 1861, and on 3 March 1862 he attained the rank of sergeant. He was appointed quartermaster sergeant on 21 December 1863. On 5 October 1865 the battalion embarked for India, where they remained until 2 January 1873. He re-engaged at Rangoon to complete 21 years' service.

It would seem that he had married at some time because his wife, Kate, died in Rangoon in December 1868. The climate had a bad effect on Joseph too as he was hospitalised on several occasions while serving at Secunderabad in 1872, with ailments such as dyspepsia, dysentery and diarrhoea. During July and September he is known to have performed literary readings to the troops.

Having returned to Aldershot, he married Annie Hannah Letitia Sullivan, on 16 August 1874, at St Giles-on-the-Field in Middlesex. He is described as being a widower, suggesting that he had married while on overseas duty. He reverted to colour sergeant on 21 June 1873, and on 4 January 1876 he reverted to sergeant, and on 14 July of that year he was appointed colour sergeant.

He was promoted to quartermaster sergeant on 17 January 1877, while he was serving at the Dover Citadel, and the following report appeared in local newspapers on 3 February 1877:

PRESENTATION–On Saturday, a very gratifying presentation was made to Quartermaster-Sergeant Joseph L Windridge, of the 24th Regiment. It consisted of a handsome 14-day drawing room clock, gilt alabaster, under a glass shade, on the base of which was the following inscription: 'Presented to Quartermaster-Sergeant Joseph L Windridge, by the non-commissioned officers and men of the A Company, 2nd Battalion of the 24th Regiment, as a mark of esteem. Dover, 16 January 1877.' The clock was supplied by Mr W A May, goldsmith and jeweller, Snargate Street.

He reverted back to sergeant at his own request on 27 April 1877, having been appointed orderly room clerk on 1 April 1877, when he was recommended for the Long Service, Good Conduct Medal.

He married for a third time at the Holy Trinity Church in Dover on 14 June 1877. His new wife was 19-year-old, Helena Catherine Rawlinson. A daughter named Helena was born to them in 1878. At the time of the defence his parents lived in Granville Street in Birmingham.

He received orders for active service in South Africa and sailed with his battalion to the Cape in February 1878. He took part in the Cape Frontier War, and during the Zulu War he was present at the defence of Rorke's Drift. He was placed in charge of some caskets of rum in the store, with orders to shoot any man who tried to get near them. However, being fond of a drink himself, he used his better judgement and delegated this responsibility to Sergeant Millne. Lieutenant Chard stated: 'Sergeant Windridge showed great intelligence and energy in arranging the stores for the defence of the

Commissariat stores, forming loopholes, etc.' He was said to have taken great satisfaction in issuing each survivor with a tot of rum when relief came in the morning. For his service he received the South Africa Medal with 1877-8-9 clasp.

On 6 July 1879, Joseph went 'absent without leave', being charged and tried on the following day. He was reduced in rank, which was remitted, but he had to forfeit his good conduct pay. On 16 November 1879, he was confined for drunkenness, and was tried and reduced to private three days later. He served at Gibraltar in 1880, before being posted to Secunderabad in India, where he reached the rank of sergeant on 3 March 1882. Sergeant Windridge was discharged at Gosport on 7 August 1883, having served for over 24 years, and during his service he had been admitted to hospital on eight occasions. He was entitled to four good conduct badges and his conduct was described as 'very good'.

He gained employment as a clerk to a lamp maker, and the family made their home at 32 Paddington Street, St George's Parish in Aston, Birmingham. Selina was born in 1881, but she died when she was eight years old. Joseph Lenford was born in 1883, but he died in 1884. Twin boys, Lenford Rawlinson and Henry Rawlinson, were born in 1885, Martha Clarissa was born in 1886, Josepha Rawlinson was born in 1888, Joseph Rawlinson was born in the spring of 1890, and in December of that year came Ann. In 1891 Joseph moved his family to live at 156 Clifton Road in Aston, where Dolly was born in 1892, followed by Amy in 1894 and William in 1895. Sadly, six of their children died of tuberculosis in March 1896.

The 1901 census shows Joseph staying with his nephew at Velos Yard in Atherstone. He died on 30 August 1902, aged 60, at the home of his sister, 59 Tower Street, Aston, Birmingham. He had suffered a stroke, and the cause of death was given as apoplexy. He was buried in an unmarked grave at Witton Cemetery in Aston (plot 97, grave 54737), where both fellow defenders Robert Cole and Samuel Parry had been laid to rest four years earlier. In 2015 memorials dedicated to Joseph, Robert and Sam were placed at the cemetery.

Marriage certificate to Annie Sullivan (St Giles in the Field–B364025)
Birmingham Mail for 15 March 1879

Caleb Wood was a survivor of the defence.

He was born on 24 April 1858, at 4 Oliver's Row in Ruddington near Nottingham. He was the second of five children to William Wood, a framework knitter, and his wife, Ellen (formerly Daft). Caleb received his education at the small village school in Ruddington, and by the time he was twelve he was working with his father and elder brother as a framework knitter.

Like Robert Tongue he left this type of work to join the army. He attested on 6 March 1877, and as 1316 Private Wood he was posted to the 2nd Battalion, 24th Regiment.

He received orders for active service in South Africa and sailed to the Cape with his battalion in February 1878. He took part in the Cape Frontier War, and during the Zulu War he was present at the defence of Rorke's Drift. He transferred to G Company on 29 January 1879. For his service he received the South Africa Medal with 1877-8-9 clasp. He served at Gibraltar in 1880, and in India, where he was appointed drummer on 1 February 1881, and from where he returned home on 1 May 1883, and took his discharge.

He took lodgings at Cambridge Street in New Radford near Nottingham. He met Emily Jones (formerly Whitworth), who had a two year old daughter, Catherine Annie, and they married at the New Radford Parish Church, on 25 December 1883.

He returned to the regular army at Newport for a short period of time, and by 1888 he had returned to civilian life and made the family home at Tibshelf, a village three miles from Hardstoft, where he gained employment as a coal miner at the number one deep pit in Tibshelf.

On 26 January of that year Caleb and Emily's first child, William John, was born. Soon after the birth, Caleb took his family to live at Lower Brook Street in Long Eaton, where he found work as a coal miner at the local pit. He then took his family to live at 7 Sawley Road, and Caleb changed his occupation to that of a twist hand in the lace industry. Arthur Charles Jepson was born in 1895, and Wilfred Roy was born in 1899. By 1900 they had moved to Cossall, near Ilkeston, Derbyshire, and Caleb remained employed in the lace making trade.

Caleb and Emily moved to Digby Street in Ilkeston, and from there to Lower Chapel Street. Caleb joined the silver band at the local church, and he also joined the Voluntary Fire Service. Caleb and

Emily were active members of the Church Army Mission, and in this capacity Caleb was invited to give a talk on Rorke's Drift to help raise money for the Church Land Fund, on 19 April 1913. An account of his service in South Africa appeared in the Ilkeston Pioneer on 26 December 1913, and he was occasionally asked to go into schools to give talks about his life and the events at Rorke's Drift. He became a commissionaire at the King's Cinema in Ilkeston in 1915. His two eldest sons served with the Sherwood Foresters during the Great War, and Arthur was awarded the Military Medal for bravery during the Somme Offensive in July 1916.

By 1922 they had moved back to Ruddington, and Caleb returned to the trade of framework-knitter. In 1934 they moved into a cottage at 2 Asher Lane in Ruddington.

Caleb attended the Northern Command Tattoo held at Ravensworth Castle in Gateshead, and the 2nd Battalion, South Wales Borderers, recreated the action at Rorke's Drift. Caleb, now almost blind and visibly frail, appeared in the arena at the end of the sketch with fellow defenders Frank Bourne DCM, William Cooper, John Jobbins and Alfred Saxty. Also in 1934 he attended the ceremony for the laying-up of the regimental colours at Brecon Cathedral.

Caleb died at his home on 20 February 1935, aged 77, and he was buried at Shaw Street Cemetery in Ruddington; where fellow defenders James Marshall and Robert Tongue had already been laid to rest. A new headstone was placed at his grave during a re-dedication service held at his gravesite in 2004. His great-grand-daughter has written a number of booklets containing biographical tributes to some of the defenders.

Birth certificate–Wilford CM289646
Death certificate–Basford HC829522
Marriage certificate–Radford PAS443264
Private Caleb Wood: Rorke's Drift: Story of Valour Retold by Ilkeston Veteran Who Was There. Ilkeston Pioneer, 26 December 1913
Private Caleb Wood: Ilkeston Hero of Rorke's Drift. Nottingham Daily Express, 23 July 1914
Derbyshire Life for April 2008–*Zulu! Rorke's Drift Hero's 150th Anniversary*

BIBLIOGRAPHY

Ancestry.com

Atkinson, C. T. (Christopher Thomas): *The South Wales Borderers, 24th Foot, 1689-1937*, 1937

Aberdare Leader for 26 February 1916

Attwood, Corporal Francis: Six letters written while he was on active service in South Africa, from November 1878 to December 1879, including one dated 25 January 1879, giving his account of the action at Rorke's Drift.

Bancroft, James W: *Rorke's Drift: The Zulu War, 1879*, 1988.

Bancroft, James W: *The Rorke's Drift Men*, 2010

Bancroft, James W: *Zulu War VCs: Victoria Crosses of the Anglo-Zulu War 1879*, 2018

Bancroft, James W: *The Rorke's Drift Commanders: Gonville Bromhead and John Chard*, 2022

Barnet Express for 17 May 1879

Baynham-Jones, Alan: Biographical records of the men who served with the 24th Foot (Later the South Wales Borderers, the Royal Regiment of Wales 4th/41st Foot, and now The Royal Welsh) in South Africa 1 February 1875 to 12 January 1880

Baynham-Jones, Alan, and Stevenson, Lee: *Rorke's Drift: by Those Who Were There*, 2001

Bennett, Lieutenant Colonel Ian H. W.: *Rorke's Drift: The Story of the Commissaries (Two Parts)*, 1978

Bourne, Colonel Frank: Letter published in the *Daily Mail* newspaper on 24 August 1932, naming survivors of the Rorke's Drift action - Public Records Office, WO 100/46 f 149A and the Museum of the Royal Welsh

Bourne, Colonel Frank: Article in *The Listener* dated 30 December 1936 taken from the BBC Radio programme *I Was There!* which was broadcast on 20 December 1936.

British Newspaper Archive

Brown, Dugald Blair, *Surgical Experiences in the Zulu and Transvaal Wars, 1879 and 1881*, published in the *Lancet* on 5 July 1879

Cantlie, Lieutenant General, Sir Neil: *A History of the Army Medical Department*, 1974

Census Returns: 1841 to 1921

Chard, Lieutenant John: His official report dated 25 January 1879. Public Records Office, WO 32/7737

Chard, Lieutenant John: An account submitted to Her Majesty Queen Victoria at Windsor Castle on 21 February 1880–Royal Archives, Windsor.

Clarke, NMP, Lieutenant Colonel W. J.: *My Career in South Africa*–The Killie Campbell Africana Library

Connolly, Private John: Statement made to Captain Liddell, Royal Navy, while on his way home from South Africa aboard the *Tamar* on 3 May 1879–Regimental Archives of the South Wales Borderers at Brecon

Distinguished Conduct Medal Register, National Archives WO146/1

Dunne, Commissary Walter Alphonsus: *Reminiscences of Campaigning in South Africa, 1877-81–Journal of the Army Service Corps*, February 1892.

Emery, Frank: *The Red Soldier*, 1977

Evans, Gunner Abraham: Letter in the *Free Press of Monmouthshire* for 18 April 1913

FamilySearch

FIBIS (Families in British India Society)

Glover, Michael: *Rorke's Drift: A Victorian Epic*, 1975

Guardian for 5 March 1879

Hall, Robert: Letter to the *Natal Witness*, 1906.

Harford, Colonel Henry: *The Zulu War Journal of Col. Henry Harford, CB.* Edited by Daphne Child, 1978

Hathorn, Michael, *Swedish Land Surveyor in Natal*, 1997

Hayes, Drummer Patrick: *Survivor Recalls Epic of Rorke's Drift, News of the World*, 22 January 1939

Hitch, Private Frederick: Statement made on his being admitted to Netley Military Hospital in Southampton, published in *The Cambrian* newspaper on 13 June 1879

Hitch, Private Frederick: Eyewitness account held in the Regimental Archives of the South Wales Borderers at Brecon, and reproduced in *The Silver Wreath* by Norman Holme in 1979

Holme, Norman, the *Noble 24th*, 1999

Holt, H. P.: *The Mounted Police of Natal*, 1913

Hook, Private Alfred Henry: *Stories of the Victoria Cross: Told by those who have won it*–published in the *Strand magazine* for January/June 1891

Hook, Private Alfred Henry: *How They Held Rorke's Drift*, published in the *Royal Magazine* for February 1905

Howard, Gunner Arthur: Letter published in the *Daily Telegraph* on 25 March 1879

Jackson, F. W. David: *Hill of the Sphinx: The Battle of Isandlwana*, 2004

Jobbins, Private John: Letter from Rorke's Drift to his father, dated 6 February 1879, published in the *Hereford Times* on 29 March 1879

Jones, Private Robert: *Stories of the Victoria Cross: Told by those who have won it*–published in the *Strand magazine* for January/June 1891

Jones, Private William: *Stories of the Victoria Cross: Told by those who have won it*–published in the *Strand magazine* for January/June 1891

Journal of the Society for Army Historical Research

J. W. B. Historical Archive

Kenworthy, J. C., *The South African Wars: The Somerset Connection*, 1994

KwaZulu Natal Archives, Pietermaritzburg

Laband, John: *Fight Us in the Open: The Anglo-Zulu War Through Zulu Eyes*, 1985

Lane, Edward 'Ted': Private letter concerning his grandfather, Sergeant Henry Gallagher, and his part in the defence of Rorke's Drift, 15 May 1994

Listener for 30 December 1936

London Gazette for 1879, including: VC citations dated 2 May, 17 June, 18 November and 2 December.

Lugg, Bryn: Private letters dated 19 May 1990 and 29 July 1991

Lugg, Harry Camp: *A Natal Family Looks Back*, 1970. Including a letter from Harry Lugg published in the *North Devon Herald* Supplement for

24 April 1879
Lummis VC Files compiled on behalf of the Military Historical Society
Lummis, William: *Padre George Smith of Rorke's Drift*, 1978
Lyons, Corporal John: Statement made on his being admitted to
  Netley Military Hospital in Southampton, published in *The Cambrian*
  newspaper for 13 June 1879

MacKinnon, J. P., and Shadbolt, S. H.: *The South African Campaign of
  1879*, 1880
Mason, Private Charles: Letter from Rorke's Drift to his family in
  London, dated 8 February 1879–National Army Museum in London
Maxwell, Lieutenant John, 2nd/3rd NNC: *Reminiscences of the Zulu War*
  in the Christmas 1879 number of the *Natal Witness*
Melbourne Argus for 21 April 1897. *The Defence of Rorke's Drift by an Old
  Soldier*
  The identity of this man is not known but the details provided in the
  narrative suggest that it may have been Corporal John Wilson (John
  B. Welson) or someone who was extremely well-informed about the
  events at Rorke's Drift on 22 January 1879
Men of Harlech: Zulu War Centenary 1879-1979, 1979
Mitford, Bertram: *Through the Zulu Country*, 1983.
Morris, Donald: *The Washing of the Spears*, 1965

New Oxford Dictionary of National Biography, 2004
Norris-Newman, Charles: *In Zululand with the British throughout the Zulu
  War of 1879,* 1880

Orchard, Private George: Letter from Rorke's Drift dated 29 January
  1879–the Bristol *Observer* on 29 March 1879
Osprey Men-At-Arms, Series 57: *The Zulu War*

Paton, G.; Glennie F.; Penn-Symons, W: *Historical Records of the 24th
  Regiment*, 1892
Penn-Symons, Captain William: His Report Written in 1879
Pitt, Private Samuel: Transcript of a Press interview published in the
  Western Mail newspaper on 11 May 1914
Public Records Office at Kew (War Office Papers–numerous)
Record of Service Ledger for the 2nd/24th Regiment
Regimental Museum of the Royal Welsh at Brecon

Reynolds, Surgeon James Henry: Account in the Appendix to the Report of the Army Medical Department, 1878–Royal Army Medical Corps Museum at Aldershot

Royal Engineers Journals for 1879 and 1897; and a special centenary edition for June 1979–*The Defence of Rorke's Drift, 22 January 1879. The Commemoration of the Centenary*

Royal Engineers Museum at Chatham

Royal Magazine: February 1905

Runcorn Weekly News for 10 June 1993

Savage, Private Edward: Transcript of an interview at Brecon published in the *Manchester Weekly Post* for 19 July 1879

Smith, Sergeant George Henry: Letter from Rorke's Drift to his wife in Brecon, dated 24 January 1879, published in the *Brecon County Times*

Smith, Reverend George: Account dated 3 February 1879, published in the *Royal Army Chaplains' Department Journal* for July 1936–Royal Army Chaplains' Department Museum at Aldershot

Smith, Reverend George: *The Defence of Rorke's Drift by an Eyewitness*–published in the *Natal Mercury* for 7 April 1879

Smith-Dorrien, General Horace: *Memories of Forty-Eight Years Service*, 1925

South Wales Borderers Publication: Historical Records of the 2nd Battalion, 24th Regiment for the Campaign in South Africa, 1877-78-79, Embracing the Kaffir and Zulu Wars, 1882

Stafford NNC, Captain Walter H., His Recollections of the battle of Isandlwana, January 1938

Symons, J. P.: My *Reminiscences of the Zulu War, 1879*. Campbell Collections, University of KwaZulu-Natal

Thornton, Neil, *Rorke's Drift: A New Perspective*, 2016

Thornton, Neil, *Henry Hook VC: A Rorke's Drift Hero*, 2024

Victorian Military History Society Journal, Soldiers of the Queen, various

War Office Army Lists

War Officer Papers, including: The Narrative of the Field Operations Connected with the Zulu War of 1879, 1881

WO 147/7 Wolseley Papers: Private journal kept while commander-in-chief of troops fighting the Zulu War; dated 8 June 1879 to 25 May

1880

WO 16–Regimental musters

WO 25–Officers' services

WO76–Officers' services

WO 25/3474–Casualty returns

WO32/7698–Reports

WO32/7793–Medical services

WO32/7737–Lieutenant Chard's report on Rorke's Drift

WO/33/34/76–Correspondence

WO33//34/831–Transport

WO97 – Soldiers' services

WO100/46 - Medals for South Africa, 1877-1879

Waters, Private John, Statement made on his being admitted to Netley Military Hospital in Southampton, and published in the *Cambrian* newspaper on 13 June 1879

Witt, Reverend Otto: Statement Given at Bramhall Hall in Cheshire in 1879

Wood, Private Caleb: *Rorke's Drift: Story of Valour Retold by Ilkeston Veteran Who Was There. Ilkeston Pioneer*, 26 December 1913

Wood, Private Caleb: *Ilkeston Hero of Rorke's Drift. Nottingham Daily Express*, 23 July 1914

Wood VC, General, Sir Evelyn: *From Midshipman to Field-Marshal*, 1906

ABOUT THE AUTHOR

Recognised for the depth of his research, James W. Bancroft has produced more than a hundred books and articles, the subjects of which reflect his varied interests. He contributed several articles for inclusion in the *New Oxford Dictionary of National Biography*, and his book *Rorke's Drift: The Zulu War, 1879* has been reprinted seven times. His J. W. B. Historical Archive, compiled over five decades, is one of the largest private collections of its kind in the world.

When he is not writing, James enjoys singing and playing music, and being with his growing family.

Also by Barnthorn Publishing:

***Henry Hook VC: A Rorke's Drift Hero* by Neil Thornton.**

Henry Hook is perhaps the most famous private soldier in British military history. It is his portrayal in the movie, *Zulu*, which has cemented this position, but the real Hook was a far cry from the hard-drinking scoundrel that he was portrayed as on screen. Unlike the character in the movie, Hook's record was unblemished, and he received excellent character references from his superiors after leaving the army.

Posted to defend the Rorke's Drift hospital with orders to protect the sick and wounded at the start of the battle, Hook stuck to his task with the utmost determination. Indeed, he was more than willing to lay down his own life in his duty to save the lives of those others who were less able.

Here, Rorke's Drift expert, Neil Thornton, chronicles Hook's life, including his early years, his turbulent marriage, and his later life, putting to bed a number of myths that have developed and grown over the years, whilst analysing Hook's part in the Battle of Rorke's Drift for which he was awarded the coveted Victoria Cross.

The Victoria Crosses of Melvill & Coghill by Neil Thornton & Michael Denigan.

As with many aspects of the Zulu War, many myths surround Lieutenants Teignmouth Melvill and Nevill Coghill, 1st Battalion, 24th (2nd Warwickshire) Regiment of Foot, both of whom lost their lives on 22 January 1879, following the Zulu attack at iSandlwana.

Melvill had died after attempting to save the Queen's Colour of his battalion, and Coghill after returning into the fray to save his brother officer. 'The Dash with the Colours' featured in newspapers and magazines up and down Britain, propelling Melvill and Coghill into legend.

The public were captivated. Yet a large amount of what was circulated was not accurate. Here, authors Neil Thornton and Michael Denigan lay out what we know, what we don't know, and what has been muddled along the way, either by fault or design.

Featuring unpublished letters and correspondence between the Coghill family, the War Office and the King amongst others, the authors also show just how and why Melvill and Coghill came to be awarded posthumous VCs some 28 years after they had lost their lives. The answers will shock and intrigue.

Lightoller: Titanic to Dunkirk by James W. Bancroft.

Charles Lightoller was one heck of a sailor, who grasped life with both hands and relished in challenging the fates; and that life was one of tragedy and perilous adventure. The son of an army captain, he was a member of a family who were prominent in the Lancashire cotton trade, and suffered several domestic tragedies in his life.

He was shipwrecked and faced near starvation on one of the remotest islands on Earth; he was caught up in a cyclone and nearly drowned, and he almost died of malaria; and he suffered a year of a harsh Canadian winter during the Klondike gold rush–and that was all before he was a senior officer on board RMS *Titanic* in 1912, when she hit an iceberg and sank with a dreadful loss of life.

For gallant service during the First World War he was awarded the Distinguished Service Cross and bar. In 1940 he took his own 18-metre boat, *Sundowner,* out to Dunkirk during Operation Dynamo, and under enemy fire he rescued over a hundred British servicemen of the stranded British Expeditionary Force; which Winston Churchill described as a miracle.

He lost two of his sons in action during the Second World War, and at the end of hostilities he and his surviving son established a boat building business which specialized in maintaining river launches for the police.